Place- and Community-based Education in Schools

"Finally! Here is a book that will help educators and parents understand the meaning of place- and community-based education and how it can enrich the lives of students and community members. I've been waiting for this kind of book that uncovers the mystery of what this approach is and the how and why of implementing it in schools. The authors really know what they are writing about because they go beyond their ivory towers and talk to teachers and administrators who are doing it."

Clifford E. Knapp, Northern Illinois University

Place- and community-based education—an approach to teaching and learning that starts with the local—addresses two critical gaps in the experience of many children now growing up in the United States: contact with the natural world and contact with community. It offers a way to extend young people's attention beyond the classroom to the world as it actually is, and to engage them in the process of devising solutions to the social and environmental problems they will confront as adults. By doing so, this distinct curricular approach can increase students' engagement with learning and enhance their academic achievement.

Envisioned as a primer and guide for educators and members of the public interested in incorporating the local into schools in their own communities, this book explains the purpose and nature of place- and community-based education and provides multiple examples of its practice. It provides models and guidance for developing lessons that give students opportunities to engage more deeply in the life of their own region and potentially participate in work that is valuable for their community. The detailed descriptions of learning experiences set both within and beyond the classroom will help readers begin the process of advocating for or incorporating local content and experiences into their schools.

Gregory A. Smith is Professor in the Graduate School of Education and Counseling at Lewis & Clark College in Portland, Oregon. He speaks nationally and internationally about place- and community-based education and is involved with efforts in schools in the Pacific Northwest to adopt this approach to teaching and learning.

David Sobel is Director of Teacher Certification Programs in the Education Department of Antioch University New England in Keene, NH. He consults and speaks widely on developmentally appropriate teaching, environmental education, and parenting with nature.

Sociocultural, Political, and Historical Studies in Education

Joel Spring, Editor

For additional information on titles in the Sociocultural, Political, and Historical Studies in Education series visit **www.routledge.com/education**

Place- and Community-based Education in Schools

Gregory A. Smith
Lewis & Clark College

David Sobel
Antioch University New England

Routledge
Taylor & Francis Group

NEW YORK AND LONDON

First published 2010
by Routledge
270 Madison Avenue, New York, NY 10016

Simultaneously published in the UK
by Routledge
2 Park Square, Milton Park, Abingdon, Oxon OX14 4RN

*Routledge is an imprint of the Taylor & Francis Group,
an informa business*

© 2010 Taylor & Francis

Typeset in Minion by Swales & Willis Ltd, Exeter, Devon
Printed and bound in the United States of America
on acid-free paper by Walsworth Publishing Company, Marceline, MO

Library of Congress Cataloging in Publication Data
Smith, Gregory A., 1948-
Place- and community-based education in schools /
Gregory A. Smith, David Sobel.
p. cm.— (Sociocultural, political, and historical studies in education)
Includes bibliographical references and index.
1. Place-based education—United States.
2. Community and school—United States.
I. Sobel, David, 1949- II. Title.
LC239.S64 2010
371.11'5—dc22
2009034063

ISBN 10: (hbk) 0–415–87518–8
ISBN 10: (pbk) 0–415–87519–6
ISBN 10: (ebk) 0–203–85853–0

ISBN 13: (hbk) 978–0–415–87518–9
ISBN 13: (pbk) 978–0–415–87519–6
ISBN 13: (ebk) 978–0–203–85853–0

Contents

Preface

Place- and community-based education—an approach to teaching and learning that connects learning to the local—has become for us an antidote to one of the most serious but generally unspoken dilemmas in American education: the alienation of children and youth from the real world right outside their homes and classrooms. What's real for many young people is what happens on their computer monitors, television screens, and MP3 players. Caught in an interior and electronically mediated world, they are losing touch with both the society of flesh-and-blood humans and the delicate natural world that supports our species. Like Richard Louv, author of *Last Child in the Woods* (2005), we suspect that American children are nature-deprived, but we would go further—they are community-deprived, as well. Schools are one of the few institutions where it might be possible to rectify this problem. This book will describe ways that educators can take on this issue.

Place- and community-based education also provides a way for teachers and communities to prepare children to become participants in the local problem-solving that we believe must become increasingly common as humanity adjusts to the consequences of climate change, economic globalization, and resource exhaustion. Negotiating the challenges of the coming decades is likely to require a level of human adaptability and creativity unmatched since the agricultural and industrial revolutions. Replacing fossil fuels and reinventing sustainable farming and manufacturing processes will demand the intelligent involvement of large numbers of widely dispersed people. An educational process that begins with the local and that draws students into real-time participation in civic life and decision-making can help children and youth begin to see themselves as actors and creators rather than observers and consumers. As the stories in this volume will illustrate, students in many communities across the United States are already demonstrating the impact that involvement in community problem-solving can have on their sense of efficacy and their academic achievement.

Some Common Misconceptions

On one level, much of the vision of place- and community-based education is attractive. It often resonates with the kinds of educational experiences that many people find meaningful. In our work with educators across the country, however, we've found that it's not long before a variety of concerns and outright objections can disrupt deeper conversations about place- and community-based education and prevent people from giving this approach the serious consideration it deserves. Five of these come up with some frequency, and we'd like to address them at the outset.

- **Misconception 1:** Place- and community-based education sounds appealing, but it's not for us. Our school has to focus on keeping our test scores improving so we can meet Annual Yearly Progress.
- **Misconception 2:** Place- and community-based education is another add-on that teachers have to shoehorn into their curriculum.
- **Misconception 3:** An educational approach that focuses on place is environmental education in sheep's clothing.
- **Misconception 4:** Place- and community-based education is for rural schools in small communities with lots of wide open spaces out the back door.
- **Misconception 5:** Place- and community-based education takes much more time and energy, both of which are in short supply for most teachers.

In response to the first misconception, place- and community-based education is both appealing and capable of enhancing student learning. Student achievement is hampered when students aren't motivated and they don't see the relevance of their learning to everyday life. Place- and community-based education makes school experiences meaningful and therefore motivates students to learn. Numerous studies over the past decade of authentic, place- and community-based education have demonstrated that students become more engaged in learning when they've been involved in real-world problem-solving, something that will be discussed at greater length in Chapters 6 and 7. Incorporating place- and community-based approaches into literacy, math, social studies, and science curricula is therefore a proven way to improve student academic performance.

Reconceptualization 1: Place- and community-based education helps motivate students to learn and can contribute to increased test scores on standardized tests.

Second, place- and community-based education is a mindset, a paradigm shift, a way of thinking broadly about the school's integral relationship to the community and the local environment. It's not a new curriculum unit. It's not like the DARE program, the new FOSS science curriculum mandated by the district, or Everyday Math. Instead, it's a new approach to all of these curricular areas. Let's take DARE for instance. The fact that the local police officer is coming into the classroom, connecting the police department and the school, is illustrative of one aspect of place- and community-based education—breaking down the walls between the school and the community. From a place- and community-based education perspective, we'd also have the park superintendent and the town recycling coordinator and the neighborhood redevelopment director in the classroom, as well. And, instead of just having the DARE police officer in the school, the fifth graders might take a field trip down to the police station, and maybe even go to court to see a trial of an adolescent DWI offender. Therefore,

Reconceptualization 2: Place-and community-based education is a new way of thinking about the school's role in society. It requires a more holistic mindset about school reform than No Child Left Behind.

Third, place- and community-based education owes much to environmental education as well as to critical pedagogy, problem-based learning, service learning, constructivism, and many other education innovations of the last half-century. Place- and community-based education is certainly about local places and the environment, but it's also about history, the arts, cultural diversity, social justice, and more. It's about literacy emerging from reading neighborhood street signs; it's about supermarket math; it's about learning history in the cemetery; it's about drumming being central to the music curriculum in a school with a majority of African-American students; it's about learning to sail as part of the science curriculum. Therefore,

Reconceptualization 3: Place- and community-based education involves using all of the environments in which students live—natural, social, cultural—as starting points to teach concepts in language arts, mathematics, social studies, science, and other subjects across the curriculum.

Fourth, it is true that much good place- and community-based education has happened in rural communities. The Rural School and Community Trust has initiated projects from Maine to Alaska, and from North Dakota to Louisiana that have resulted in community revitalization and school improvement. But cities are places, too. And some of the most exciting examples of place- and community-based education are flourishing in inner-city schools. Most interesting is to see the coming together of critical pedagogy, with its emphasis on social justice, and place- and community-based education, with its emphasis on learning the neighborhood. This results in curriculum initiatives that focus on access to green space as a social justice issue, homelessness, the bathrooms in substandard school buildings, learning the history of community revitalization, and including local African-American, Asian, Cape Verdean, and Hispanic artists in the art curriculum. Therefore,

Reconceptualization 4: Place- and community-based education is alive and well in urban and rural, Northern and Southern, liberal and conservative communities and schools.

Finally, place- and community-based education requires a different approach to planning and teaching than an education centered on textbooks, lectures, and classroom demonstrations. It doesn't necessarily take more time. In effective place- and community-based educational settings, teachers and students become co-investigators of issues and concerns, with students taking increasing responsibility for their own learning. Teachers no longer must prepare all of the content that students are to master. They instead assemble materials, human resources, and inside- and outside-of-classroom experiences that serve as the foundation for student learning. When this happens and the work students are asked to complete is vital and meaningful, young people take control of their own education. Teachers not uncommonly experience professional revitalization and an increase in energy. Teaching in this way does not become a source of exhaustion but a source of vocational meaning. Therefore,

Reconceptualization 5: Place- and community-based education relies upon learning experiences that require teachers to use their time in new and often invigorating ways.

We are discovering that in schools where teachers, students, and community members have embarked on the process of integrating the local into educational activities, teaching and learning become dynamic for both young people and adults. What had been abstract and seemingly irrelevant becomes as immediate as the dangerous railroad crossing on the way to school or stories about the heroism and activism of children's neighbors and ancestors. More students find reasons to become involved in school, and their achievement begins to demonstrate the attention and commitment they bring to their studies. Many teachers rediscover the possibilities and ideals that drew them into education as a vocation and become energized and passionate about their work with the young. And community members realize that schools can be more than they ever imagined and that students are capable of making extraordinary contributions to their common life.

An Overview of What Is to Come

We have envisioned this book as a primer and guide for educators and members of the public interested in incorporating the local into schools in their own communities. Each of us has been involved in writing or editing other volumes that have explored place- and community-based education, but in different ways. We hope that what we have assembled here will provide readers with information and tools that will allow them to persuade other people about the value of this approach and to implement some of their own place- and community-based units or projects.

We begin in Chapter 1 with a case study of an urban school that serves diverse students in Boston that has been actively diminishing the boundaries between school and place for a number of years. The Young Achievers Science and Mathematics Pilot School exemplifies many of the characteristics of this approach to teaching and learning and demonstrates the ease with which they can be implemented in a setting dominated more by humans than by nature. Chapters 2 and 3 discuss definitions of place- and community-based education, antecedents to this approach, and a rationale for moving curriculum development and instruction in this direction at a time when many school reform efforts are pointing more toward the abstract and national or international than the concrete and local.

Chapters 4 and 5 explore ways that educators in numerous communities across the United States have been adopting place- and community-based educational strategies. Chapter 4 considers the way some educators have embarked on this process by identifying relevant local cultural, environmental, economic, or governmental issues as topics worthy of students' attention and energy. Student work in these instances has generally been focused more on problems or questions than traditional academic disciplines. A number of the examples in this chapter have grown into school-wide projects that at the outset may intimidate readers. It is important to realize that all began as single units or projects that evolved over time into something more substantial. Chapter 5, in contrast, shows how teachers can use the traditional academic disciplines as a starting point for place- and community-based learning. Many of these examples are more self-contained. This chapter also includes a set of guidelines educators can keep in mind while crafting units that draw upon learning resources just outside the classroom or school.

Chapters 6 and 7 consider research studies that point to the impact of place- and community-based education on student learning, initially on academic engagement and achievement and then on students' attitudes and behaviors related to environmental stewardship and community participation. Studies about this approach to teaching and learning have been growing in number over the previous decade, although they remain primarily small-scale in nature. It is also possible to draw upon larger research efforts that have explored closely related concepts and practices such as authentic instruction or service learning to posit the potentially comparable impact of similar educational approaches. Research to this point is promising and strongly suggests that place- and community-based education positively impacts student learning as well as stewardship and citizenship behaviors. A side benefit has been the way that this approach has often become a source of professional regeneration for educators.

Chapters 8 and 9 look at the role of community partners and school leaders in advancing an educational agenda aimed at grounding more learning in the local. Teachers and school principals on their own will generally have neither the knowledge nor the energy to sustain place- and community-based learning. When they are able to draw upon the knowledge and energy of people beyond the school, however, a synergy is created that can become a source of motivation and meaning for everyone involved. Teachers begin to experience a sense of meaning and purpose that can often become scarce in the face of a recurring curriculum and disengaged students. And community members come to see themselves as contributors to the education of the young and participants in the completion of socially valued projects. Children, youth, and adults all benefit when they attach their lives to work that they and others perceive as contributing to the health, welfare, or beauty of what they experience in common.

School leaders can either open or close the door to this kind of teaching and learning. Chapter 9 draws upon the thoughts of six principals or central office administrators who have been active proponents of place- and community-based education. They share useful lessons about how they have been able to support this work through staff development, the cultivation of partnerships and resources, the shaping of new organizational frameworks and schedules, or the adoption of philo-sophical perspectives more in line with an approach to learning that values the communal benefits of education as much as its benefits for individuals. School leaders are often instrumental in making this approach work, even though teachers and their students are the people who enact it.

Chapters 10 and 11 recapitulate themes and images that have been presented throughout the volume. A case study of the K–12 Vinalhaven School is the focus of Chapter 10. It demonstrates the way that place- and community-based education has evolved in a school that serves children on an island off the coast of Maine in Penobscot Bay. The Vinalhaven School has been actively reshaping its curriculum over the past few years to help connect its students to their island home. Building on the educational practices encountered on Vinalhaven, Chapter 11, the final chapter of the book, pulls out threads from earlier chapters in an effort to reiterate and solidify understandings we believe to be especially helpful in thinking through and then adopting place- and community-based educational approaches.

Our biggest hope is that you will steal the ideas we present in this book and make them your own. We want you to transform your schools into living laboratories for democracy, places that can reinvigorate the neighborhoods and communities that surround them. This is the education we believe can help twenty-first-century human beings find our way through the difficult dilemmas of the present to a more sustainable and equitable future.

Acknowledgements

We wish to acknowledge our gratitude to the growing community of educators, scholars, agency and business people, and citizens who are committed to revitalizing American education by connecting schools more firmly to their places and communities. Our conversations with people in our own regions and in other parts of the United States and the world about the possibilities we raise in this book are an ongoing source of inspiration and encouragement for us. We wish to thank in particular our colleagues at Antioch University New England and Lewis & Clark College who have provided time and resources for this work, and organizations like CO-SEED, the Promise of Place, Place-Based Education Northwest, the Place-based Education Evaluation Collaborative, and the Rural School and Community Trust that work shoulder to shoulder with us to advance these possibilities.

This book could not have come into being without the visits and talks we regularly have with teachers and administrators in schools that are finding ways to get their students out of classrooms into communities and to bring community members into their schools. These educators have given us untold hours of their time, and their willingness to stretch the boundary of educational practice has given us the stories that now fill our writing and talks. We offer particular thanks to Jinny Chalmers, Robert Hoppin, Leslye Grant, Heidi Fessenden, and Nicole Weiner for participating in conversations at the Young Achievers Science and Math Pilot School. Similar thanks are due to Kathy Warren, Margaret Qualey, Yvonne Thomas, Gloria Delsandro, Mark Jackson, and Tristan Jackson at the Vinalhaven School. We offer additional thanks to Sue Dempster, Mike Felton, and George Joseph from Vinalhaven for reading drafts of the manuscript and providing valuable feedback. We're also grateful for the insights of school leaders Ed Armstrong, Brian Goodwin, Tom Horn, Sarah Taylor, Jon Yoder, and Joyce Yoder, whose interviews form the basis of Chapter 9.

We wish to especially thank Delia Clark for her primary authorship of Chapter 8 about school–community relations. Delia's ground-breaking work in conducting community vision-to-action forums has played a major role in the evolution of the school–community change work in New England. Her zest and charisma as a facilitator come through in the writing in this chapter.

Finally, thanks are due to Naomi Silverman and Joel Spring—our editor and series editor at Routledge—who believed this book was worth publishing; our partners, Rebecca and Jen, for their willingness to put up with the time we spend with our noses behind books or computers; and our children, Ethan, Paul, Eliot, Tara, and Eli, now all young adults, whose bright lives motivate so much of our own work and commitments.

Chapter I

The Young Achievers Science and Mathematics Pilot School

Step in the door at Young Achievers and you can feel the vibe. In the teachers' room you're greeted heartily with broad smiles. The building, though old and well worn, is pristinely tidy, conveying the sense that it is well cared for by staff and students. The main hallway is lined with framed posters proclaiming: National Hispanic Heritage Month, National Black History Month: We Are All Equally Different, National Asian American Heritage Month, and National Native American Heritage Month. The assistant principal strolls the halls and projects authority. He's dressed in a sharp green suit, silk tie, beaded necklace, well-coiffed dreads. A teacher confided to Sobel that one of her young students thought he was the president. "Of what?" Sobel asked naively. "The president of the United States, of course," she responded. Names on the lockers read Jahzell, Mykayla, Tyriq, Alyria. Definitely not Kansas, but the power of the ruby red slippers is at work here. This is an academically together, happening place. The teachers are "a bunch of intellectual artists," one staff member described. One external evaluator of the school concluded that:

> Extremely high aspirations and deeply rooted values tangle with the reality of the logistical, personal, political constraints that are inherent in an urban school setting. The overall sense is that Young Achievers is on the edge of something really big, riding an exhilaratingly tall wave that could break at any moment.
>
> (Duffin and PEER Associates, 2007)

The Young Achievers School is one of Boston's original pilot schools, founded in response to the Massachusetts Education Reform Act of 1993. Now there are 20. The goal of the pilot school program is to develop pioneering models of education within the Boston Public School District and to disseminate best practices to other schools. The school was created by community activists from Roxbury and Dorchester who believed that schools were not providing adequate literacy in math and science to students of color. The school aspires to a curriculum based on active learning that is culturally relevant and free from cultural biases and that concentrates on addressing individual needs. The student population is 67 percent African American, 23 percent Latino and Hispanic, 6 percent White, 2 percent Asian, and 2 percent Native American. Owing to Boston's school choice program, students come from many Boston neighborhoods, including Dorchester, Mattapan, Hyde Park, Roxbury, Jamaica Plain, Roslindale, and others. Over 65 percent of the students receive free or reduced-price lunch.

In 2002, the Young Achievers principal, Jinny Chalmers, and her staff expressed interest in participating in the Antioch University New England-based CO-SEED program, a school improvement/community development initiative grounded in the principles of place- and community-based education. The program, funded by regional foundations, supports school improvement through providing professional development in many forms, a professional facilitator, a community vision-to-action forum for engaging community members, grant money for the school to disburse to appropriate projects, and a half-time place-based educator from a local community organization.

Prior to this time most CO-SEED projects had been in towns and small cities in New Hampshire and Vermont, with the exception of the Beebe School in Malden, Massachusetts, the organization's first urban site. All of the lead community partners had been environmental organizations such as the Harris Center for Conservation Education, New Hampshire Audubon, the Appalachian Mountain Club, and the Stone Zoo. These partners were referred to as Environmental Learning Centers or ELCs. Young Achievers and other Boston CO-SEED schools were invited to participate in choosing their own community collaborator. Young Achievers' decision to partner with the Dudley Street Neighborhood Initiative (DSNI), a prominent social justice organization in Roxbury about two miles from the school, is an indicator of how place- and community-based education can evolve in urban settings.

Roz Everdell, education director of DSNI, was enthusiastic about the possibility of working with Young Achievers. One of the goals of the neighborhood association has been development without displacement and gentrification, something local residents have accomplished through sustained participation and engagement. As Everdell says, "Our goal is for students to understand that positive change happens because local citizens make it happen. Then perhaps they'll understand that they're the change agents that will keep the improvements happening."

At the Young Achievers School, the tenets of "critical pedagogy" are married to the tenets of place- and community-based education. The purpose of critical pedagogy is what Paulo Freire calls *conscientizacao*, which involves "learning to perceive social, political, and economic contradictions and to take action against the oppressive elements of reality" (Gruenewald, 2003, p. 5). The Young Achievers School seeks to do this by improving science and math instruction for students of color so they can compete and succeed in the high-technology businesses in the greater Boston area. The Dudley Street Neighborhood Initiative does this by making it possible for African-American, Latino, and Cape Verdean residents to shape the destiny of their own community. The Young Achievers School has provided an opportunity to discover how to nurture academic achievement through an educational focus on social justice in places traditionally underserved urban students call home. What does such an education look like?

Bringing Community Members into the School

It is not uncommon for teachers in many of the nation's inner-city schools to have little if any connection to the neighborhoods where their students live. Their lack of direct knowledge of students' experience makes the crafting of appropriate place- and community-based learning opportunities difficult. Class, racial, and ethnic differences can compound this challenge. In an effort to overcome these difficulties, administrators and teachers at the Young Achievers School are working to create new roles for community members to give them more responsibility for the education of their own and their neighbors' children.

One of these roles has emerged as a result of a distinctive feature of the Young Achievers School, a Seamless Day Program that provides educational offerings from 7:30 a.m. to 4:45 p.m. each day. This came about in part to serve working parents who either had to leave children supervised by siblings at home after school or faced the challenge of getting children to childcare or after-school programs during the work day. The before- and after-school components of the day are not considered childcare, but instead are considered additional opportunities for extending the curriculum and learning. Therefore, the school day runs from 9:00 to 4:45, and the period of time from 3:15 to 4:45 provides more open-ended time for clubs, field trips, and in-depth explorations. To staff this long school day, each classroom has both a classroom teacher and a community teacher. Classroom and community teachers collaborate and overlap during the middle of the school day, with the classroom teachers arriving and leaving earlier and the community teachers arriving and leaving later.

Principal Jinny Chalmers provides a convincing rationale for why incorporating community members in this way may be important to urban place- and community-based educational efforts that aim to address social justice issues:

> Environmental education has not historically taken on the issue of social justice. Here, we work at the intersection between critical pedagogy and environmental justice. All of our community teachers except one are going to the summer institute [a professional development training in place- and community-based education]. The community teacher role is a sustainability piece because it links us to the actual communities where students come from. They're really core because you can't just have only the professional class understanding the issues. It's also core to our inclusion model.
>
> (Duffin, 2005)

Originally, the community teacher was identified as a teacher aide. But, as place-based education and connecting the curriculum to the community became a more salient feature of the school, it made sense to change the title of this position. Additionally, the titles of classroom teacher and teacher aide implied a hierarchical relationship. The administration and the staff wanted to find a way to suggest greater parity and more of a collaborative relationship—hence the switch from teacher aide to community teacher. Although vestiges of the previous distinction still exist, more and more, classroom and community teachers are perceived as co-teachers. Much professional development is targeted for community teachers and seeks to support those who want to gain further credentialing.

To achieve equity, a number of strategies have emerged. A conscious attempt has been made to raise the salaries of community teachers to bring them closer to the salaries of the professional staff. Specific professional development just for community teachers is being provided, and they are also being supported in their desire to pursue formal teacher certification. Community teachers are being encouraged to participate in leadership roles such as being workshop leaders at the CO-SEED summer institute. One year, community teachers trained classroom teachers and community members from rural Maine in curriculum planning. Being recognized as experts by credentialed colleagues has had an impact on their sense of competence and their contributions to the improvement of their school.

Community teachers have also had the opportunity to learn from local leaders during the community vision-to-action forum, a community/school planning session to envision the future of the school. Part of the forum included a presentation by the activist founders of Young Achievers, all African-American and Latino community members. One of the founders, Julio Henriquez, made it clear that, "If you have great expectations of children, it inspires them—they feel like they can take on any challenge." The founders' energy provided a role model for how community teachers can themselves become leaders in the school and community. It is this kind of inspiration, responsibility, and leadership that adults at Young Achievers seek to cultivate among their students, as well.

Finding Nature in the City

In an article entitled "Learning to Read Nature's Book: An Interdisciplinary Curriculum for Young Children in an Urban Setting" (2006), Young Achievers kindergarten teacher Alicia Carroll and art teacher Bisse Bowman describe the rationale for a year-long curriculum that uses field trips to Forest Hills Cemetery:

> Founded on our belief that outstanding curricula and competence in math and science, supported by a strong literacy program, are vital for our urban, culturally and ethnically diverse student population, our school is committed to social justice. These experiences are crucial in laying the foundations for learning scientific methods through firsthand experiences, an introduction to inquiry-based research, data gathering, recording, interpreting, and drawing conclusions. ... Children in urban settings often do not have access to firsthand experiences with regional flora and fauna in natural settings, and therefore find it difficult to feel truly connected to nature, to be able to analyze and understand the natural and scientific world in which they live, and to understand their place in it. Our visits to the field study site provide our students access to all of this.

(Carroll & Bowman, 2006, p. 19)

They bundle up the children, cross Hill Street, stroll up a side street, and slip through a hole in the fence to a 10-foot square study site on the wild fringes of the cemetery. They remove the turf, set it aside, and then look for creatures.

Golden leaves rustle gently as the breeze moves through the trees in our urban forest. The children are squatting in the deep green star moss, poking their trowels underneath the moss with great care. Suddenly, a voice is raised in excitement. "Look, Ms. Alicia! Look what I found! What is it?" The excitement was catching, and the rest of the children gathered around Amir, looking into his cupped hand.

(Carroll & Bowman, 2006, p. 19)

Such investigations are the crucial first step in a comprehensive literacy and science program for these young children. From the investigations, new vocabulary lists are developed: puddingstone, moss, acorn, rustle, daddy longlegs, path. These words are incorporated into books that children write. When the children have questions about the centipedes, worms, or pupated beetles that they're finding, these creatures are placed in a collector terrarium and brought back to the classroom. Then the teachers introduce the idea of "research," looking in books to figure out what they've found. The Research Center is supplied with nonfiction insect books, Science Rookie Readers, magnifying glasses, paper, pencils, and modeling clay. During one study session, Rosa suddenly called out, "I found it. I found it! What does it say in the book? What does it say? I found it!" And sure enough, she has found an image of the mealworm pupa that Amir had discovered in the cemetery. Her enthusiasm for extracting meaning from text, illustrated in her query "What does it say in the book?," is a perfect illustration of the power of the natural world to provoke academic learning.

For a time, the Research Center becomes "The Mealworm Research Center." Each child set up a mealworm habitat in a petri dish and fed them not too much (which would result in rot and mold), but not too little (which would impede the development of the larvae). Students named their mealworms, watched them change, learned more new vocabulary—larva, pupa, exoskeleton, beetle, emerge— and created careful observational drawings and life cycle charts.

Carroll and Bowman place their curriculum within a broad context, touching on the possibilities of *conscientizacao*:

Paulo Freire, the Brazilian educator, said that authentic knowledge transforms reality. Knowledge of the word is not the privilege of the few but the right of everyone. We want to broaden our students' scope of the world. Our students—Black, Asian, Latino/a, and White, should have the right and freedom to know the world, beginning with themselves. ... When this is so, they will be able to step into the shoes of others, begin to construct knowledge that is authentic, and thereby a new reality. This is the real standard we should meet.

(Carroll & Bowman, 2006, p. 32)

Food, Farm, and Shelter

Heidi Fessenden and Nicole Weiner, first-grade teachers, conduct a year-long study of food, farm, and shelter. Though the unit evolves from year to year, it usually starts with classroom investigations of food and its sources. What kind of food do we eat? Where do we get it from? How does it get to the store? Visits to an apple orchard, a farmers' market, and a local farm then connect students to the real world of food production. Students choose topic groups and do focused studies of bees, apple production, compost, greenhouses. They write, draw diagrams, make models, read nonfiction literature. All of this is straightforward place- and community-based curriculum grounded in real-world experiences. But, each year, there's a twist.

Part of visiting the apple orchard involves talking to migrant workers, usually Jamaican men. The teachers use this encounter to delve deeper into the lives of these people who help bring food to children's tables. Teachers' guiding questions in the design of the unit are: Who are migrant farmworkers? What is hard about their lives? What rights are they fighting for? After conversations with the farmworkers and reading of related literature, students generate their own questions:

- Do they ever get fired?
- Do they have their own houses?
- How do they travel around?
- Where do they come from? Where were they born?
- Where do they bring the produce after they pick it?

Figure 1.1 Student work from the first-grade food, farm and shelter unit

These questions guide classroom presentations, conversations with classroom visitors, and the children's reading. One year, a visit to a migrant worker exhibit at the National Heritage Museum in Lexington led to a study of Cesar Chavez and the farmworkers' movement. This then grew into a comparison of the non-violent protest strategies adopted by Mr. Chavez and Dr. Martin Luther King, as well as a visit from a local community activist. To culminate the study, children developed displays for local stores about what they had learned. One class presented information about migrant farmworkers at the Harvest Co-op in Jamaica Plain. The other class focused on portraits of activists and shared their work at Jamaicaway Books and Gifts.

In the fall of 2006, the unit took a different direction. Nicole and Heidi describe the authentic way this unit emerged:

> We were looking for a field trip site in our neighborhood and came upon ReVision House, a shelter for homeless women and children that was also an urban farm. There was so much cool stuff there—organic gardens, beekeeping, a greenhouse with a compost heating system, huge aquaculture tanks where they were raising tilapia, a farm stand. And they were really interested in developing more community connections. They were excited about using our visit to train the residents in being field trip leaders. At first we were concerned about the homeless aspect, but the more we thought about it, the more appropriate it seemed. Each year, there's usually a homeless child in each of our classrooms, and children always encounter homeless people on the street. Homelessness is a reality here, so it makes sense to look at it.

In the classroom, they prepared the children by reading Jeannie Baker's book *Home* (2004) and having children write about places where they feel safe. Then they talked about people without homes—people affected by Hurricane Katrina, people without jobs, people who are just arriving in a new place. The teachers constructed guided dramatic play scenarios for the students. In one scenario a family is in their home and the landlord comes to demand rent. Since the mother is unemployed, they can't stay and the children have to talk about where they might go. These conversations prepared the children for their visit to ReVision House.

The curriculum focused both on the food systems at the shelter and on what the shelter was doing to help women and children find new homes—job training, skill development in food production, money management. Heady stuff for first graders, but not completely beyond them.

There were many unanticipated outcomes. A child who was living in a shelter got the opportunity to open up and talk about her experiences; she was particularly interested in the differences between her shelter and ReVision House. On the street, children's attitudes towards homeless people changed. When walking by a homeless man sleeping by the subway station, the children, instead of making fun of him as they'd done in the past, encouraged each other to be quiet so they wouldn't wake him. Other children wondered why he didn't go to live in a shelter. And, noticing that the daycare center at ReVision House had a paucity of books, the children

Give Away Some of the Food You Grow

Figure 1.2 A page from the Twelve Things calendar
Calendar created by Nicole Weiner and Heidi Fessenden

decided to organize a book drive to collect books to give to the center. More recently, the teachers and children have created a calendar titled "Twelve Things You Can Do to Help Everyone Have Enough Healthy Food" based on what they've learned from spending time at ReVision House.

Through the use of a local resource, and through the teacher's willingness to confront an uncomfortable social justice issue, a unique curriculum project emerged that involved not only a focus on homelessness, but also writing, the creation of mini-aquaculture systems in the classroom, the preparation of pesto and apple sauce, and the organization of a classroom farmers' market where the pesto and apple sauce sold out in 20 minutes. Perhaps the most important outcome of the unit was the way it helped children gain a sense of how they can make a difference in their community.

Breathing and Exercising in Roxbury

The science curriculum at Young Achievers is able to take advantage of a variety of valuable neighborhood assets including the Boston Nature Center, the Arnold Arboretum, a nearby cemetery, and other pocket green spaces within walking distance of the school. Another feature of Jamaica Plain and Roxbury, however, is low air quality—which has become an additional topic for scientific inquiry. Only three or four minutes by foot from the school is the Forest Hills Subway Station, the terminus of the Orange Line and the site of a large Massachusetts Bay Transit Authority bus station. Heavy traffic on Washington Street a block away and idling buses at the Forest Hill Station generate an unhealthy brew of air pollutants. The students wondered, "Why is it that the air quality is worse in this neighborhood than in richer neighborhoods?"

Fourth- and fifth-grade teacher Michael Dower collaborated with Roxbury-based Alternatives for Community and Environment (ACE) and had his students research the effects of air pollution. Students interviewed ACE staff about the topic and then, with the support of technology educator Robert Lamothe, filmed related footage around Boston. The children next produced and distributed four 60-second public service announcements (PSAs) on the effects of pollution on the environment and on health. In producing the PSAs, students learned how to use specialized applications for professional audiovisual scripts and shot their PSAs against a blue screen, using a computer as a teleprompter. Michael Dower commented that "This was a great example of technology being a vehicle for the curriculum. The students were very motivated by being able to use the high-quality video camera and production software" (FOYA News, 2005, p. 4).

The next example is also grounded in the neighborhood, but in a different way. Last spring, one of the programs developed by after-school coordinator Evan

Figure 1.3 Fourth/fifth graders producing air quality public service announcements
Photo by Bo Hoppin

Franchini was a club for people interested in riding bikes. Just like access to green spaces, biking is one of those activities that is less available for inner-city children because there aren't many safe places to ride. To give students this opportunity, the Bike Club was created. Evan collected bikes from Bikes Not Bombs and other community organizations, fixed them, and then was working out where to go when he got a call from the executive director of Forest Hills Cemetery. A parent had contacted the director to tell him about the Bike Club, so he was calling Evan to encourage him to use the roads and paths in the cemetery. "It's a great, safe place for kids to bike," he offered. Evan had been worried about even asking. Most of the students had never ridden a bike before, and parents were thrilled with their children's opportunity to learn to ride a bike and get more exercise.

During the same period Evan had been working with a couple of fourth-grade boys with learning disabilities and behavioral problems. "One of them is probably in the office for something as we speak," speculated Evan. Both of the boys were overweight, and both needed things to keep them busy. Dwayne knew how to ride a bike; the other, Isaac, didn't. To make matters worse, Isaac's older brother continually ridiculed him because of his ineptitude. After a couple of practice sessions in which Evan and Dwayne worked with Isaac, he was ready to show off his new skill. While Evan's back was turned, Isaac decided to ride his bike past the whole middle school class, which at the time was standing out in front of the school. When Evan saw what was happening, he imagined catastrophe: Isaac crashing and all the older students pointing and laughing. Instead, Isaac rode his two-wheeler perfectly, and the whole middle school, led by Isaac's brother, gave him a big round of applause.

Both of these examples illustrate the diverse ways in which Young Achievers teachers are utilizing community resources to level the playing field and expand students' horizons.

Cleaning Up the School Environment and Beyond

Middle school students at Young Achievers are given multiple opportunities to exercise leadership at the school, in their neighborhood, and in and around Boston. At the same time, they are invited to consider how social justice and environmental issues play out on the global stage. Eighth-grade students, for example, must meet a graduation requirement for community activism by participating in the Making a Difference program. The program links them to a variety of local community organizations where they participate in or develop a project that has some positive impact on the school, neighborhood, or social issue. At the conclusion of the project they must complete a presentation that documents their activism and reflects on their experience and knowledge they've gained. Students interview with representatives from the organizations as a prerequisite to being chosen. Internships are available at organizations such as the Boston Nature Center, Bikes Not Bombs, the Boston Housing Authority, the Patriots' Trail Girl Scouts, the Robert F. Kennedy Children's Action Corps, and the Computer Learning Center.

One of the internships in the past few years led to the provocative "bathroom project." During a summer institute for teachers, administrators, community members, parents, and students coordinated by CO-SEED (the school improvement/community development collaboration with Antioch New England mentioned earlier), students were charged with brainstorming an action project to improve their school. As it turned out, students were dismayed with the condition of the bathrooms in the school, and rightfully so. The bathrooms weren't standing up to the intensive use brought on by the extended day program, and maintenance was casual. This is a great illustration of how, especially in cities, "place" is as much buildings as it is green space. And, in schools, a significant feature of "place" is bathrooms.

So the students launched into a campaign to get the bathrooms upgraded, to get them better maintained, and to get their fellow students involved in keeping them clean. The first step was a student-designed PowerPoint about the state of the bathrooms. It wasn't pretty. The PowerPoint laid out the problem in no uncertain terms:

- **The smell of the bathrooms is disgusting:** People do not like going to the bathroom unless they really have to go because of the smell. People leave urine in the toilet, so when the next person comes they can't use that stall. Some people miss the toilet and don't even clean up after themselves.
- **There is rust on the side of the walls:** The rust is on the wall and the soap dispenser. It is nasty and people don't want to use a bathroom with rust on the wall.
- **The doors are broken or there are no doors:** There are some stalls that don't have a door in the girls' bathroom, and that's taking away the privacy from that person when they have to go to the bathroom.

The students then laid out an action plan aimed at their classmates that they believed would help correct part of the problem:

What We Want From You!
We Want You to Help Keep the Bathrooms Clean:

- If you see someone messing up the bathrooms, don't be afraid to tell your teacher or the principal.
- If you notice that there are no paper towels, soap, or toilet paper, tell Mr. Cobb [the custodian].
- **CLEAN** after yourself: Wipe yourself. Flush the toilet. Wash your hands. Throw the paper towels away.

The PowerPoint was the student behavior prong of their three-pronged approach. The second prong involved working with the principal to get the custodial staff to take better care of the bathrooms. Lobbying the Boston Public Schools Facilities Department to renovate the bathrooms was the final prong, and the students were successful in getting the bathroom project moved up on the priority list for maintenance monies.

Leslye Grant, a community teacher at the school and the mother of a former eighth grader, described her daughter's engagement in the project:

She wrote all these letters and she showed me the big list of telephone numbers that the teachers gave her to call. Some days she'd be on the phone all day from 9:00 to 4:00. They'd give her the run-around, put her on hold. She said, "Sometimes I wanted to quit, but then I just knew someone else would have to do it." Finally they got some new paper towel holders, but that wasn't enough. They even went down to the BPS [Boston Public Schools] Facilities office a couple of times to get some action. And in the end, they fixed those bathrooms, because the students weren't going to stop until they saw results.

Now, my daughter's a student at Boston Arts Academy and she describes the other students saying, "There's three groups of students. One group's into partying and getting high; the other group's just into being with their boyfriend or girlfriend; the third group is into getting some education. I'm in the third group, and I just go to those other kids and say, "You just better wake up and take advantage of what this place has to offer." That's what my daughter got from being at Young Achievers. She's awake.

Seventh and eighth graders encounter another form of awakeness in their exploration of the link between environmental activism and social justice. Although this connection is implicit throughout their learning experiences as younger students, it is made explicit before they leave Young Achievers. As eighth graders they investigate the environmental degradation of three post-colonial countries in the developing world, Haiti, Kenya, and Sudan. Deforestation, in particular, is investigated. Forests in both Haiti (the home of one of their teachers) and Sudan have been devastated as a result of human activity. The result is growing impoverishment and misery as people are exposed to the consequences of deforestation: flooding, siltation of rivers and streams, diminished access to firewood, loss of wildlife, and falling water tables, among others.

Forests in Kenya had been similarly threatened, but women throughout that country, inspired by the work of Nobel Prize-winning activist Wangari Maathai, have for more than two decades planted millions of trees and reversed the trend that continues in Haiti and Sudan. Eighth graders participate in reforestation activities at the nearby Boston Nature Center and are given the chance to see themselves as members of the community of people worldwide who are involved in the work of restoring damaged ecosystems. As a graduation requirement, students must create a PowerPoint presentation about the relationship between deforestation and socioeconomic conditions that gets presented to a panel of community partners.

Another community-based partnership may at the outset seem unlike many other Young Achievers offerings; it, however, simply addresses issues of empowerment and action from another direction. This is the school's relationship with the firm of PricewaterhouseCoopers (PwC). PwC is one of the world's largest professional services organizations, providing assurance, tax, and advisory services. The partnership provides an excellent model of the usefulness of strong math skills.

PwC employees have volunteered for school fix-up events, as participants reviewing eighth-grade portfolios, and for weekly MCAS (Massachusetts Comprehensive Assessment System) tutoring programs. One of the central features of the partnership is Shadow Day, where seventh graders travel downtown and get paired one on one with a professional staff member. There students learn about filing taxes, interest income, and the way companies sell shares to stockholders. The partnership is coordinated by Ann Ulett in the Center for an Inclusive Workforce at PwC. She observed that:

> You can see how just a few hours can really change the students' perceptions about the accounting industry and increase their awareness of what it's like to work in a big building. We're really able to show the students what opportunities exist at PwC and act as role models for them.

Even some of the top brass are involved in the program. Michael Costello, one of the managing partners of the firm, noted:

> I think of PwC staff's time with Young Achievers as an investment in our future. Young Achievers teachers and parents, through their mentoring and encouragement, are enabling students to imagine a successful future and giving them the tools to realize their dreams. We are proud of our involvement and whatever small part we may play in students' development.
>
> (FOYA News, 2004, p. 5)

There's no contradiction between learning accounting and learning to advocate for better bathrooms or wiser forestry practices. In fact, the synergy across these endeavors is the beauty of what's going on at Young Achievers. The students are motivated to develop academic skills because they see the real-world application of what they're doing—their teachers are always providing opportunities to share, apply, and demonstrate their learning. And they're developing social consciousness and an understanding of how to make change in the world. These are the keys to improving their own lives and their own places. As principal Jinny Chalmers observed about the impact of place- and community-based education at her school, "We are invigorated about how the use of local places, organizations, and the environment has made the curriculum come alive in the past three years."

What's the Difference? Preliminary Results

Our conviction is that place- and community-based education is a much more holistic, vital, effective model for school improvement than the current No Child Left Behind, test-till-you-drop, paradigm. Academic achievement is important, and particularly achievable through this approach, but it is only part of the mission of schools. Schools should also be able to increase parent satisfaction, community improvement, environmental health, and social justice. Although we'll discuss impacts in greater depth later in the book, we'd like to briefly address ways in which place- and community-based education is making a difference at Young Achievers.

Academic Achievement

The 2007 evaluation completed at the conclusion of CO-SEED's formal involvement with the Young Achievers School could not yet point to a direct relationship between students' participation in place- and community-based learning activities and statistically significant gains in student achievement. The evaluators did note that:

> What can be said with confidence, however, is that the body of quantitative and qualitative evidence for Young Achievers (and other CO-SEED sites as well) suggests clearly that the reported benefits of CO-SEED and similar place-based, experiential learning programs can certainly occur without compromising performance on typical standardized assessments of student academic achievement.
>
> (Duffin and PEER Associates, 2007, p. 14)

Outcome measures from student surveys at Young Achievers that do demonstrate statistically significant gains include student satisfaction with the school, their belief that learning in place and community enhances their grades, their enthusiasm for learning, and their sense of connection to the community (Duffin and PEER Associates, 2007). Such gains suggest that over time this foundation will grow into the positive attitudes toward formal education and its implications for personal well-being that undergird school success.

Teachers at Young Achievers are able to point—right now—to the high quality and rigorous nature of student work produced for family night presentations, often scheduled at the end of major academic units. Although these examples of student work do not always translate into higher scores on standardized tests of academic achievement, they are reflective of forms of competence and learning that are meaningful to parents and students, themselves. As such, they affirm the value of academic effort. These culminating celebrations—with their combination of support and accountability—also give focus to student learning. When students know that their academic efforts will be displayed before their parents and other community members, they are motivated to do their best. In addition, these projects provide a tangible goal around which teachers can organize their daily and yearly curricular activities (Duffin and PEER Associates, 2007).

Change in Environmental Attitudes

With regular and recurrent outdoor experiences at Young Achievers, children's attitudes towards and comfort in the natural world has changed. Teachers recently commented:

> In the beginning, I think the kids felt like visitors. When walking around the forest, they were out of their element. Now they walk around like it's their forest. It's really amazing to me how they have gone from "This is somebody else's

space, this is not my space" to "This is my space. I know how to get around here. I know what lives here."

During the presentations about the community activism work, one student said that he used to walk home and throw things at birds. Then his job at the Boston Nature Center was to feed and interact with the birds. Now he says, "I sometimes have extra seeds in my pocket; I feed the pigeons." He's going to get the eighth-grade award for community activism because he's ... changed the way he looks at other things as well.

(Tso & Hill, 2006, p. 15)

Teachers' attitudes about nature were also affected by the program. Teachers who come from an urban environment and have had less exposure to nature get the biggest benefit. One community teacher shared this observation:

I noticed that the kids were going on these naturalist trips and digging up compost heaps so they could see all the stuff that was living there. Then one day, I showed up, and I was teaching and I had on my teacher clothes and teacher shoes and I didn't expect it. I'm thinking, "nature walk and observe nature," but it was hands on, and I thought, "Oh I'm gonna fall; I'm gonna mess up my clothes." I was just watching the kids, and they knew what certain things were. They looked at certain plants and they knew that trees were dying because of a particular disease. They saw how I was estranged from nature, so they started taking care of me. They said "Ms. X, you stay down there, don't go where we're going." I realize that they're not going to be the way that I am—even though we all grew up in the city. Their relationship with nature will be different than my relationship with nature because of these outdoor programs.

(Tso & Hill, 2006, p. 15)

This community teacher is now one of the leading enthusiasts for outdoor programming.

Parent Satisfaction

All public schools in Boston are part of a choice system allowing parents to request that their children attend any school. One indicator of the school's success is that Young Achievers is one of the most requested public schools in the city and often has the highest number of children on the district waiting list. In addition, Young Achievers has one of the higher attendance records, an indicator of parent and child investment in education. One result of the school's popularity is that it is moving to a much larger new school facility for the 2009/2010 school year so the school can accommodate more students.

Although it is commonly thought that city dwellers—like the community teacher described above—are alienated from the natural world, this stereotype neglects the environmental heritage of many newly arrived families in Boston. During a recent "cultural competency" assessment of the CO-SEED program at Young Achievers, two different parents commented:

As I explain to my daughters, we grew up in the West Indies where everything was outdoors. I said, "You need to know where the tomatoes came from."

I'm from the southern part of the U.S., and the geography is very different. I grew up able to roam around, to go from house to house, to go in the cow pasture with friends and race through the woods. My children, because we're in Boston, don't have that opportunity and what I see is them becoming more separate from the environment and not having a sense of the interrelation between who they are and the environment. In more traditional African-American or African culture, people view themselves as part of the environment. And I like your word "steward." We're stewards of the environment. I think those are important lessons for my kids.

(Tso & Hill, 2006, p. 14)

Educators have always assumed that the role of ecology education is to connect urban kids with the environment. But they've had it wrong in two ways. First, as the parent above says, in traditional African-American culture people already view themselves as part of the environment. Connecting students with their neighborhood environments is just reconnecting them with their roots. Moreover, the environment in the city isn't just birds, bunnies, and trees; it's also bathrooms, air quality, and neighborhood revitalization. It's about the school in the community and the community in the school. These are the connections that place- and community-based education strives to affirm and extend.

Laying the Foundation for Place- and Community-based Education

The Young Achievers School demonstrates a number of ways that educators have sought to make the wall between schools and their communities more permeable and to draw students into a sense of social membership and environmental responsibility. Although unique to the possibilities of the Jamaica Plain/Roxbury neighborhood where the school is located, these approaches could be implemented anywhere. Their adoption requires, more than anything else, a change in perspective and the recognition that educational standards and requirements can be met in a variety of ways, including the opportunity to engage in meaningful place- and community-based investigations and projects. By starting small and building on small successes, educators can grow themselves into this new perspective and do so in their own time. The elements described below include a collection of principles that can guide teachers anywhere in initiating their own opportunities, shaping their efforts to match the characteristics and possibilities of their schools and surrounding neighborhoods.

Bringing Community Members into the School

Creating the role of community teacher for individuals more typically viewed as aides has proven to be an especially creative way to bring people knowledgeable about local issues and resources into the Young Achievers School. This strategy honors local expertise and connections, especially when community teachers are given the opportunity to participate in professional development activities, including opportunities to teach other educators. The hiring of teacher aides from the local community and the incorporation of parent or community volunteers could potentially achieve the same end in other schools, although doing so would require teachers to rethink the role of these additional classroom adults and increase the instructional responsibilities of people whose work is generally supplemental rather than central to fundamental educational goals.

Forming Partnerships with Community Organizations

Establishing a long-term working relationship with an organization committed to ameliorating local social or environmental conditions can also provide teachers with an inroad to community members knowledgeable about issues and projects. This should be a pivotal element in all place- and community-based education school change initiatives. That the Young Achievers School is able to work with the Dudley Street Neighborhood Initiative, one of the more dynamic community development organizations in Boston, offers it a rich set of opportunities for service as well as a chance to interact with a group of committed social justice activists. Young Achievers also works with a broad collection of other groups, including Alternatives for Community and Environment, the Harvard Arboretum, Boston Nature Center, ReVision House, and Forest Hills Cemetery, among others. The formation of multiple partnerships is commonly encountered in schools that are striving to implement place- and community-based education approaches.

Initiating School/Community Planning Activities

When a group of partners has been brought together, CO-SEED's community vision-to-action forums can provide a venue for identifying important community needs that might dovetail with curricular needs. Finding community-based learning opportunities can be difficult for teachers whose regular responsibilities can be both compelling and time-consuming. Meetings that bring teachers and community people together to brainstorm and then refine action plans can alert them to exactly the kinds of outside-of-classroom projects that will be valued and strengthen the relationship between the school and the community. Not all place- or community-based learning activities need to have an action component, but, when some do, the rewards for students can become much more meaningful and public.

Grounding Curriculum in the Community

If place- or community-based learning opportunities are to become well established, they must be linked in a substantial rather than tangential way to the curriculum. Without this curricular validation, outside-of-classroom activities will be perceived as add-ons or as an instructional approach associated with a few idiosyncratic teachers, easily dispensed with in the face of new demands or changed priorities. Faculty at the Young Achievers School are working to create exactly the kind of intellectual foundation to their work that will make place- and community-based education central to the school's identity. Alicia Carroll and Bisse Bowman's year-long study of flora and fauna at Forest Hills Cemetery addresses important curricular goals while at the same time giving children the opportunity to get outside and study the natural world. Similarly, the investigations of local food production, homelessness, or the relationship between deforestation and poverty are associated with commonly agreed-upon academic goals and objectives. When experiences in the community become firmly connected to the way that teaching and learning happen in a school, then changes in personnel or district and state mandates will be less likely to disrupt the incorporation of the local into students' school experiences.

Allowing Teachers to Be Curriculum Designers

At Young Achievers, the role of the teacher is reconceptualized to include the design of innovative, new curriculum projects. One of the necessary characteristics of this approach is a curriculum that is finely suited to particular places. For this to happen, teachers will need to reach beyond pre-packaged curriculum to become involved in the creation of at least some of the lessons and units they present to their students. As with Carroll and Bowman's unit, this will require educators to draw upon their own creativity, intelligence, knowledge, and passion. Teachers need to become learners themselves. Rather than presenting themselves as experts, dominating conversations and taking primary responsibility for conveying content and skills, they work shoulder to shoulder with their students while sharing their more mature abilities as researchers, writers, and presenters.

Giving Students the Chance to Be Knowledge Creators

Similarly, students in schools that have adopted place- and community-based practices are no longer perceived to be primarily consumers of knowledge, but creators as well. Students are invited to observe the world, draw some conclusions, and then see how well their understandings match the understandings of others. After visiting a local farm and speaking with the primarily Jamaican farmworkers who worked there, students tackled a set of difficult questions aimed at exposing them to the political economy of food production in the United States. In a college sociology course, this might be expected. But, at Young Achievers, questions about job stability, home ownership, mobility, and origins create an opportunity for a kind of learning born from personal experience that is rare in most American schools. A similar kind of learning happens for students who investigate the topic of homelessness. In this instance, their experiences led to a shift in not only understanding but also empathy. Knowledge for students at Young Achievers becomes immediate and concrete rather than distant and abstract.

Nurturing Student Capacity and Voice

But this immediacy of knowledge—especially in a social setting characterized by poverty and discrimination—needs to be presented with care. Sobel (1996) has written about the danger of exposing children and youth to information about environmental problems without having first established a satisfying connection with the natural world and offered them opportunities to develop a sense of agency and voice. At Young Achievers this dilemma is addressed by encouraging students to take on activities that show them that they can make a difference. The bathroom clean-up proposal mirrors in a small way what adults in Roxbury have been doing with regard to the community as a whole for more than a generation. Along the same lines, during the 2008/2009 academic year a second-grade class investigated air quality and asthma rates, challenges faced by residents of Boston's Chinatown, the need for more academic learning space in their school, and the beneficial impact

Figure 1.4 Student radio production at WBUR studios
Photo by Bo Hoppin

of public murals. The teachers and students created oral presentations and then traveled to the WBUR studios to work with a producer and technicians to record segments for a long-running program entitled *Con Salsa*. For young students, the demands of radio production create authentic high academic expectations of their speech and reading skills. This cultivation of voice and agency is furthered through teachers' intentional effort to expose students to the work of change-makers like Nobel Peace Prize laureate Wangari Maathai and others. Students are shown how people like themselves can spark national or even global movements to address important environmental or social issues.

Linking Students to Adults outside the School

Finally, the boundary between school and community can be diminished by providing students with opportunities to interact with a broader range of adults outside the school. Participating in internships in businesses and governmental or non-governmental agencies gives young people a chance to see how they can link their own lives to purposes and causes bigger than their own immediate needs or desires. The Shadow Day that brings students to institutions like PricewaterhouseCoopers similarly demonstrates possibilities for community contributions that might otherwise go undiscovered or unacknowledged.

In a variety of ways, then, educators can take steps to extend learning experiences beyond the classroom into the life worlds of students. Not all of these elements need to be incorporated into a school's offerings, but, as more are, the deeper will be its connections to both place and community. By bringing community members into the school, forming partnerships with local organizations, initiating joint planning activities, grounding curriculum in local knowledge and issues, becoming curriculum designers, giving students the chance to create knowledge, nurturing their agency and voice, and linking children and youth to adults outside the school, it becomes possible for schools to become vital centers of community learning and activity, institutions worthy of both children's attention and adults' support. These elements will appear again and again in later chapters as we describe the work of educators in other schools across the United States.

Chapter 2

Place- and Community-based Education

Definitions and Antecedents

The Young Achievers Science and Mathematics Pilot School in Roxbury exemplifies many of the ways that teachers who have adopted place- and community-based education deal with curriculum development, teaching, and school–community collaboration. Eleven or twelve years ago when we began speaking and writing about the potentialities of this approach, we spoke primarily in hypotheticals. Since then, we have learned of, studied, and on occasion helped create or reshape schools where teachers have begun to diminish the barriers between classrooms and the school grounds and communities that lie beyond them. In the past, students and teachers at the Young Achievers School would have been a rare exception; today they are part of a growing vanguard of educators and young people who are demonstrating a powerful way to construct formal learning and link it to life outside the classroom.

In this chapter we will present definitions that practitioners and supporters of place- and community-based education are developing to guide teachers and school leaders interested in moving in this direction. We will also explore other educational approaches that have anticipated the possibilities of place- and community-based education. In many respects, this approach is a synthesis and extension of a broad range of educational innovations that have been developed throughout the preceding century. What sets place- and community-based education apart is the way that it strives to bring all of these strands together into a common framework for curriculum thinking and school design aimed at deepening students' connection to their communities in ways that make those communities better places to live.

Definitions

Place- and community-based education has much in common with other contemporary efforts to link schools more firmly to their communities—efforts such as civic education, contextual education, service learning, environmental education, and workplace education. We have chosen to hang our hats on place- and community-based education because it is the only term that allows for the inclusion of both the human and the more-than-human, something we believe is essential if educators are to help students grapple with the messy and cross-disciplinary nature of humankind's current dilemmas. There is no particular reason that service learning or civic education, for example, should address environmental concerns, although some projects may from time to time focus on natural resource issues or ecological restoration projects. Similarly, the disciplinary preoccupations of environmental educators can lead them to attend less to people's social and economic needs than the needs of other species. What place- and community-based education seeks to achieve is a greater balance between the human and non-human, ideally providing a way to foster the sets of understanding and patterns of behavior essential to create a society that is both socially just and ecologically sustainable.

Although we will later argue that this approach has been around as long as human beings have been inducting their children into local cultures, attention to place and local communities by contemporary educators is a moderately recent phenomenon. C.A. Bowers is perhaps one of the first people to write about the importance of the local in a chapter about bioregional education that concludes his 1987 volume *Elements of a Post-liberal Theory of Education*. Bioregionalists are noted for their belief that human cultures and economies should be grounded in the characteristics of particular places and communities. Smith followed up on this theme in an article published in 1993 in the *Whole Earth Review* entitled "Shaping Bioregional Schools." David Orr refers explicitly to the importance of place in "Place and Pedagogy," a chapter in his 1992 book *Ecological Literacy*, and devotes significant attention to this issue in *Earth in Mind* (1994). There he argues that "the preservation of place is essential to the preservation of the world" and goes on to say that:

> A world that takes its environment seriously must come to terms with the root of its problems, beginning with the place called home. This is not a simple-minded return to a mythical past but a patient and disciplined effort to learn, and in some ways, to relearn the arts of inhabitation. These will differ from place to place, reflecting various cultures, values, and ecologies. They will, however, share a common sense of rootedness in a particular locality.
>
> (Orr, 1994, p. 170)

The belief that being rooted has value and deserves the attention of educators is one of the things that sets place- and community-based education apart from many other contemporary school reforms that focus primarily on the cultivation of individual talents and career trajectories rather than on the benefits that individuals might bring to their communities and regions.

In 1998, the Orion Society published *Stories in the Land: A Place-based Environmental Education Anthology*, the first time the term "place-based education" appeared on the cover of a book. That same year, rural educators Paul Nachtigal and Toni Haas's volume *Place Value: An Educator's Guide to Good Literature on Rural Lifeways, Environments, and Purposes of Education* was published by the ERIC Clearinghouse on Education and Rural Schools, extending the definition of place to something more than the environment. The language of "place" was clearly beginning to insert itself into the discourse of educators.

At about the same time, Nachtigal and Haas became co-presidents and David Orr a board member of one of the earliest U.S. proponents of place-based education, the Rural School and Community Trust. Started as the Annenberg Rural Challenge in the mid-1990s, this organization distributed in its first five years approximately 50 million dollars to educators and community organizers in rural towns and villages across the United States. The Rural Trust's definition continues to inform many of the best place-based educational initiatives in the United States.

> Place-based education is learning that is rooted in what is local—the unique history, environment, culture, economy, literature, and art of a particular place. The community provides the context for learning, student work focuses on community needs and interests, and community members serve as resources and partners in every aspect of teaching and learning. This local focus has the power to engage students academically, pairing real-world relevance with intellectual rigor, while promoting genuine citizenship and preparing people to respect and live well in any community they choose.
>
> (Rural School and Community Trust, 2005)

This definition points to two critical aspects of place-based education. The first involves its applicability to all disciplines. Place can be drawn upon to teach any subject area. This approach can also encourage educators to look beyond the language and methods of their own fields to explore problems and projects that open the possibility of cross-disciplinary dialogue. A second important aspect of place-based education illuminated by this definition involves the role played by community members in the delivery of education to the young. Rather than seeing teaching and learning as being located primarily within the school, place-based education requires potentially all mature citizens to take responsibility for inducting children and youth into the obligations and possibilities of adulthood. Agencies and workplaces become potential sites for student learning, and adults who possess expertise in a multiplicity of areas can be invited to share their knowledge and skills with young people as well as their peers.

In his work with schools throughout New England, co-author David Sobel has crafted a definition that provides additional insight into what place-based education involves. For Sobel,

> Place-based education is the process of using the local community and environment as a starting point to teach concepts in language arts, mathematics, social studies, science, and other subjects across the curriculum. Emphasizing hands-on, real-world learning experiences, this approach to education increases academic achievement, helps students develop stronger ties to their community, enhances students' appreciation for the natural world, and creates a heightened commitment to serving as active, contributing citizens.
>
> (Sobel, 2004, p. 7)

Seeing place-based education as a starting rather than ending point—as Sobel suggests here—can reduce the chance that focusing on the local will encourage parochialism and a disregard for the national or global. Once children have had an opportunity to learn more about things with which they are already familiar, they can then be directed to phenomena that are more distant and abstract. To some extent, the K–12 curriculum in many schools is already organized around this principle—with the local being considered most frequently in the early elementary years. What a K–12 place-based educational approach can foster is an incorporation of the local throughout a child's school experience, so that older students can bring their increased maturity, creativity, and skill to bear on the study of issues that are of importance to their own families and neighbors. With its incorporation of hands-on learning experiences, place-based education also gives students from kindergarten through high school the chance to apply what they are learning to significant community problems.

This opportunity to participate in efforts to address important local issues is central to a definition developed of community-based learning by the Coalition for Community Schools. Drawing on contributions from organizations that run the gamut from the National Environmental Education and Training Foundation to the National Service Learning Partnership, their definition of "community-based learning" is in many respects comparable to place-based education in its concerns and dimensions:

> [C]ommunity-based learning helps students acquire, practice, and apply subject matter knowledge and skills. At the same time, students develop the knowledge, skills, and attributes of effective citizenship by identifying and acting on issues and concerns that affect their own community. When implemented thoughtfully, these strategies create a pedagogy of engagement. Students invest time and attention and expend real effort because their learning has meaning and purpose.
>
> (Melaville, Berg, & Blank, 2006, p. 3)

The promotion of citizenship has been an element in all three of the definitions presented here. The definition from the Coalition for Community Schools emphasizes even more strongly the creation of learning opportunities that allow students to apply what they encounter in disciplinary courses to local issues and concerns, and the meaning and purpose that can inhere in these activities. Not all place-based educational experiences necessarily involve problem-solving or action, but those that do can have a profound impact on young people's sense of self-worth and efficacy.

In this volume, we have chosen to conjoin place- and community-based education to emphasize even more clearly our commitment to both the human and the natural environments in which children and their teachers live. For us, place- and community-based education is characterized by a focus on local knowledge, issues, and phenomena and is potentially relevant to all subject areas. It seeks to expand the range of adults who can serve as instructors and mentors and to build strong collaborative relationships between community members and their schools. Place- and community-based educators see learning about the local as a starting rather than ending point, but a starting point that remains significant throughout a child's—or an adult's—educational experiences. Finally, place- and community-based education often engages students in projects that require them to apply their knowledge, skills, and energy to community issues or problems. In doing so, it demonstrates to young people the value of their own efforts and helps cultivate a taste for civic participation.

Antecedents

In many respects, it is important to acknowledge there is nothing new about place- and community-based education. Those who practice it simply do what adults concerned about inducting children into membership in their surrounding social and natural communities have done for millennia: they provide opportunities for the young to engage in the common life of older and more experienced people. Even as late as the 1970s, Tlingit residents of Sitka, Alaska encouraged their children to visit adults in their villages to learn about the activities they performed. Children would spend time with the fisherman, the bentwood box maker, the cook, the storyteller, the herbalist. If a child came back a number of times to the same person, the adult would give him or her simple tasks to complete. As the child continued to return, he or she would gradually acquire the knowledge base and skills that gave the adult his or her unique position in the community. In this way, the culture replicated itself from one generation to the next without forcing anyone into tasks to which he or she was not attracted.

Dewey and the School's Isolation from Life

Even among Euro-Americans, similar approaches to cultural transmission remained common throughout the nineteenth and early twentieth centuries, when formal schooling was little more than a supplement to the informal educational experiences from which children learned how to support themselves as farmers, tradespeople, homemakers, or industrial workers. As access to desirable jobs has become tied to high school and now college graduation, however, these contextually rich educational settings have given way to classrooms where learning is typically divorced from the lives children lead when they aren't in school. In the late 1890s John Dewey warned of this emerging disconnect in *School and Society* and sought in his own educational approach to recover the relationship between formal learning and community life that had been disrupted in most schools:

> From the standpoint of the child, the great waste in the school comes from his inability to utilize the experiences he gets outside the school in any complete and free way within the school itself; while, on the other hand, he is unable to apply in daily life what he is learning at school. That is the isolation of the school—its isolation from life. When the child gets into the schoolroom he has

to put out of his mind a large part of the ideas, interests, and activities that predominate in his home and neighborhood. So the school, being unable to utilize this everyday experience, sets painfully to work, on another tack and by a variety of means, to arouse in the child an interest in school studies.

(Dewey, 1959, pp. 76–77)

During Dewey's tenure at the University of Chicago, he and his colleagues created a model of an educational process that sought to immerse children in those fundamental community activities from which the contemporary academic disciplines have emerged. Using such perennial vocations as gardening, cooking, carpentry, and clothing manufacture, students at the Laboratory School were drawn into the forms of problem-solving and investigation that led to the invention of biology, mathematics, chemistry, and art. And by transforming the school into a small, interactive community, Dewey was able to induct students into the kinds of thinking and decision-making that underlie the disciplines of economics and political science. Students at the Lab School learned not for some future purpose but to be able to address issues that were compelling to them in the present, issues that were comparable to those they saw adults encounter in the broader society beyond the school.

Kilpatrick's Project Method

In the years following World War I, William Heard Kilpatrick, one of Dewey's colleagues after he became a professor at Columbia University's Teachers College, proposed the project method as a more open-ended way to connect formal education to children's lives. Central to Kilpatrick's definition of this approach is his assertion that it should consist of "wholehearted purposeful activity proceeding in a social environment" (Kilpatrick, 1918, p. 320). He argued that projects most likely to inspire deep learning were those chosen by individual students or groups of students and not simply handed to them by their teachers; effective projects necessarily reflected students' purposes. Such projects must furthermore be worthy of students' time and attention and important in some way for the life of both the individual and others around him or her. Jack Shelton, a leading place-based educator in Alabama, currently calls such learning *consequential* (Shelton, 2005). Kilpatrick contended "that wholehearted purposeful activity in a social situation as the typical unit of school procedure is the best guarantee of the child's native capacities now too frequently wasted" (1918, p. 334). He believed that learning in this manner would serve as effective preparation for life in a democratic society. Although Kilpatrick and his approach to project learning remain little more than minor topics in the history of American education, his vision and the rationale behind it have remained in play in at least some U.S. schools ever since.

Counts' and Rugg's Social Meliorism

Later in the 1930s, the work of two other Teachers College professors anticipated additional dimensions of place- and community-based education. In the midst of the Great Depression, George Counts (1932) delivered a keynote speech to the annual meeting of the Progressive Education Association in which he asked whether schools should dare build a new social order. He answered his own question in the affirmative, asserting that educators must play a role in extending a vision of America in which the lives of common people are made physically easier and at the same time ennobled. Counts' fellow professor at Teachers College, Harold Rugg (1939), took this vision of social reconstruction seriously, and for the next decade wrote curriculum and textbooks that made it possible for teachers across the country to draw their students into exactly the kinds of social analysis that Counts called for. These volumes stressed the interdependence of industrial nations and encouraged the development of a more cooperative society in the United States; by the late 1930s volumes from Rugg's textbook series were used in approximately half of the social studies classrooms in the country (Riley & Stern, 2003–2004). Although not explicitly focused on local issues or place in any way, Counts' and Rugg's work does point to the way that schools could potentially serve as a vehicle for problem-solving and analysis aimed at social improvement.

Service Learning

Such direct involvement in local social problems can be seen in the history of the service learning movement in the United States, another antecedent of place- and community-based education. Although generally more focused on action than analysis, service learning has sought to involve young people in work explicitly aimed at enhancing community and social conditions. From the late nineteenth century on, educators and social philosophers such as Dewey and William James have encouraged community service as means to engage young people in meaningful activities. As early as 1915, folk schools in Appalachia based on the Scandinavian model became two- and four-year colleges where students combined work, service, and learning as part of their degree programs. Service, itself, received national recognition and support through the creation of the Peace Corps and VISTA (Volunteers in Service to America) in the 1960s, and a White House Conference on Youth in 1971 emphasized the value of linking service to learning. Throughout the 1970s and 1980s, community service programs became more common in U.S. schools, and in 1990 the U.S. Congress passed the National and Community Service Act, legislation that authorized grants to schools to support service learning (National Service Learning Clearinghouse, 2007). This widespread adoption of service learning has without question been extraordinarily valuable, although the movement has yet to become widely integrated into the primary course requirements students must fulfill to graduate. More often than not, service learning is extra-curricular rather than curricular, an additional requirement or special activity instead of a substantial part of students' educational experience. It connects students to their communities without intentionally deepening their understanding of the unique characteristics and dynamics of their home places.

Nature and Environmental Education

The construction of this deeper understanding of place has been a defining characteristic of the work of some environmental educators, especially those who are inclined to take their students beyond the classroom into the field and community. The roots of environmental education can be located in the late-nineteenth- and early-twentieth-century nature study movement that grew out of the work of Wilbur Jackman (1904) at the University of Chicago and Liberty Hyde Bailey (1915) and Anna Botsford Comstock (1986) at Cornell. All encouraged public school teachers to make use of the local environment as a basis for scientific investigations, arguing that an approach that included object lessons and direct experience was superior to one limited to textbook learning. Although nature study has waxed and waned in its prevalence in U.S. classrooms, it has continued to be an element in the work of at least some teachers. Conservation and outdoor education later in the twentieth century also sought to connect students to local issues and places. Then, in the 1960s and 1970s, environmental education emerged as a legitimate field of study, encouraging a resurgence of nature study coupled with a new focus on environmental problem-solving. Although courses in environmental studies can be restricted as much to textbooks and distant issues as any academic subject, it is not uncommon for teachers to engage students in learning activities that are grounded in the local, and that combine academic investigations with service projects located in the community.

Cultural Journalism

Another recent antecedent to place- and community-based education can be found in the work of language arts and social studies teachers who have adopted the practices of cultural journalists, anthropologists, and historians. An outgrowth of the work of educators associated with the Foxfire project that took the nation by storm in the 1970s and 1980s, this approach focuses on involving students in fine-grained investigations of the lives of people in their own communities, both in the present and in the past. The Foxfire journals and books explored the unique characteristics of Appalachian culture in northern Georgia. They inspired the development of similar journals and books across the United States and became the basis for an educational model that affected hundreds if not thousands of teachers through Foxfire training institutes; these institutes continue through the present, albeit in a much reduced format. Although the great majority of Foxfire activities centered around the collection of oral histories, under the leadership of Hilton Smith and others the program also investigated contemporary community issues and involved students in local decision-making processes. In this, it set the stage for place- and community-based educators like those at the Young Achievers School who invite their students to look critically at their own communities and uncover issues—like air pollution or homelessness—and then participate with others to rectify these problems.

Local Entrepreneurialism

One final antecedent to place- and community-based education involves efforts to deal with not only environmental or social issues but also economic. Critical to the long-term well-being of any community are the business and employment opportunities that are available to local citizens. Organizations like REAL Enterprises— Rural Entrepreneurship through Action Learning—have since the mid-1970s been providing training for secondary and now elementary students aimed at helping young people gain the skills necessary to create their own businesses so that they do not have to be dependent for employment on jobs created by others (information retrieved on January 16, 2007 at http://www.cfed.org/focus.m?parentid=32&siteid =341&id=341). They also are an important antecedent to place-based education. Over the 30 years that it has been in existence, REAL Enterprises has extended its range of operations to urban areas and to community colleges and community development organizations. Like many of the other educational approaches discussed above, REAL Enterprises emphasizes the importance of experiential learning. By providing young people and others with the skill sets required to operate successful businesses, start-up loans to get those businesses going, and support for novice entrepreneurs, REAL Enterprises has given invaluable aid to people in low-income and sometimes isolated communities where opportunities for economic development are not obvious.

Reintegrating Children into their Worlds

In the Preface, we suggested that place- and community-based education is a way of thinking about the school's role in society that involves using rural, urban, and suburban communities and environments as the starting place for teaching the academic disciplines. It requires a reformulation of the school's relationship to other social institutions and people, and a reimagining of what education might be. In contemporary societies, schools have become the equivalent of age-based ghettos in which children are removed from the lives of adults as well as the lives of the other-than-human beings that make up their world. Dewey's concern about the separation of the school from the life of the child is as much a worry today as it was a century ago. Place- and community-based education as seen in places like the Young Achievers Science and Mathematics Pilot School seeks to create a bridge between the classroom and students' lives that will make their learning both natural and meaningful, natural in that it emerges not so much from force and direction as from curiosity, and meaningful because it is connected to activities valued by both students and those they love.

The common school arose in part because of a perceived need on the part of community leaders and policymakers to get immigrant children off the streets and to socialize them to mainstream American expectations and values. When the communities from which those children came retained their vitality and the environs in which many lived, their open spaces, connections to children's social and natural worlds could still be maintained. As American communities have become more attenuated and the natural world more distant and inaccessible, our society runs the risk of losing its coherence and its understanding of natural limits. American children furthermore run the risk of losing a sense of what it means to be a member of a larger social collective responsible to its members and responsible for its actions. In the following chapter we will consider in more detail why it seems especially important to revive place- and community-based education during this moment of our national experience.

Chapter 3

Why Worry about the Local in the Era of No Child Left Behind?

A Rationale for Place- and Community-based Education

Despite the degree to which an education that focuses on place and the local resonates intuitively, it is important to acknowledge that public education has from the beginning been more concerned about diminishing community ties than strengthening them. Public schools from the 1800s through the present have been positioned to serve other purposes (Church & Sedlak, 1976). In the United States and elsewhere, state-supported education arose to redirect children's attention away from the local to the national and now the international. Loyalties to specific regional, ethnic, or religious groups competed with loyalties to emerging nation states and needed to be made secondary if national governments and commercial markets were to become the primary organizing structures of modern societies.

For more than a half-century, schools have furthermore been seen as the key vehicle for developing a society's human capital, the skills and knowledge required to participate successfully in modern economies (Inkeles & Smith, 1974). In the post-World War II era the dramatic expansion of post-secondary education in countries like the United States was accompanied by an equally dramatic increase in economic productivity and wealth. American innovations in science and technology helped to contribute to the United States' emergence as an undisputed superpower. Spurred by the role of weapons research and development during the previous world war as well as the emerging space race, the National Defense Education Act in the 1950s recognized the important role that the development of intellectual skills must play in the future military security of the country. This led to the willingness on the part of Congress to invest federal resources in what up to that point had been a locally supported and controlled enterprise.

When the U.S. economy began to be threatened by German and Japanese competition in the 1980s, policymakers more explicitly argued that educational achievement in the United States was tied to the country's ability to maintain its position of economic dominance, as well. Drawing freely upon military metaphors, *A Nation at Risk* (National Commission on Excellence in Education, 1983) argued that student school performance in the U.S. did not measure up to the performance of their peers in countries that were competing for the same markets. Their failure and the failure of their schools and teachers were said to be jeopardizing America in the same way that a failed defense policy would endanger the country. From this perspective arose the standards and accountability movement with the advent of widespread student testing and school evaluation, and with this, the further diminishment of local authority over the nation's schools. Concerns about the competitiveness of U.S. workers continue to dominate conversations about education, although with the 2001 reauthorization of the Elementary and Secondary Education Act, No Child Left Behind, the human capital focus has broadened to include a concern about the performance of diverse populations, marrying the rhetoric of the Civil Rights Movement to economic security.

Early in the history of the common schools, the requirements of nation building thus led to the development of educational experiences divorced from the life students encountered outside the school. In the past half-century, the requirements of international military and economic competition have resulted in the same thing: a preoccupation with the preparation of individuals whose central loyalties are not to their families and the communities into which they are born but to the nation state and a competitive job market. To some extent, an institution capable of muting group loyalties and patterns of mutual support was necessary to induct young people into the requirements of industrial societies where economic welfare for both individuals and communities is tied not so much to the work of families as to individual participation as wage earners in business and other enterprises owned or controlled by others. In a country like the United States made up of immigrants from diverse ethnic and religious groups, the replacement of narrower sources of personal identity with a set of values and expectations aimed at transcending such differences also seemed essential as a preventative to the forms of inter-group strife that still remain the stuff of daily news throughout the world.

This is the institutional and policy environment with which advocates of place- and community-based education must contend. Why, given these demands and realities, should educators or the communities that support them be willing to entertain an approach that varies so significantly from what schools up to this point in the nation's history have been? And, given the limited success of comparable efforts such as those described in the previous chapter, why is there any greater likelihood that the implementation of place- and community-based education will become more widespread now?

The answer to these questions is fourfold. First, educational practice largely divorced from children's direct experience of the world is failing to engage large numbers of students. Second, the absence of an institution aimed at drawing young people into the experience of social affiliation is resulting in a form of civic withdrawal that threatens the long-term viability of democratic institutions. Third, the sustainability of contemporary societies requires the development of an ethic of environmental stewardship that places the welfare of future generations and natural systems over short-term profits. Finally, the economic, social, and environmental challenges of the twenty-first century are unlike those known in any earlier period of human experience. Addressing them will require a multiplicity of diverse responses from people where they live rather than from large centralized institutions unable to adapt with enough speed or specificity to changing economic, political, or environmental conditions.

Giving Young People a Reason to Invest Themselves in Learning

Widespread public and political concerns about student achievement speak to the degree to which many young people are failing to learn at levels seen as desirable by either policymakers or their communities. After two decades of the accountability movement and the adoption of state testing standards, however, low performance on the part of a significant proportion of American students continues to be a national preoccupation. The problem of student motivation that John Dewey identified in *School and Society* is rarely addressed in either public pronouncements or policies. The theory of human learning encountered in most contemporary reform efforts appears to be dominated by the belief that fear of failure and institutional censure will lead teachers to do a better job and students to apply themselves to their studies.

Nearly everything about the No Child Left Behind Act is punitive in nature. Schools are held up for public scrutiny and then derided in the press for their inability to meet goals set by others. Teachers are condemned by their administrators if their students do not display "adequate yearly progress," and administrators are fired or moved to less desirable buildings if their schools consistently fail to measure up. With regard to students, they face a battery of examinations from kindergarten forward that inevitably lead them to compare and evaluate their own performance to the performance of others. Early on, some come to see their test scores as indicators of superior capacity and intellect, while many others are led to believe that they possess fundamental inadequacies that will prevent them from ever enjoying the benefits of social and economic success (Wilkinson & Pickett, 2009). This situation is not unique to schools at the beginning of the twenty-first century, but it has been exacerbated by No Child Left Behind and the standards movement that preceded it.

Many students who define themselves as losers eventually resign themselves to their own exclusion from the school's and society's rewards despite repeated messages about the tie-in between educational attainment and earning power (Sennett & Cobb, 1972). That resignation manifests itself in their unwillingness to invest attention or energy in the hard work of learning. Recent meta-analyses of research regarding student engagement suggest that approximately 40 to 60 percent of U.S. students are minimally involved in their education (Blum, 2005). It is not surprising that other studies suggest that approximately 30 percent of students fail to graduate from high school in four years (Barton, 2005). The proportion of Latino, Native American, and Black students who do not graduate on time is even higher. Although many of these students will earn a diploma or complete a G.E.D. before they are 24 (Bracey, 2006), this rate of four-year non-completion clearly demonstrates the extent to which a vast population of young people does not perceive formal education to be in their own best interest.

In the late 1980s, co-author Gregory Smith participated in a U.S. Department of Education-supported study of programs that were experiencing some level of success in helping students who were potential dropouts to graduate from high school

(Wehlage, Rutter, Smith, Lesko, & Fernandez, 1989). What this research team's investigation of 14 schools and programs across the country demonstrated is that an agenda based upon constant evaluation, fear, and exclusion has little in common with the kinds of educational practice capable of actually re-engaging otherwise alienated youth to the demands of formal learning. What did characterize successful programs was a willingness to welcome young people into a community where adults and adolescents cared for and supported one another, and where teachers constructed learning activities whose meaning and purpose were evident to students.

The Media Academy at Fremont High School in Oakland, California was one of the most successful of these programs. Initially the only small school-within-a-school in a large urban high school that primarily served Black and Latino students, it more recently has become one of several separate academies all located in the Fremont building. The Media Academy was created in the mid-1980s in an effort to give low-performing but promising adolescents a chance to experience what it would be like to work as media professionals. At the time it was started, similar "partnership academies" with different occupational foci—electronics, health sciences, banking, catering—were being established in other schools across California. The academy model stressed the formation of partnerships with local businesses or agencies, paid and unpaid internships, the integration of professional issues across as much of the curriculum as possible, and the cultivation of mutually supportive relations among all academy participants. The model—with its effort to diminish the boundary between schools and communities—displays many of the characteristics of place- and community-based education. A central aim of the partnership academies was to encourage as many graduates as possible to go on to community college or university in the pursuit of professional possibilities they might not have otherwise imagined for themselves. For students in academies that focused on electronics, graduates were often hired for higher than entry-level positions in the local computer industry.

An especially notable feature of the Media Academy was the way that students were inducted into a peer culture in which intellectual work was valued. For many of them, this was a new experience. In the Media Academy, ninth graders saw juniors and seniors fulfilling leadership roles tied to the production of the school's newspaper, yearbook, and a community newspaper. Older students served as mentors for the younger, teaching them the ins and outs and expectations tied into the creation of quality writing and quality publications. One of the reasons that the Media Academy has worked as well as it has is the result of its teachers' willingness to allow students to pursue topics that are of importance to them, even if these topics sometimes run counter to the positions and beliefs of school administrators. Students believe that the publications are their own, and that there is a place for their voices and concerns in the issues they choose to investigate. The result has been higher grades, higher graduation rates, and a greater likelihood that students pursue post-secondary education. For students at the Media Academy, academic achievement results not from fear and a steady diet of academic testing but from the opportunity to participate with peers and supportive adults in meaningful and authentic learning experiences valued by themselves and others.

Place- and community-based education programs like the Media Academy are premised on a theory of human learning that is very different from the one that seemingly underlies the standards movement and No Child Left Behind. Rather than assuming that learners are primarily motivated by external controls and judgments, teachers focus more on the creation of attractive opportunities: the chance to explore personally meaningful issues, to join a high-energy group of committed peers, to develop unique talents and contribute them to group efforts, to gain broader recognition from school and community members, to gain skills that could potentially be translated into eventual employment, and to have a chance to make a positive contribution to their school, neighborhood, and city. Students' own curiosity and desire for purposeful activity, social membership, and the experience of competence become the central motivators for learning. An education grounded in place and community is connected to what is important in students' own lives. In such schools and classrooms, educators do not have to resort "to other means," as Dewey noted, to gain the involvement of young people in the tasks and opportunities of learning.

Growing Social as Well as Human Capital

The development of human capital is a perfectly legitimate educational aim. Varied talents cultivated to a level of competence are essential to the maintenance of human communities. The difference between the way that these talents are nourished in many pre-industrial societies and our own is that, instead of being perceived as the means by which individuals support the long-term welfare of their families and neighbors, talents are seen as the primary vehicle by which individuals vie with others for the rewards of a competitive labor market. Social patterns characterized by mutuality, trust, and cooperation are replaced by others that focus more on individual striving, independence, and competition. None of these attributes in themselves is necessarily bad. There is without question a place for the kind of individual striving, independence, and competition that have become so central to life in the United States. The problem is that, when these attributes come to dominate human interaction, societies can become less able to support the needs of all of their members and fail to help their citizens experience the meaning and sense of purpose associated with social affiliation.

Over the past few decades, American sociologists have directed their attention to this issue. In the mid-1980s bestseller *Habits of the Heart*, Robert Bellah and his associates (Bellah, Madsen, Sullivan, and Swidler, 1985) chronicle the impact of the American preoccupation with individual success and mobility. The pursuit of opportunity and happiness defined personally rather than collectively has brought with it the growing isolation of American citizens and a diminished commitment to the welfare of others outside immediate families and lifestyle-oriented communities. In *Bowling Alone* (2000), Robert Putnam documents a similar phenomenon, focusing on the declining importance of informal groups that once brought Americans together with people who would have otherwise remained strangers. It was exactly such groups that the nineteenth-century French commentator Alexis de Tocqueville (1904) saw as the most distinctive and promising element of social and political life during the first decades of the American democratic experiment.

In a subsequent volume, *Better Together* (2003), Putnam and Feldstein describe numerous examples from contemporary U.S. communities where people have joined together to address common issues in ways not dissimilar from what de Toqueville had observed more than a century and a half before. They suggest that underlying the success of these various efforts is a kind of broad interpersonal trust they call social capital. This trust stands in contrast to the competitive individualism celebrated in contemporary economic institutions; it is generally disregarded as an externality by classical economic theory. Democracies, however, depend on the widespread diffusion of social capital throughout the body politic. Without it, citizens withdraw from community life and fail to invest the time and energy essential to maintain democratic institutions.

One of the chapters in *Better Together* is devoted to a description of an after-school program in Waupun, Wisconsin. Two teachers interested in engaging their students in community service activities became connected to a national organization called the Do Something League that supports and encourages educators and activists in their efforts to link young people to meaningful work in their neighborhoods and towns. The teachers asked their sixth-grade students about community problems or issues they would like to address. After listing a variety of options during a brainstorming session, students zeroed in on a railroad crossing in the center of town they felt was especially dangerous. They approached city leaders about working on this issue and learned that adults had been attempting to rectify this situation for years. Undeterred, students wrote a letter to the state's railroad commissioner, asking him to investigate the crossing. He did. Although he indicated that the level of traffic at the crossing did not warrant the expense of a signal, he did authorize funding to improve its visibility.

Encouraged by their partial success, students decided to take on another issue. The children of Waupun enjoyed playing in two parks located on the Fox River, a city park in town and a county park a few miles away. They felt that a bike path between the two parks would improve their recreational opportunities. When they began the project, the only way they could get to the county park on their own required a bike ride on a dangerous county road. Once they started pursuing this topic, students learned that county officials had also been attempting to create such a bike path and had been granted easements by all but one property owner along the proposed route. The students prepared a presentation and arranged to meet with the property owner, who found their plan persuasive and agreed to allow the path to be built across his land. The county was then able to seek funding for the path, which has now been constructed.

Projects like these as well as the efforts of students at the Young Achievers School in Boston to address air pollution issues and homelessness demonstrate to children and youth the value of collaboration and civic involvement. They come to see that joining with others to address community problems can lead to positive results and that such efforts are worth their time and energy. Such processes also take them beyond their own immediate family and friends and engage them in conversations with agency and civic leaders. These experiences show them that their ideas have merit and that they possess the capacity to voice their concerns in ways that are capable of gaining the ear of decision-makers. Alienation is commonly associated with the experience of political disenfranchisement. When people feel as if their actions are incapable of improving the quality of their lives, withdrawal from civic involvement is not far behind. Creating opportunities that allow children to become change agents in their own communities is likely to inspire a taste for such involvement and encourage the formation of the social capital and sense of common identity so essential to the maintenance of a democratic society.

Inspiring the Desire to Steward and Preserve

In addition to social affiliation, human happiness is also often tied to a deep sense of relationship to a particular place. When they are anchored in both human and natural communities, people can experience a sense of contentment, meaning, and purpose that has become increasingly rare in modern societies. Nature writer Barry Lopez in his long essay *The Rediscovery of North America* (1990) talks about the absence of this relationship throughout much of the European settlement of this continent. According to Lopez, the resources of the New World tended to be seen by many of its new residents as little more than means for the achievement of personal wealth. Rather than being treated as a home for oneself and one's descendants for generations to come, the land was treated as a resource mine.

Unable to find an English word to describe a person's apolitical affiliation with place, Lopez adopts the Spanish term *querencia* to capture what he has in mind. *Querencia* denotes an abiding love for a place that leads to its care and stewardship as well as a desire to assure its beauty and integrity for generations to come. Lopez asserts that a mature and sustainable culture will reemerge in North America when the continent's more recent inhabitants realize and then act upon this understanding. By connecting children to their geographic as well as social locales, place- and community-based education holds out the promise of inducing *querencia* in addition to the forms of interpersonal trust associated with social capital.

As with social capital, *querencia* is not entirely foreign to the American experience. Its generation does not require the introduction of something new to our common life but the restoration of an orientation to place and the natural world that has become secondary to the demands of a market society. In his novel *The Big Rock Candy Mountain*, Western writer Wallace Stegner (1957) identifies two character traits that can be observed throughout the European settlement of North America. Those who primarily displayed one of these traits he called the boomers; the other, the stickers. Boomers included people who were always questing for the next economic opportunity that would allow them to strike it rich. They were and are the people who, drawing on Lopez's analysis, see this continent as little more than a resource mine; staying put in one place would have prevented them from fulfilling their vision of economic comfort, privilege, and security. In contrast, stickers were people interested in putting down roots in one place and creating their wealth and security through sustained labor and human interaction.

Although poet Gary Snyder (1980) argues that one of the most radical things a person concerned about contemporary environmental and social issues can do is to stay put, the kind of affiliation with the natural world that leads to responsible stewardship called for by Lopez is not necessarily an outcome of rootedness. Locally based ranchers, farmers, fishermen, and loggers have engaged in practices that have also resulted in environmental degradation even though they may feel a sense of intergenerational responsibility to the land. *Querencia* requires the willingness to limit short-term profits for long-term sustainability and is reflective of an orientation to the world that is tied more to a love of place and people than any form of economic calculus. Its enactment does not demand the elimination of economic concerns—concerns that must be honored if fundamental human needs are to be met. As with the tension between social affiliation and independence noted in the previous section, however, at issue is how these equally compelling issues are balanced.

Conventional educational practice does little to ensure that such a balance is likely to be achieved, in part because so little attention is paid to the natural world. Students are generally given few opportunities to learn in any deep way about the locales that are their homes or to experience those places directly. Parental concerns about children's safety and compelling forms of indoor electronic entertainment have also reduced the amount of time that young people devote to exploring their neighborhoods and regions on their own. As mentioned earlier, the result is what Richard Louv (2005) calls nature-deficit disorder, a condition that he links to the problem children often experience paying sustained attention to many non-electronic activities. Nature writer Robert Pyle (1993) associates what he calls children's "extinction of experience" of natural places to a declining willingness on the part of American citizens to care for the land. If people are not familiar with the beauty of their environs or the diversity of species that surround them, why should they work to protect them? And the absence of such experience is true not only for children growing up in urban and suburban settings. Plant ecologist Gary Nabhan (1997) has found that a reduction in children's experience of the outdoors is as much an issue in rural settings as in contemporary cities.

Addressing young people's diminished encounters with the natural world will require the active intervention of some institution, and there is no reason that schools cannot take on some of the responsibility for doing so. Although, at the outset, teachers in urban settings may assume that this is something beyond their means, many cities still provide rich opportunities for investigations of the natural world. A teacher who worked with two of Smith's sons in a suburban Portland school regularly incorporated locally relevant lessons into her curriculum in ways that helped nurture *querencia* in her second- and third-grade students. In the fall she and her students would visit a fish hatchery outside of Portland where they learned about the life cycle of salmon. They returned to the classroom with gestating salmon eggs that they placed in a large aquarium. They watched the salmon develop throughout the winter and spring, and then released the fish into the mouth of the Tualatin River in a park a couple of blocks from the school. Not long after this event one year, a drain in the playground became clogged. Workmen were called in to clear it, and as they did so threw cigarette butts into the drain. Knowing that the storm sewers emptied into the river, the students became upset—"all in a lather" was the phrase their teacher used to describe them. The students didn't want anything harming their fish "babies." She spoke with the principal, who then asked the workmen to be more careful about their litter. The teacher also mentioned having conversations with students at the end of the next summer about reports of pollution in the Willamette River into which the Tualatin empties. She observed that this learning experience had developed in the children she taught a personal connection to their place that she found to be striking and that she suspected they would not forget. Without knowing about *querencia*, she was cultivating it, potentially preparing her students to be thoughtful advocates for the maintenance of healthy ecosystems as they grow into adulthood.

Developing the Capacity for Local Problem-solving

Humanity is experiencing one of the most dynamic and dangerous periods in our species' tenancy on the planet. During the past century, our numbers have quadrupled and are projected to increase by another third by 2050. Technological advances have allowed a significant proportion of citizens of the developed world to live with a degree of physical comfort and security unheard of for all but social elites in previous eras. These advances coupled with population increases, however, have resulted in the expropriation of one-third of the planet's net primary productivity from photosynthesis and now threaten the stability of many marine and terrestrial ecosystems as well as the climate as a whole (Vitousek, Mooney, Lubchenco, & Melillo, 1997). The globalization of the economy has furthermore diminished the integrity of national economies and the influence of local decision-makers. The events of 9/11 and its aftermath have also clearly revealed that the United States is no longer isolated from the social inequities and enmities that continue to lead to violence in other parts of the world. All of these issues suggest that, rather than focusing on the local, schools should instead be developing among their students a deep awareness of the global.

We would not disagree with the assertion that attending to the global is critical. Given human numbers and the degree to which international political and economic relationships are now intertwined, there is no way that any locale can presume to be independent from every other community across the globe. Parochialism is no longer an option anywhere. There is furthermore no way that the fundamental problems facing humanity can be dealt with in an isolated fashion. Successful responses to contemporary challenges must take place throughout human-created systems from top to bottom.

What is problematic today is that national and international institutions have become so dominant that local populations are becoming less able to respond to events that disrupt their lives. When non-local institutions are unable or unwilling to respond to catastrophes like Hurricane Katrina, the South Asian tsunami of 2004, or the unraveling of local economies set in motion by the North American Free Trade Agreement, people on the ground are left initially in peril and then over the long term in poverty. The multiplicity of challenges now facing the human species will require something different.

Children everywhere need to be prepared to become collaborators in the creation of communities where economic, social, and political practices enhance the welfare of the human inhabitants and the integrity of the natural systems that support them. Children must understand how many of the practices of the twentieth century have resulted in our current dilemmas and require transformation. One of the contributing factors to contemporary crises is the common assumption that single, universal responses are desirable. When energy is cheap and widely available, for example, it becomes possible to allow people to live in the same way in central Alaska or southern Nevada as people in more moderate climates. When energy is expensive and less accessible, this will necessarily change. Then, as throughout the preceding millennia, human beings will need to craft cultural responses that are uniquely suited to the particularities of local geographies. This does not mean that commonalities cannot be identified across specific places; such sharing is bound to be possible. But projections of energy costs and availability suggest that a one-size-fits-all model is no longer appropriate.

Conscious of what is happening globally, people at the local level need to be able to invent solutions to their own dilemmas while remaining in conversation with people from other locales about their inventions and experiments. As challenges become increasingly difficult, it will become imperative that people believe that they have the capacity to address their problems. Knowing about efforts in other parts of the world could potentially give them heart and allow them to persist in their own activities (Hawken, 2007). Children now need to be educated to believe in their own ability to address local problems and to think about these problems in fresh and innovative ways.

Although drawn from a third-world setting half a world away, a Sri Lankan model of school–community collaboration that was started in the late 1950s called Sarvodaya Shramadana provides an example of the possible (Macy, 1983). A.T. Ariyaratne, a high school teacher in Colombo, the Sri Lankan capital city, was concerned about the degree to which his upper-class students were cut off from the life of common citizens throughout their country. He decided to rectify this situation by creating a voluntary workcamp organization that took them into rural villages where they met with local residents to identify projects that would benefit the community. They would often begin by asking about unanswered requests sent to government officials. Such requests would generally focus on the building of a school or clinic, road repairs, or the construction of cisterns or wells. Students would ask residents about the number of people needed to complete these projects, the amount of money necessary to purchase materials, and the time required to get the job done. They would then help organize a workcamp in which they and local people would contribute their labor.

Over time, Sarvodaya became one of the premier community development organizations in Sri Lanka and its leader recognized globally for his innovative work. It currently reaches 15,000 villages in Sri Lanka and employs 1,500 staff. An American acquaintance who serves as a consultant to Sarvodaya noted that, in the aftermath of the 2004 tsunami, individuals who had worked with the organization were often the people who assumed leadership roles in helping fellow-villagers rebuild their lives following this disaster (Abdullah, 2005). They would be the ones who gathered clothing for individuals who had lost everything or created systems by which food was collected and distributed to those who had nothing.

Educators like those at the Young Achievers School or Waupun, Wisconsin who invite their students to participate in community problem-solving are laying the groundwork for the kinds of collaborative invention that could make the difference between supportive and sustainable communities in the future or those that are good for neither people nor the planet. It is not clear at all whether students raised on a diet of standardized tests will possess the knowledge, skills, or dispositions required to join in this process. In contrast, place- and community-based education alerts young people to their own capacities, the assets and needs of their communities, and the importance of their willingness to become involved in the shaping of both individual and collective responses to the demands of the future.

Educating for the Common Good

In societies prior to the modern era, the process of cultural transmission and education was primarily aimed at ensuring the long-term viability of the community as well as the acquisition of skills and knowledge essential for individual survival. As schools have become one of the central vehicles for sorting and selecting students for varying economic roles, the contribution of education to community health and stability has been reduced (Spring, 1976). Thanks to lowered external expectations and diminished self-esteem, the very act of sorting has also meant that many individuals categorized as less able by the school fail to gain the competencies required to become economically and socially successful. Although contemporary schools do a commendable job of preparing a proportion of their students to compete effectively in the labor market and make significant contributions to our common life, they are poorly serving millions of American students and the communities in which they live. Reform strategies like NCLB that reify the sorting mechanisms of conventional schools without addressing the meaning and purposes of education promise to make this problem more severe rather than solve it.

Reestablishing the relationship between classroom, community, and region offers a way out of this conundrum by reclaiming the good sense displayed by our human ancestors. Over the generations they came to understand that children are drawn into the experience of social membership and participation not by being removed from their communities but by being immersed in the world of adults. They understood that children are motivated to master new knowledge and skills because doing so allows them to display their competence and make contributions to the lives of those they love and respect. Learning in such settings took place within a rich social and natural context that made its significance self-evident. Adults furthermore knew that any child who did not gain the skills necessary to support himself or herself and give back to the community would become a drain on everyone's resources and energy. They could not allow failure to become widespread without endangering themselves.

By resituating instruction in the world beyond the classroom, place- and community-based education gives students a reason to invest themselves in learning, and communities a reason to support their schools. Education becomes not merely a vehicle for advancing the interests of individuals but a means for sustaining neighborhoods and towns in ways that will advance the common good. During an era in which individuals are likely to find it increasingly difficult to carve secure places for themselves and their families alone, an approach to teaching and learning that enhances collaboration, people's sense of shared purpose, and the knowledge of what it means to live successfully in a particular region could do much to enhance their connection to one another and the Earth, as well as their capacity to meet the challenges of the coming decades. In the chapters that follow we will describe more schools where place- and community-based education is being practiced, its impact on students and their communities, and what it may take to make this approach more the rule than the exception.

Chapter 4

Place- and Community-based Education in Practice

Starting with Local Knowledge and Issues

One of the challenges facing educators interested in encouraging their colleagues to implement place- and community-based approaches is that there is no play- or recipe book available that can be picked up to guide the design of lessons or units. The current trend in curriculum development is to create common scripts or syllabi that can be used anywhere. Teacher compliance with prescribed plans is often monitored by their superiors to assure the "fidelity" of program implementation. Even some environmental educators rely heavily on curriculum guides produced by Project Learning Tree, Project Wet, and Project Wild (Krafel, 1999). Such materials do provide a means for disseminating concepts and pedagogical practices viewed as desirable by their proponents; place- and community-based education, however, requires something different. By its very nature, it cannot be standardized or centralized; it must instead reflect the unique circumstances encountered in specific schools and communities. This means that teachers must take the initiative in developing lessons and plans responsive to the circumstances and opportunities that exist beyond their classrooms.

The prospect of engaging in this kind of activity can be intimidating. Few teachers have been prepared to embrace this task, and the demands of teaching an increasingly prescribed curriculum leave educators with little time to experiment with an approach to learning that is more complex and more difficult to control. Fortunately, their colleagues in numerous schools across the United States have been breaking a path that demonstrates the possibilities and doing so in ways that are meaningful for themselves as well as their students. Although what they have accomplished cannot be simply transported from one place to another, their approaches and processes can serve as both imaginative stimuli and guides.

Their work often focuses on a set of common themes or issues that can serve as a starting place for teachers interested in incorporating place- and community-based education into their own classrooms. These themes include cultural aspects of a community's life, environmental issues, economic development, and civic involvement. This chapter will describe each of these domains in more detail and offer examples of what educators are doing to use them as a means for connecting classrooms more firmly to their communities. It will conclude with a discussion of common principles of place- and community-based education drawn from the examples. Chapter 5 will, in contrast, consider ways these principles can be put into practice when traditional school subjects are used as the starting place.

Cultural Dimensions of Community Life

As indicated in Chapter 3, public schools have tended to devote little attention to local issues of any sort, especially after primary school. Smith recalls three lessons in junior and senior high school that took him outside the classroom and into the community: a visit to a tree farm when he was in the eighth grade, a walk around the neighborhood to observe trees in the springtime as a sophomore, and a local government day as a senior spent at the wastewater treatment facility. Aside from a unit about introducing a bill into the state legislature in a high school civics class, no other units focused on information about the Pacific Northwest or the community where he grew up in southern Oregon. What he discovered about his place came from independent investigations as a young adult returning home after living elsewhere. It was then that he read about the Indian wars that had decimated local indigenous populations, learned the names of local flowers and shrubs and trees, and became familiar with Northwest literature.

One of the primary reasons for incorporating local culture and history into children's school experience is because it is potentially familiar and accessible; it furthermore helps young people to see what is valuable and worth preserving in their home communities. In a society dominated by media that originate in New York and Los Angeles, it is easy to believe that the important work of American culture happens not in the country's small towns and cities but in the large urban centers of the East and West Coasts. When schools reinforce this message by ignoring the communities where students live, it is not surprising that out-migration has become the problem it is in rural towns across the country. If young people think that nothing of significance can happen outside the Beltline, Manhattan, or the computer capitals in the Bay Area and Puget Sound, why should they stay? Why should they put down roots and invest their lives in supporting the well-being of the people who supported them during their early years? Why not be boomers rather than stickers?

Francisco Guajardo is an educator who could have left the community where he grew up in south Texas (Smith, 2002). His parents had migrated to the Edcouch-Elsa region from Mexico when he was a small child. He had grown up in a community of low-income Mexican Americans where many residents continue to harvest crops around the United States as a means of livelihood. Although poor, the community had a history of activism and was one of the places where people of Latino ancestry fought to be given the same rights as their Anglo counterparts. Guajardo was a successful student and was able to parlay that success into a university education and a teaching license. Instead of seeking a position in a more comfortable urban district, he decided to return home with the intention of persuading more young people to find ways to serve their natal community.

He began his career just when the standards movement was gaining steam. Texas had developed a common statewide curriculum, and teachers were expected to

Figure 4.1 Conducting an interview with a local elder
          Photo by Francisco Guajardo

deliver this to their students. Guajardo realized that for most of the Latino students in his classes this would be a recipe for failure. He set the curriculum on a shelf and directed his attention to the unrecognized riches of his own community. He believed that introducing students to the assets that existed around them among their families, friends, and neighbors would potentially trigger a desire to maintain their connections to the region. Because what they learned in school would also be tied to their own identities, they might also become more willing to invest themselves in the enterprise of formal education.

He began by inviting his students to collect oral histories of older residents of the region. This gave them the opportunity to learn about the qualities of persistence, care, and generosity that are so essential to the maintenance of positive social environments in the face of limited resources. It also gave them insights into the heroism that lay under the surface of the lives of people they might otherwise disregard as uninteresting or of no account. In the early years, students would gather their interviews, transcripts, photographs, and video recordings and present them to community members in a museum format. The community and the students loved it. Guajardo found that incoming students who had heard about these projects wanted to do more of the same. And other community members wanted to participate in the interview process. In the mid-1990s he successfully wrote a grant proposal to the Annenberg Rural Challenge to enhance student achievement, community development, and cultural pride through the creation of the Llano Grande Center (see www.llanogrande.org for more information). The additional resources allowed him to expand the program, gain national recognition, and come to the attention of other philanthropic organizations.

In the years since Guajardo began teaching in his hometown, over 80 students (from a high school whose student population is 1,400) have gone on to Ivy League and other top-flight universities. They are among the 65 percent of graduates from Edcouch-Elsa High School who pursue post-secondary studies. This rate of college attendance is exceptional for students from Latino backgrounds and speaks to the power of an educational process that focuses on the strengths of their own families and culture rather than the disadvantages of poverty. Guajardo bristles at the notion that people from his community are limited in any way by their own experiences, arguing instead that they are privileged. The power of his message can be seen in the fact that numerous graduates from Edcouch-Elsa High School have returned after earning their degrees at institutions such as Yale, Tufts, and Brown to work with him to strengthen their own community.

Among more recent projects taken on by students and teachers as this work has evolved are regular television productions featuring interviews with local residents and a Spanish-language school that was for four years marketed to people from outside the region and state. Working with the regional public access station, students are acquiring video production skills that both open new career possibilities for themselves and knit together the region thanks to the stories they are able to share through electronic media. The Spanish-language school created more immediate economic rewards. Students and their families opened their homes to paying guests interested in immersing themselves in another language. Like immersion programs in other countries, home stays were combined with intensive language instruction. These activities confirmed the value of students' cultural identity and provided them with a way to translate assets into economic opportunities, as well.

For Guajardo, such an education is at base liberatory because it challenges assumptions often encountered in the dominant society about the academic and occupational potential of non-White and non-middle-class students. The efforts of educators associated with the Llano Grande Center and the Edcouch-Elsa High School demonstrate the talents that lie just beneath the surface in schools that would otherwise be seen as low-performing and among students often consigned to low-track and remedial classes. Not all place- and community-based educators who focus on local cultural issues have adopted a stance as explicitly political as Guajardo's, but the aims and consequences of their efforts could also be described as liberatory, as well.

Attention to local historical and cultural issues does much to dispel the notion that young people are responsible for little beyond the development of their own talents and the pursuit of economic independence. It can affirm their relationship to others whose welfare is at least partly tied to the decisions they will make about their own life directions. Understanding these relationships can make a significant contribution to the restoration of the forms of trust and mutual support so critical to the experience of social capital. When students embrace rather than ignore or deride their own ancestry and traditions, they will be more likely to commit themselves to the difficult but rewarding work of making their communities good places to live. Even when they move to new communities, they will at least have a sense of the importance of social capital and may become more likely to make sure they cultivate relationships similar to those they encountered in the places where they grew up.

Environmental and Natural Resource Issues

It can be argued that one of the primary reasons for incorporating more educational experiences in the local environment is to acquaint young people with the non-human assets encountered in their home places. Once children and youth value those assets, they will more likely be disposed to care for and protect them. This is certainly the point that Robert Pyle makes in his essay about the extinction of experience described in the previous chapter. Paleobiologist Stephen J. Gould (1991) makes a similar argument, suggesting that human beings protect and preserve what they love; if they don't know something, they don't attend to it. Teachers who engage their students in scientific field studies, join with them in the restoration of places degraded by human misuse or the introduction of invasive species, study the principles of ecology and the operation of complex systems as witnessed locally, convey a knowledge of the unique geological and biological attributes of a particular place, or simply open students' senses to the beauty out of doors encourage the development of the kind of responsible stewardship that Barry Lopez associates with *querencia*. Again, there can be no simple guidebook for the development of a curriculum that explores these issues, but there are certain foci and approaches that describe the possible.

The Sunnyside Environmental School, a K–8 school in Portland, Oregon, has been striving to create educational experiences directed toward this end since the fall of 1995. Initially created as a middle school, Sunnyside is the brainchild of a former elementary school teacher, Sarah Taylor. Taylor had been enrolled in an educational administration program at Portland State University, where she was asked to design a school as a requirement in one of her courses. The mother of her own teenage sons at the time and adoptive mother to more than a dozen immigrant children, she had become acutely aware of how ill matched many middle schools are to the developmental needs of young adolescents. While walking along a forested trail close to her home one day, she developed a vision of a school that was more responsive to middle school students' needs for social interaction, hands-on learning experiences, and the opportunity to situate themselves in both the human and the natural contexts of their own lives. When she described it on paper, her professor encouraged her to share it with the then superintendent of Portland Public Schools, Jack Bierwirth. Concerned about the out-migration of middle-class families following the passage of a state initiative that significantly reduced school funding and local control, Bierwirth and the school board gave her the go-ahead to transform her vision into reality, hoping that her school would keep more students in the district.

Figure 4.2 Preparing the soil at Jean's Farm in Portland, Oregon
           Photo by Gregory Smith

Taylor quickly assembled an advisory group of teachers and community members who helped her decide on a building where the school could be located, recruit 180 sixth through eighth graders from across the district, and hire six faculty. Taylor and the new teachers crafted a curriculum and schedule whose outlines have remained constant from that first year. They decided to work in "blended" classrooms with sixth through eighth graders together for all subjects with the exception of math and Spanish. They would structure their teaching in the core classes of language arts, social studies, and science around the broad themes of rivers, mountains, and forests for each of the years that a student attended the school. The creation of a core class incorporating three academic disciplines gave them the option of going on day-long trips to environmental or community service sites every Tuesday or Thursday. Finally, each morning would begin with a community meeting during which students would be introduced to individuals and groups who were contributing to social and environmental health in Portland and elsewhere.

In the spring of 2002 Smith had the opportunity to spend one day a week at the then Environmental Middle School. Although he had been involved in the school's creation and served on its site council for a number of years, time commitments elsewhere had prevented him from immersing himself in its offerings over a sustained period of time. Anecdotes described below are drawn from that period.

The curricular theme for the 2001–2002 academic year was rivers, and a wide range of academic and off-campus activities served to deepen students' understanding about the function of rivers in ecosystems and their importance to human life both in northern Oregon and in other places. In the fall, students studied the features of riparian environments and constructed wall-sized murals in every classroom that captured what they had learned about rivers' physical and ecological characteristics. This process gave graphic expression to the vocabulary and concepts they were acquiring. After becoming acquainted with local streams and rivers they conducted independent research projects describing rivers in other parts of the world. In December, the school sponsored an open-house called the River Festival that was attended by several hundred people. During this time, family and community members were able to observe students' work from the previous three months displayed in classrooms and hallways.

In January, core classes spent a day or more learning about Portland's water system, which starts in the foothills of the Cascades Mountains at the Bull Run Reservoir and ends at the Portsmouth wastewater treatment facility on the Willamette River. During one lesson, they tracked water from the reservoir to pump stations to purification facilities to the storage ponds in Mount Tabor and Washington Parks. Another day they focused on the history of the Bull Run watershed and how the foresight of city leaders in the 1800s had contributed to some of the purest urban water in the United States. These lessons were followed by field trips to Bull Run Reservoir as well as the wastewater treatment facility, where students had the opportunity to stand in the middle of a 14-foot pipe the same size as those that carry sewage into the facility.

These activities were accompanied by monthly field trips via city bus to the Brookside Wetlands, public property managed by the Portland metropolitan area's regional government. The wetlands are in the Johnson Creek drainage and are part of a long-term reclamation project aimed at restoring indigenous salmon runs and minimizing flood damage. During their monthly trips to Brookside, students tracked seasonal changes, monitored water temperature and turbidity, identified macro-invertebrates, observed local birds, checked for animal tracks, played games, and recorded their thoughts about being in nature during quiet times after lunch. They got to know this particular place well, and data they collected were regularly submitted to the city's Bureau of Environmental Services in an effort to alert natural resource professionals to anomalous events. Preparation for field trips included the development of hypotheses about what they were likely to see and why; follow-up meetings in the classroom focused on discoveries and the importance of standardizing data collection procedures.

The school ground provides an additional site for environmental lessons. Students in earlier years had planted vegetable, flower, and native species gardens. These require ongoing maintenance and become the source for lessons about plant identification and food cultivation. Students and teachers at the school also run an extensive composting program and maintain worm bins, all of which contribute to garden efforts. Students take such learning into the neighborhood around the school as well, sponsoring native plant sales or constructing raised vegetable beds at the city-sanctioned Dignity Village for homeless people.

Some years, students investigate controversial environmental topics. In the spring of 2005, for example, one core class decided to learn more about efforts to develop a policy to govern the likely migration of wolves into Oregon from Idaho. Students linked this topic to the idea of manifest destiny that had governed the settling of North America by people of European descent. When a legislative hearing about the wolf plan was scheduled in East Portland, their teacher, Jan Zuckerman, decided that this was a good opportunity for them to learn about public decision-making processes. She invited interested students to write statements and then chaperoned them during the hearing. Since student opinions tended to favor the reintroduction of wolves, their comments sparked a temporary outcry from ranchers and their elected representatives from eastern Oregon. Their teacher, however, had been careful to include multiple viewpoints about the issue and not to intentionally sway students in one way or another, so concerns about possible indoctrination quickly dissipated. A positive outcome was that a class conversation with a state judge from a ranching community resulted in invitations for this teacher's students to visit families in the eastern part of the state and learn about their life ways and perspectives. Political activism as well as observation, restoration work, and gardening are thus part of students' experience at the school.

Three years ago, the middle school became a K-8 school in an effort to respond to long-standing district pressure to enroll more students. Taylor and her teachers developed new curricula that continue to draw heavily upon the local environment as a basis for learning experiences, incorporating activities like a morning walk into children's daily schedule and assigning one teacher to be responsible for instruction in art and gardening, assuring that students across all grades have the opportunity to observe and learn from nature. Elementary students, like their middle school counterparts, also participate in the investigations of rivers, forests, and mountains that lead to the school's public festivals.

Teachers at the Sunnyside Environmental School speak explicitly about connecting students to the region and developing a commitment to care about their home place. That students evolve in this direction can be seen in their willingness to spend time outside in inclement weather, engage in the work of soil preparation and weeding, and master information about local flora and fauna about which their

peers in other schools often remain ignorant. Although the data are purely anecdotal, some high school biology teachers speak of the way that students from
Sunnyside know what they are doing when involved in field studies and that they
really care about the natural world. Graduates of the program are also drawn to
environmental fields when they get to college and display a willingness to become
politically involved. An educational experience that incorporates ecological information about the students' region, that takes them regularly into the natural world,
and that asks them to contribute their labor to restoration and gardening projects
provides an opportunity for young people to become acquainted with where they
live and to move beyond the limitations of a human-centered culture that tends to
disregard its roots in the physical world.

Exploration of Economic Possibilities and Entrepreneurialism

Educational experiences that draw students into a meaningful relationship with the
human and natural communities that surround them may do much to engender
social capital and Lopez's notion of *querencia,* but if they do not also help students
grapple with economic issues they will be useful only for the independently
wealthy. Young people must also gain an understanding of what is required to make
a living in the places where they live. Unfortunately, in many rural and inner-city
communities, viable economic opportunities are in short supply, and the result is
that students—regardless of how much they may love and be committed to their
home places—will be forced to move elsewhere to support themselves once they
graduate from high school and are expected to achieve some degree of financial
independence. One of the strengths of the Llano Grande Center described earlier is
that teachers found ways both to attract college graduates back to south Texas and
to create meaningful employment for them. Educators have rarely considered the
role that they might play in community development, perceiving their own responsibilities to lie primarily with individual students. Some place- and community-
based educators, however, are demonstrating ways that schools can become
genuine contributors to the economic well-being of the communities whose tax
dollars support them.

In the mid-1990s, Randy Parry was the business teacher and basketball coach at
Howard High School in Miner County, 65 miles northwest of Sioux Falls, South
Dakota (see www.mccr.net for more information). The town of Howard, like many
towns throughout the upper Midwest, had experienced decades of out-migration.
After peaking in the 1920s and 1930s, population in Howard—the county seat—
had declined to 1,000 people; Miner County, itself, had only 1,000 registered voters.
Mr. Parry was determined to see what he could do to turn this around and believed
that young people could become a critical element of this process.

With the Program for Rural School and Community Renewal at South Dakota
State University, he wrote a grant to the Annenberg Rural Challenge to support
projects aimed at connecting rural schools and communities. The aim of the grant
was to develop sustainable communities that met the needs of local residents for

food, water, shelter, clothing, and jobs while at the same time keeping that growth within the region's ecological limits.

One of his students' first projects was a community cash flow study that involved surveying all 1,000 of the county's registered voters to find out where they shopped and which improvements in local businesses might lead them to spend more of their dollars in Miner County. Students found that about half of all respondents were primarily going to larger towns outside the county for most of their shopping needs. They shared this information with the community as well as suggestions about businesses staying open later and people's desire for a local ATM machine. They also let county residents know that, if they spent only 10 percent more of their disposable income close to home, seven million additional dollars would be added to the regional economy and more sales tax revenue would be available for local government. People listened and, over the next year, taxable sales in Miner County increased by $15.6 million—41.1 percent—and then gradually stabilized at this level. Other projects included student-taught adult computer classes, the construction of a greenhouse and community garden supported by a U.S. Department of Agriculture grant, and a student study of cancer clusters in the county.

Fired up by the success of these early projects, Parry and his students began sponsoring community vision meetings during the fall of 1997. People from all walks of life were invited to these gatherings, including youth, the elderly, farmers, business

Figure 4.3 Planning with community members
Used with permission of Jim Beddow

people, clergy, teachers, and low-income and high-income residents. Large meetings were generally attended by about 150 people. Discussions focused on identifying Miner County's assets, its weaknesses, and strategies for creating a community capable of creating enough high-quality jobs to prevent a further population decline. Focus groups studied and then developed recommendations about housing, employment, health care, and education. Out of these discussions evolved the Miner County Task Force made up of 22 members from a variety of different constituent groups including young people and the elderly.

This work was substantive enough so that, when Parry applied to the Northwest Area Foundation, Miner County was selected out of 197 communities of comparable size to receive a grant of over $4 million to give legs to the ideas residents had been discussing over the past two years. This grant was supplemented by $2 million more from the nonprofit South Dakota Community Foundation, allowing for the creation of a new organization, Miner County Community Revitalization (MCCR). In the years since MCCR has been in existence, the organization has supported county-wide beautification efforts, the creation of a revolving loan fund to help business start-ups, the conversion of a vacant school into a wellness center, and the establishment of a daycare center. The county is also beginning to attract new businesses, including a factory that manufactures state-of-the-art turbine blades for the burgeoning Midwest wind power industry and an organic beef packinghouse. Together, both enterprises now employ over 200 people.

Throughout this period of time, student researchers have continued to play an important role supporting the work of MCCR. Although Parry took over the reins of MCCR once it was formed, he did not forget his ties to education. In 2000, a recent graduate of Howard High School was hired to investigate population loss, transfer payments, future trends in agriculture, land ownership in agriculture, sales in agriculture, and personal income. Stories based on his research were published in two of the county's local papers. During the summer of 2002, six more Howard High School students were hired by MCCR to update research in these areas as well as the status of elderly residents, free and reduced lunches, income and poverty, wind energy, and social capital. More recently, a nearly $50,000 grant from the South Dakota Department of Health and Humanities will support student research in Howard and Corsica, another small town, but in Douglas County to the south of Howard. This grant will allow students to investigate such issues as town design, entrepreneurship, and new strategies for supporting community development. As a research associate for MCCR observed, "We will take what we learn and change and modify it into something that will work for rural America. We can't afford not to engage youth. That's how things change here" (Sand, 2006).

Schools and communities that engage students in work as important as that provided for them in Miner County and the counties where this model is spreading both demonstrate to young people their capacity to make real contributions to the welfare of their families and neighbors and exhibit to them possibilities for meaningful and financially viable employment they may have never imagined. The success of MCCR and the activities associated with this organization are tied to a belief that average people are capable of taking care of their own lives and of creating their own opportunities. In this sense, efforts there are as liberatory as those in the Llano Grande region of south Texas even though these students in Iowa are as mainstream as it gets. They are learning that, despite the messages of the urban media that there is little of value in rural America, they and their fellow citizens can craft good lives for themselves if they join together to gather data, to learn, to analyze, to imagine, to invest, and to build.

Induction to Citizenship

The fourth approach to place- and community-based education focuses on activities aimed at inducting young people into the give and take of local decision-making. Civic education has long been one of the goals touted by American schools, but actual instruction has tended to focus more on abstract discussions of forms of government than on experiences that give children and youth the opportunity to hone the skills associated with effective citizenship. A partial list of such skills might include the ability to research and analyze an issue, to educate and organize the public, to write and deliver statements at hearings or events, and to use the media to advance one's cause.

One of the grandfathers of the place- and community-based education movement is a retired science teacher from Seaside, Oregon named Neal Maine. Maine has long argued that students need to be seen as intellectual resources, and the Annenberg Rural Challenge was quick to grasp the value of his perspective during the years he served on its board of trustees. Maine went on to suggest that, if children and youth are to fulfill this role, they need something like the equivalent of Little League Baseball to help them gain the appropriate abilities and confidence. Kids don't learn to play baseball by reading books or watching videos—although these activities can help; they become baseball players by playing baseball—often in modified form with shorter baselines and more forgiving rules. Growing citizens requires the same kind of support.

Maine worked to form cooperative agreements between city and county governments to engage students in research activities—like those in Miner County—aimed at bettering their community. Over the years, students in Seaside have investigated such things as their own buying patterns and then shared this information with members of the Chamber of Commerce, catalogued native species on an old lumber mill site that was the object of an urban renewal grant, took measurements of all buildings on the city's tsunami plain so that emergency planners could make use of a software program aimed at anticipating damage caused by different-sized waves, and made recommendations about playground equipment needs in the county's parks. In each of these instances, the focus of students' activities was bounded, and they received plenty of support from their teachers and members of appropriate agencies or committees as they developed their reports or presentations. What they learned was that they could speak in a public meeting like any other citizen and engage in activities that had real value for the community. They began to develop a taste for participation and a sense about how best to make contributions to community life.

In many instances, students' introduction to democratic participation can be structured in ways that are non-controversial. Democracy, however, tends to be characterized by disagreement and controversy. Educators who venture into issues around which people do not agree must be thoughtful about how they proceed. As with the example from the Sunnyside Environmental School, it is important to leave space for students to make up their own minds and not be swayed by their teacher to believe and act in one way rather than another. There are circumstances, however, when the issue of community harm is so clear cut that engaging students in efforts to correct the situation can be justifiable.

Elaine Senechal worked for nearly a decade as a science teacher at the Greater Egleston Community High School (GECHS) in Boston, Massachusetts (Senechal, 2008). The high school was initially created in the 1990s by a group of parents worried about the attractions of street life for their primarily Black, Latino, and Cape Verdean children. They hoped that a school experience aimed at preparing them to become community leaders might be more attractive than gang membership. GECHS operated for a few years as a charter, but then like Young Achievers became a pilot school. Thanks to an agreement between the district and the teachers' union, pilot schools—like charter schools—have more flexibility over hiring, curriculum, and budget, giving them the ability to respond more immediately to the needs and interests of their teachers, students, and community.

When Senechal began teaching at GECHS, she wanted to find some way to integrate the school's mission about community leadership into her science program. She decided that whatever project she embarked upon would be more successful if it were clearly linked to concerns already identified by local residents. Her investigation surfaced a nonprofit organization called Alternatives for Community and the Environment (ACE) that was working with low-income people in Boston to correct environmental inequities. Two community organizers at ACE were very interested in youth development. When Senechal met them, she realized that she had found just the people she needed to create a science elective that focused on environmental justice.

At that time, ACE was investigating on air quality issues in Roxbury. Asthma rates were soaring, and diesel exhaust was suspected of being the cause. One of Senechal's students' first projects involved simply counting the number of diesel-burning vehicles that passed the front door of the school in an hour. In that period of time, over one hundred trucks or busses drove by, many of them empty busses on the way to the Massachusetts Bay Transit Authority (MBTA) terminal located in the neighborhood. Working with the community organizers from ACE, students learned that excessive idling by diesel-burning vehicles is a major contributor to diminished air quality. They also learned that a Massachusetts statute theoretically prevented vehicles from idling for more than five minutes at one stop; the statute, however, was rarely enforced.

This understanding resulted in the initiation of a six-year campaign to pressure public officials to enforce the law. Different groups of students in Senechal's environmental justice class helped to organize public rallies and demonstrations that gained the attention of the media and decision-makers. Presentations made at such

Figure 4.4 Demonstrating for clean air
Used with permission of Elaine Senechal

events eventually included data from research about levels of local air pollution students had completed in Roxbury. At the time, air quality for the Boston region was only being monitored by the Environmental Protection Agency (EPA) from a high-rise building in the center of town. Students learned how to use soil samples to assess pollutant levels and at one point were able to borrow air-monitoring equipment from the EPA to measure CO_2 levels both in and around their school. EPA officials were shocked to see how serious the problem was. This, coupled with growing public awareness, helped contribute to the community's success in gaining grants to purchase air quality monitors that would provide hourly feedback about pollutant levels. Students also worked with Roxbury Community College and researchers from the Harvard School of Public Health to compare medical records regarding asthma conditions and air quality records from the community's new monitoring station.

This growing body of data coupled with the attention now directed to air quality and environmental justice issues by the public culminated in 2004 in a court ruling that resulted in a decision against the MBTA. The MBTA was required to pay a fine, reduce the amount of time their busses idled, and continue converting diesel-burning busses to less-polluting natural gas. In this instance, students involved in place- and community-based educational projects over several years made a notable contribution to their families' and neighbors' quality of life.

Air quality was not the only issue to gain the attention of students in the environmental justice class. Students were actively involved in campaigning for the creation of a light-rail service to their neighborhood, resisting the siting in Roxbury of a level 4 biolab that would study some of the world's most dangerous communicable diseases, and supporting a Massachusetts bill aimed at giving human beings the same protections as endangered species. They also responded to requests to help organize against a proposal by the superintendent of the Boston Public Schools to require students to pay for bus and subway passes (these had historically been issued at no charge) and to investigate and then present their findings to the Boston City Council about job opportunities, pothole repairs, affordable housing, and youth programs. Students in the environmental justice class became recognized as skilled researchers and effective spokespersons for their community—both by members of the community, themselves, and by decision-makers in their city. As Senechal notes in a chapter she wrote about her experiences at GECHS (Senechal, 2008), the students who were gaining this respect and recognition were the same kids who had nearly dropped out of other schools. What made the difference was that they were able to find ways to contribute their intelligence and energies to projects that were genuinely worthwhile. They rose to the occasion and both they and their community were the beneficiaries.

Common Elements

In all of the foregoing examples, educators created learning opportunities that were unique to the circumstances of their own communities and regions. They did not rely on lesson or unit plans developed by others, but took advantage of possibilities that lay beyond their classroom door. They and their students looked for topics that are common to human experience: culture, the natural environment, making a living, handling the challenges of governance. Although unique to each community, the teaching practices encountered here demonstrate many of the characteristics of place- and community-based education seen at the Young Achievers Science and Mathematics Pilot School. Not all of these elements need to be present in every lesson or unit, but including more rather than fewer of them seems likely to lead to projects that have the capacity both to engage students in learning and to do so in ways that elicit positive responses from people outside the school.

In each of these communities, the **curriculum was clearly grounded in local issues and possibilities**, be they stories from people's past, data gathered about the condition of nearby streams and forests, buying habits of county residents, or air quality and its effects. That these topics were brought into students' school experiences was a result of the **willingness of their teachers to step beyond the lessons presented in generic texts and workbooks and to design instructional plans on their own or with others**. There was no prescribed plan that Elaine Senechal could have drawn upon to develop her lessons on air pollution and its solution, just as there was no guide that would have told the teachers at the Sunnyside Environmental School what aspects of their community ought to be included in their exploration of rivers, forests, and mountains. Their skill as educators lies in their ability to learn, synthesize, and make sense of new information, modeling what it means to engage in inquiry, to present findings to audiences beyond the school, and to become involved in efforts to improve the lives of people in their home communities. By working in this way, educators tend to act more as co-learners and facilitators than subject matter specialists.

Place- and community-based teachers furthermore embrace an educational model based more upon inquiry and action than memorization and recitation. In doing so, they **invite students to become knowledge creators and to exercise their own voices** as they share their findings and understanding with people beyond the classroom. Such activities have been termed "authentic" by educational researchers and are seen as an important aspect of classrooms in which students are genuinely engaged in academic work (Newmann, Secada, & Wehlage, 1995). When students know that the products of their investigations will have an audience besides their teacher—in the form of museum displays, PowerPoint presentations, or public testimony—they tend to invest more of their attention and energy into the tasks at hand.

Much of this happens because **teachers provide opportunities for other adults to share in the education of their community's children**. They do not try to fulfill this critical social and cultural function by themselves. At the Sunnyside Environmental School, morning meetings offer children an ongoing source of information and stories about the kinds of things that caring adults do to enhance the quality of community life or the natural environment. In south Texas, high school students interview community residents in their own homes to gain this kind of knowledge. And in Howard, South Dakota, students have played a central role as researchers and meeting facilitators, interacting with their elders as fellow citizens with an equal stake in the long-term health of their region.

Partnerships with local agencies also provide young people with access to adults outside the school. In Portland, teachers work with professionals from the Bureau of Environmental Services, volunteers at local soup kitchens, gardeners at Jean's Farm, and numerous organizations to expand the range of learning experiences they can offer their students. Similarly, at the Greater Egleston Community High School, youth were able to benefit from the knowledge and skills of community organizers who rarely have the opportunity to work with young people in formal educational settings. Establishing such partnerships greatly extends the range of expertise to which students are exposed and allows teachers—especially those new to a particular community—to acquaint their students with information and skills that may be unfamiliar to themselves, as well.

Finally, **place- and community-based educators design learning activities that could potentially engender a sense of appreciation or positive regard about students' home communities and regions.** This occurred in all of the sites described in this chapter. Students in Edcouch-Elsa became acquainted with the deep personal strengths of their relatives and neighbors. At the Sunnyside Environmental School, children came to know the natural features of their homes in ways rarely encountered by young people growing up in modern societies. In Howard, students got to know their neighbors and to recognize the economic and social potentials of their home county. And, in Boston, adolescents at the Greater Egleston Community High School were able to see that, despite the challenges faced by people in Roxbury, coalitions existed that could bring about positive change even when faced with seemingly intractable technological or social problems. One of the central aims of place- and community-based education is the cultivation of the experience of connection. Exploring community problems is certainly important, but it is also important to acquaint students with what is worth preserving, transmitting, and growing.

Drawing upon experiences and issues shared among all human communities and engaging students in work that has meaning beyond the classroom, teachers can diminish the boundary between school and place, enlivening the curriculum and demonstrating to young people the immediate importance of what they are learning. In the examples described in this chapter, educators used as their starting point the community itself. But, with an understanding about the value of incorporating the local into the classroom, teachers can also ground their curriculum development efforts in specific school subjects. How this can be done will be the focus of the next chapter.

Chapter 5

Place- and Community-based Education in Practice

Starting with the Traditional Disciplines

Most of the examples of place- and community-based education we have shared to this point have been chosen because they grew out of local concerns and carried real significance for the teachers and students who participated in them and real significance for their communities. They were, to use once again place-based educator Jack Shelton's terminology (2005), "consequential." But place- and community-based education does not always have to be earth-shaking. It can be as simple and uneventful as giving elementary school students an hour each week to write poetry in the school garden. This doesn't require extensive planning or any additional funding, but such repeated experiences can have a profound effect on students' experience of where they are and what is worthy of their attention.

The ideas we present below are organized according to subject matter as a means for inviting the reader into this material. Many of the projects we will describe could be attempted at different grade levels. At issue are the depth and complexity of the investigation and the products associated with these studies. We have collected these units and lessons from a variety of sources, including the websites of former Rural Challenge sites (listed at the conclusion of this chapter), the Rural Challenge evaluation (Rural Challenge Research and Evaluation Program, 1999a, 1999b), Michael Umphrey's account of the Montana Heritage Project (Umphrey, 2007), and our own observations in schools with which we are familiar. What we present here should be seen as imaginative stimuli, ticklers to get readers to envision previously unconsidered possibilities in their own schools and communities. Our descriptions will be brief so that we can broadcast as many ideas as possible.

Art and Music

The kindergarten through eighth-grade students at the Grizzly Hill School have for more than a decade been sharing their creative juices with their Yuba County neighbors in the Sierra Nevada foothills of northern California. One of their early projects involved recording a compact disc of holiday songs, including two they had written with their teacher. The title song, "Winter on the San Juan Ridge," was especially popular:

The roads are rutted.
The Yuba's flooded.
The trees are creaking, loaded heavy with snow.
My daddy's truck died,
Down by the creekside.
We've got to walk wherever we go.
But Mama's singing
Just as she's bringing
Fresh homemade cookies, piping hot from the stove.
I'm happy to the bone
In my foothill home.
It's winter on the San Juan Ridge.
                (Rural Challenge Research and Evaluation Program, 1999b, p. 7)

Students at Grizzly Hill have also turned to the visual arts, creating a permanent mural at the school honoring elders in their community who have worked to preserve the natural environment, and another at the Malakoff Diggins State Park (a site of placer mining in the nineteenth century) depicting wildlife of their region. The school regularly distributes students' individual artwork throughout neighboring towns. At the county courthouse in Nevada City, for example, two student pastel drawings of animals are hung in the room where judges hold mediation meetings with parents involved in domestic disputes, and an ever-changing collection of student artwork is displayed at the North San Juan Post Office. Art is also used as a tool for evaluation across the curriculum. After learning about the different regions of California, third and fourth graders drew mandalas depicting their knowledge of each of the region's characteristics with an accompanying description of what they had created. Their teacher said that this provided all the information he needed to know whether or not they had mastered this state standard.

Art has also been the focus of much place- and community-based educational activity in the coastal California town of Laytonville. High school students there painted a six-panel mural on the north-facing wall of Foster's Market, visible to travelers heading south on busy Highway 101. After interviewing community members and gaining permission from businesses and property owners, ninth-grade English classes took the lead in placing "historical monuments" around the community that include murals and descriptions of events associated with different locales. At the Laytonville Middle School, students created a quilt made up of images from historical photographs. As in North San Juan, this piece of art has been displayed at various locations in town, including the Long Valley Health Center. Musicians participated in these community-oriented activities, as well. The Laytonville High School developed a "Band on the Run" that performed contemporary and classic rock music and traveled to venues around town and to schools in the region, helping to contribute to the community's pride in the talents and skills of its young people.

A final example of a musical project that was played out in numerous Rural Challenge sites bears mentioning. Larry Long, a songwriter, singer, and guitarist, was hired by districts across the country to spend a week or more in different communities. Prior to his visit, Long asked school staff to identify a group of three or four "elders"—individuals who had made real contributions to the quality of local life—and then invited these people to the school to be interviewed by students and himself about their lives and dreams and activities. Long would then work with students to shape their interview notes into the lyrics of a song he would later compose and teach to the students. At the conclusion of Long's stay, a community dinner would be held to celebrate the elders who had been interviewed, and the songs written in their honor would be performed. Although this activity was dependent on the skills and talents of Larry Long, local musicians can be tapped to continue this process. After hosting Long in Spearfish, South Dakota, school principal Hank Fridell enlisted the support of songwriters he knew to establish a yearly tradition that brought new elders into the school and resulted in songs that recounted their life stories and contributions to the community.

Art and music have received minimal attention from the framers of the standards movement. Activities tied to imagination and creativity, however, are often central to the process by which human beings make meaning of their own experience and celebrate their lives. Art can serve as a powerful vehicle for knitting together individuals into communities where people share a common identity and sense of purpose. These examples demonstrate the way that schools can contribute to the generation of this sense of commonality and strengthen the interpersonal ties so essential to well-functioning societies.

Social Studies

Communities are also sustained through the passing down of stories about their former and current residents. This aspect of cultural transmission has also tended to be ignored in conventional classrooms and standardized tests. Social studies teachers interested in incorporating place into classrooms need look no further than the history of their town or region. Doing so does not require the elimination of courses that focus on American or world history; it simply starts the study of broad historical and social trends in the local and provides students with the opportunity to learn the research and writing skills associated with the production of historical texts or social science as they investigate their own communities.

Such work can begin close to home. At the Greenwood School in northern California, elementary school students one year wrote a history of their school. They interviewed alumni from representative decades in an effort to determine what their experience of the school had been like and how things had changed between then and now. Some of the questions posed for people they interviewed were: Why universal education? What was deemed important 50 years ago? Now? Why? Were girls and boys treated differently then? Are they now? Questions they asked themselves included: What surprises you about what you are learning? What did you expect? Such school histories do not necessarily need to go as far back in time as five decades. In the 1980s, for example, students in a middle school in Louisville, Kentucky interviewed alumni who had been at the school only a few years before. When combined with opportunities to reflect on what is being learned, investigations like these allow young people to step back from their own immediate experience and begin to grasp how they are part of a social continuum.

Cemeteries, as well as schools, can provide a rich source of accessible information for historical investigations. In Guilford, Vermont, another elementary school teacher makes use of gravestones to teach her students about the Civil War. Working with materials in the local historical society, she prepares for this unit by conducting her own investigations about the soldiers buried there. She collects information from town histories and accounts of Civil War battles and then presents this to students. She also instructs them in how to use U.S. Census data available on the Internet. The students are then asked to recreate the life of these people in as much detail as they can, speculating to whatever extent possible about the nature of their family and work experiences, as well as their personalities. This unit requires students to engage in the process of evidence-based inference that lies at the heart of the discipline of historical writing and connects them in a personal way with individuals who before would have only been names written on granite or slate.

Thetford Academy, an independent school that serves public secondary students from three designated Vermont communities, has initiated student-generated geography projects that have explored a variety of local historical and contemporary issues. Small groups of students decide on an area of interest, investigate the topic over an eight-week period, conduct a spatial analysis of their data, develop a written report or documentary video, and then present or exhibit their findings at the annual Thetford town meeting. Titles of geography projects in recent years reveal some of the topics students have chosen to explore:

- Movement of houses in Thetford caused by construction of I-91
- Analysis of the location of motor vehicle accidents in Thetford
- Changes in general stores in Thetford
- Water mills in the history of Thetford development
- Business changes in East Thetford, 1800–1990
- Analysis of solar power houses in Strafford, VT
- What happens to your soda can? Current recycling realities in Thetford

Local geography projects are aimed at achieving three goals: to serve the informational needs of local communities, to enhance students' connectedness to the community, and to reinforce and enhance student understanding of the geography curriculum through fieldwork—observation, investigation, and inquiry. They meet a range of Vermont Framework Standards including service, understanding place, geographical knowledge, and relevance. Part of an eleventh- or twelfth-grade course on human geography, the local geography projects give students an opportunity to apply what they are learning about broad issues such as population, migration, economic development, and natural resources to their own communities and regions, grounding what could otherwise be abstract and potentially meaningless to topics that are both personal and of local concern.

Another approach to the study of human geography can be found in schools that were associated with the Montana Heritage Project (Umphrey, 2007). Although this project stopped being funded in 2006 after a decade of productive activity, the ideas it seeded continue to send out roots into Montana and beyond. A number of communities associated with the project embraced what is called the Montana Study as a model for community investigation. Related to community study, a common mid-twentieth-century sociological research approach, the Montana Study was developed by Ernest Melby, Chancellor of the University of Montana during the 1940s. Like John Dewey, Melby held that democracy and education depend on one another. After the Great Depression and in the midst of World War II, he believed his state would be strengthened from a democratic and social stand-point if people began to think of education not as the sole responsibility of the school but of the community in its entirety.

In the mid-1990s Jeff Gruber, a Libby High School social studies teacher, joined the Heritage Project and invited his students to read *Small Town Renaissance* (Poston, 1950), a history of the Montana Study. It caught their attention. Libby at the time was experiencing the forms of economic disruption that have been so difficult for resource-based communities throughout the United States. As in many places, conflicts and fears were so deep that civic leaders avoided calling a public meeting. Gruber and his students did what others could not. They invited adults and young people to begin a long-term conversation about questions that people in communities rarely ask of one another. These included: What kind of people are we? Why do we live here? What cultural resources do we have? How can we make life better? How does Libby fit into Montana? How does Montana fit into the nation?

Gruber's students then embarked on an investigation that continued for many years. One of their first projects involved collecting thousands of photographs from Libby and assembling them as an extended photo essay about their town's future. Other projects took students to the local plywood plant, where they interviewed millworkers about their jobs and learned first-hand about the steps that transform trees into wood products. They wrote a pamphlet about what they learned, which to their and the millworkers' surprise became an historical document, itself, when the mill was closed by Stimson Lumber in 2003.

Now deeply committed to their place, students were not prepared to take this event sitting down. With their teacher, they prepared a presentation summarizing what they had learned about their community and took it to the headquarters of the Stimson Lumber Company and the Plum Creek Lumber Company in Portland, Oregon. Although the mill has not reopened, the process young people initiated led to the formation of a group of people who raised $2.1 million to remodel a school gymnasium into the Libby Memorial Center for the performing arts, a testament to the community's faith in their town's ability to persist. Before concluding the most recent community study, its participants composed an "insight statement" that captures the spirit behind this successful project:

If we lose faith in each other and in our institutions, we become a collection of individuals surviving in the same space, but if we grow in our faith in each other and in our institutions, we become a community of people thriving in the same place.

(in Umphrey, 2007, p. 81)

If one of the primary aims of social studies education is the cultivation of informed and responsible citizens, the work of the Heritage Project in Libby as well as other small towns across Montana is demonstrating how teachers can achieve this end.

Natural Sciences

In the twenty-first century, being an informed citizen requires a working knowledge of scientific principles and insight into the way that human activities can impact the quality of a community's health and long-term well-being. Unfortunately, much science education has become so preoccupied with the mastery of terminology that the links between the study of biology, chemistry, and physics and children's lives outside of school have become attenuated. Environmental education has sought to bridge this gap and in many instances has served as a forerunner for place- and community-based educational activities related to other subject areas. The examples of curriculum development described in this section are all drawn from the life sciences, the field of scientific endeavor that lends itself most easily to place-based pursuits. This does not mean, however, that teachers have not been seeking ways to link the study of chemistry or physics to activities that have clear applications to meaningful life experiences beyond the classroom. This is especially true of educators involved with the contextual learning movement, who have developed a variety of textbooks that demonstrate ways that chemistry and physics teachers can tie concepts in their disciplines to students' local community (see www.cord.org for more information).

Since the 1980s, a growing number of teachers at the elementary level and beyond have begun to incorporate school gardens as a means for teaching the scientific method and central principles of biology. In early 1991, the Denali Elementary School in Fairbanks, Alaska was the recipient of a three-year $750,000 grant from the RJR Nabisco Foundation to create a curriculum that focused on science and math through an investigation of the local environment. Denali was called Alaska's "Discovery School," and its teachers incorporated a sizeable school garden into many of their year-long activities. During Alaska's long and dark winter, they used classroom grow-labs to experiment with different varieties of seeds, assessing their germination and growth rates in an effort to determine which should be used in the garden. Children tracked this information, recorded it on graphs, and used it as a basis for decision-making. Throughout these and similar investigations, students would observe; question; predict; hypothesize; measure; collect, organize, interpret, and present data; and apply their findings (Hagstrom, 1993, p. 78). During the very late spring, they would plant the community garden located on the school grounds and grow flowers, cabbages, carrots, beans, peas, potatoes, pumpkins, and melons, all of which would be taken care of by the school's 4-H club and interested neighbors during the summer.

Students from elementary school on can also be encouraged to investigate environmental issues that may be affecting their own communities. Entering into this domain requires tact and finesse, since such issues often are associated with community controversy. Environmental educators John Ramsey, Harold Hungerford, and Trudi Volk (2001) have developed a process for exploring such issues while minimizing conflict. Called Investigating and Evaluating Environmental Issues and Actions (IEEIA), this approach provides a systematic approach to issue analysis that includes an exploration of a condition that places someone or something at risk (the problem), different ideas and values about the problem and its potential solutions (the issue), individuals or organizations who have a stake in the problem (the players), attitudes of the players regarding the issue (positions), true or false ideas about the issue held by the players (beliefs), the relative importance of beliefs in a particular situation (values) and strategies available to resolve the issue (solutions).

IEEIA has been successfully used from upper elementary to secondary classrooms. An especially successful program on the Hawaiian island of Molokai called PRISM (Proposing Resolutions with Integrity for a Sustainable Molokai) has been in operation for more than a decade (Volk & Cheak, 2003). At the beginning of each year, upper elementary and middle school students identify a problem they wish to explore that relates to the local environment. They then investigate its components for several months with the help of local documents and resource professionals. Their study concludes in a day-long symposium in the spring during which they present their findings and offer their solutions. Problems explored have included topics such as solid waste disposal at the school and on the island, habitat destruction associated with ecotourism developments, the restoration of traditional Hawaiian fishponds, and emergency preparedness. Students took the lead in starting an island-wide recycling program, wrote a bottle bill (for recycling beverage containers) that was introduced into the state assembly by their legislator, and have played a role in the repair of fishponds; they also write regular news articles in the local paper about their findings.

Restoration ecology is another science-related activity that has attracted the attention of educators interested in localizing the curriculum. In the mid-1990s, Laurette Rogers, a fourth-grade teacher in California's Marin County, embarked on a small project that has spread throughout the Bay Area. In response to her students' desire to do something to preserve endangered species, she began the shrimp project, an effort to improve the habitat of a species of freshwater shrimp threatened by habitat loss in the San Francisco Bay Area. She approached a rancher about planting willows and blackberries on the banks of a creek running through his property. He was amenable, and students began a project whose results would probably not be fully realized for decades. Willows, however, grow fast, and within the span of students' school career they would become sizeable enough to be noticed. In addition to planting, students studied scientific reports about *Syncaris pacifica*, analyzed data from each of the 15 creeks where the shrimp lives, did drawings about the shrimp, wrote poems, and even made up shrimp fairy tales. They also wrote letters to and testified before government officials, spoke at educational conferences, and painted a 6-foot-long shrimp mural at a local ferry terminal (Stone, 2005).

Support from the Center for Ecoliteracy and the Bay Institute (an organization formed in the early 1980s that has worked to preserve and restore the entire delta/bay watershed) resulted in an expansion of the project to more schools and teachers. Now called the STRAW (Students and Teachers Restoring a Watershed) Program, its participants number 80 to 100 teachers in three dozen suburban, rural, and urban schools. One of the most significant results of this program can be found in the message these activities send to students. Michael Stone finishes his chapter about the project with a quote from fourth grader Megan:

> I think this project changed everything we thought we could do. I always thought kids mean nothing. I really enjoyed doing this, it was fun and I felt like our class just knew exactly what to do. I feel that it did show me that kids can make a difference in the world, and we are not just little dots.
>
> (in Stone, 2005, p. 174)

Local natural science projects do not need to involve field trips away from the school building. As with gardening, simply going out onto the school grounds can be enough. Paul Krafel in Redding, California has developed curriculum units built around species like California live oak that are common in school grounds in the northern part of the state. Units focus on topics such as oak galls or leaf transpiration, engaging students in a variety of observational and experimental activities aimed at both teaching scientific principles and acquainting students with natural phenomena accessible to them in their own neighborhoods. Similar units could be developed by teachers in other regions of the country focusing on species common to their own areas. Krafel has also written units about ants or the pond life that will begin to grow in a plastic swimming pool left outside in the sun, learning activities again easy to accomplish on school property.

In Laytonville, California, teachers chose to participate in the Cornell University Laboratory of Ornithology feeder watch (http://www.birds.cornell.edu/pfw/). In addition to being responsible for filling and maintaining feeders and then watching them and recording data, students were expected to develop their own questions about birds and then use standard procedures to determine their answers. Issues students considered included the following:

1   Why are birds important?
2   What kinds of birds visit your classroom feeders?
3   How many different species live in the area?
4   How do changes in the environment affect feeding habitats?

Projects like this or the Harvard phenology study (http://harvardforest.fas.harvard.edu/museum/phenology.html) or Project Budburst (http://www.windows.ucar.edu/citizen_science/budburst/) that examine the time that plants bud out in the spring or drop their leaves in the fall give students the chance to collect data that are then contributed to national and international studies often retrievable online. They also give students an incentive to look carefully at elements in the natural world that are often easily overlooked when young people are drawn from one indoor activity to another or to formal outdoor activities that offer little opportunity to actually attend closely to nature.

The value of this kind of science education cannot be overstated. In the spring of 2007, the *Oregonian* reported that Gresham High School to the east of Portland was one of three finalists for a national award for science excellence sponsored by Intel. The science department chairperson at the school said that the school's success in improving test scores and increasing enrollment in advanced science courses in recent years is tied to the way that "We are doing science outside the classroom. Content is still our big push, but we get what the process is for real. Before we were doing book questions in class, now we are doing cutting-edge research" (*Oregonian*, April 25, 2007, p. B3). This is the kind of outside-of-classroom learning that students in all of the examples described above are engaged in. Linking science education to students' direct experience of the world provides a powerful vehicle for demonstrating the relevance of this knowledge and through the process of application and repetition a way to help young people grasp and retain it.

Mathematics

Arithmetic, algebra, geometry, trigonometry, and calculus can provide the means for recording and expressing lessons students learn from studying both the social and the natural environments around them. All could be tapped in units associated with the natural and social sciences, as well as art. Mathematics teachers can also incorporate local phenomena into the teaching of central skills and concepts associated with their discipline. The Alaska Native Knowledge Network has made exceptional strides in developing math curricula that reflect the concerns and interests of people living in rural Alaska. In his book *Village Math*, Alan Dick (no date) presents a variety of story problems students would recognize as relevant to their own experience. One set of problems, for example, asks them to determine how much it costs to run different common household appliances such as a coffee maker or skill saw. Another considers the amount of fuel consumed by different kinds of outboard engines. A third provides information about mixing oil and gas in two-cycle engines and then asks students to determine how much oil per gallon should be used if the ratio is 20:1, 50:1, and 100:1. A fourth compares the advantages and disadvantages of chartering a plane to fly from a student's village to Anchorage compared to the fare for a seat on a mail plane. Similar kinds of problems could be developed for circumstances students in other locales would be likely to encounter in their out-of-school lives. Figuring car or insurance payments, for example, would be likely to find interested students in most urban and rural high schools in the lower 48.

In their edited volume *Rethinking Mathematics: Teaching Social Justice by the Numbers* (2006), Eric Gutstein and Bob Peterson present other ways that teachers can incorporate local concerns into the teaching of math. One of Gutstein's lesson plans, for example, focuses on whether or not racial profiling is taking place in Chicago. Students initially review basic probability ideas such as randomness, experimentation, and sample size, and then conduct simulations regarding the number of Latinos, for example, pulled over by the police for discretionary traffic stops. They take colored cubes (black for African Americans, tan for Caucasians, red for Latinos, yellow for Asians/Native Americans) that have been distributed in a bag according to the racial breakdown in Chicago. They then compare their findings to the actual number of Latinos pulled over by the police between 1987 and 1997 and discuss whether the results from their simulation support the claim of racial profiling. Other problems ask students to consider issues that although general in nature are immediately related to their own lives. This, for example, is a story problem presented by Marilyn Finkelstein in a chapter entitled "Reading the World with Math":

> A full scholarship to an out-of-state, four-year, major university like the University of Wisconsin-Madison—including dorm fees, food, books, tuition, and other fees—is worth about $27,000 a year. Calculate how many high school seniors could receive a fully paid four-year college education if the monies spent on the Iraq war—as of March 2005—had been set aside for college scholarships instead.
>
> (Finkelstein, 2006, p. 30)

Strategies such as these can connect the learning of mathematics to experiences that are familiar and understandable to students and then stretch their thinking about the disciplinary implications of those experiences in ways that foster both conceptual understanding and interest.

Language Arts

The skills of reading, writing, speaking, and listening come into play with all of the subjects described so far. When students engage in historical or scientific research, interview experts, write reports, or deliver presentations before the public, they engage in a variety of literate practices. From this perspective, place- and community-based learning opportunities can do much to extend and solidify young people's ability to communicate through print as well as oral expression. There are also good reasons and a variety of strategies for incorporating the local into students' experience of the language arts.

An elementary school teacher in Tillamook, Oregon structures nearly all of her third-grade writing assignments around experiences that students have shared outside the classroom. She observed that teachers cannot assume that all children have done the same kinds of things. Even in a town that is only a few miles from the ocean, she said that many students have never gone to the beach. Lower-income families often don't perceive such activities to be a form of entertainment, and more well-to-do families go elsewhere when they have the chance. A seemingly approachable writing prompt may therefore be inaccessible for many students. She has found however that, when she takes students outside into the school's natural area or on field trips, everyone has an equal chance to describe what they have seen and felt and smelled. Writing then becomes a vehicle for telling others about something a child has directly encountered, a form of communication that is much closer to the kind of talk that kids engage in otherwise, making the process of putting pen to paper less intimidating and more likely to be successful.

Writing can also grow out of children's contact with other people in their community. Many schools are now finding ways to bring students and older citizens together, benefiting both children and people too often isolated from younger generations. Another Laytonville, California project involved supporting multiple programs that brought children of all ages together with their elders. Primary school students participated in a pen pal program that linked them with seniors who were members of the Grange, the Garden Club, and other community organizations. Students were encouraged to ask seniors about what things were like when they were children. A year of letter writing culminated in a classroom tea party during which students met their pen pal and played a small concert on song flutes. Middle school students prepared and served a monthly elder luncheon and then listened to stories about artifacts that elders were invited to share with them. Some of these stories were then written up and published in the local paper, the *Mendocino County Observer*. At the senior high school, students from a humanities class interviewed elders about their life experiences and then published a 130-page book entitled *Through the Eyes of the Elders*. Writing in such circumstances emerges naturally from what people share orally.

In some schools, students and teachers have transformed stories learned from informal sharing and interviews into dramatic productions. In Henderson, Nebraska, for example, students learned about a blizzard in the late 1800s that had resulted in the deaths of several children from families who still lived in their community (Rural Challenge Research and Evaluation Program, 1999a). They investigated this event, gathering as much information as they could from town elders, and then wrote and produced a play entitled *Jacob Friesen and the Blizzard of 1888*. Their performance was attended by approximately 400 people, many of whom were related to the people depicted in the play.

In small rural towns, in particular, students can also provide a valuable service to their fellow citizens by taking responsibility for writing and publishing community newspapers. In early-twentieth-century Alabama, for example, more than 1,000 newspapers were in circulation, presenting information needed at the local level to make informed decisions. In the mid-1990s, this number had dropped to 100. One of the consequences has been that the only news printed about these localities tends to focus on scores from athletic contests and incidents of criminal behavior. Under the auspices of the Program for Academic and Cultural Excellence in Rural Schools (PACERS), high school students in over 20 communities sought to rectify this situation. Their language arts and journalism classes started collecting news from not only their school but the surrounding region. With the help of professional journalists and a grant that allowed them to upgrade computer hardware and software, they began running small community newspapers, reporting on stories, seeking advertisements, and publishing articles that sought to present balanced and well-written accounts of important local issues. In these circumstances, writing becomes not something that a student does for his or her English teacher but a way of achieving both voice and citizenship in the broader community. Such endeavors need not be consigned to only rural places. The Media Academy, mentioned in Chapter 3, published a Spanish–English paper for Fremont High School's neighboring community as well as the school newspaper and yearbook.

Finally, language arts teachers can seek to incorporate more regional literature into the curriculum. At Oregon City High School south of Portland, for example, one elective class focuses entirely on literature from the Pacific Northwest. *Ricochet River* (Cody, 1992), a contemporary novel about inter-racial relationships in a small logging town 30 miles away, is a popular selection among students, who enjoy reading about places with which they are familiar. Similar literature can be found in any part of the United States, but it is rare for this material to make it into classrooms, where the national canon continues to dominate the selection of novels, short stories, essays, and poems. Sharon Bishop (2003), a high school language arts teacher from Henderson, Nebraska, has gone so far as to focus solely on the literature of the Midwest in her course for high school juniors. Although drawing the line between local and national literature in this way may spark controversy, her approach demonstrates a possibility that is hardly ever considered but in fact better reflects the role storytelling about local people in local places once played in earlier societies. Stories that resonated with place were in some societies a central means for socializing the young into a sense of common identity, purpose, and ethics (Basso, 1996). For these communities, commonly shared stories helped achieve social cohesion and long-term survival.

Transforming Ideas into Practice

We hope that the ideas encountered in this and the previous chapter will inspire readers to explore ways to incorporate local knowledge and issues into their own curriculum. Before concluding this discussion of place- and community-based education in practice, however, we want to suggest a sequence of questions that teachers and other curriculum designers can consider as they embark on this process. These questions are:

- Do you wish to begin your design process with an idea primarily grounded in local knowledge or issues, or from the traditional curriculum? If the former, what topics or issues are likely to be meaningful for your students and to give them an opportunity to participate in learning activities that will be valued by others? If you start with the traditional curriculum, what topics could be easily explored at the local level in ways that allow students to experience the relevance and importance of this approach to learning and knowledge generation?
- What additional subject areas could be fit within this topic or under this project umbrella? List specific sub-topics that could be explored for each of these subjects, including those incorporated in the curriculum you teach now.

- What four or five overarching questions could guide you and your students' study of this topic or participation in this project? What issues or understandings should students be able to address at length as a result of their inquiry or work?
- What specific learning standards (knowledge, skills, or dispositions) associated with each of the subject areas you have identified could be addressed during this curriculum unit? Add to these any other learning goals not included in district or state documents you believe could be addressed as well.
- How will you go about assessing learning? List possible strategies, including some culminating projects, as well as a discussion of ways you will scaffold the learning of specific skills needed to successfully complete projects (e.g., interviewing techniques, video editing, environmental monitoring, data analysis, etc.).
- What community partners could be brought into the classroom to help teach this unit or provide support in the community or during field studies or activities? What specific forms of expertise will you need to tap to bring this unit to a successful conclusion? Are there equipment or resource needs that could also be met by community partners?
- What kind of field studies, monitoring, or other inquiry activities could students engage in outside of the classroom? How will you arrange for transportation to field sites? What kinds of additional adult support will you need to chaperone students when they are away from school? How much outside-of-classroom work can students be expected to complete on their own?
- What community needs might be addressed as part of this project? What service learning opportunities does it afford? How could you publicize the contributions that students make in association with this project?
- How might students become involved in community governance activities related to this project? Are there ways they could participate in data gathering, reporting, or other forms of public participation, such as organizing and facilitating meetings or planning and orchestrating public demonstrations?
- What additional opportunities for reporting their work beyond the school could be tied into this project? What venues might you pursue that would allow students to make public speeches or PowerPoint presentations or write news articles or press statements?
- What creative possibilities could be associated with this idea especially with regard to art or music or dance or theater? What about vocational opportunities or internships? Or the use of information technologies?

Answering as many of these questions as seem relevant to specific projects could open possibilities for curriculum development and instruction that might otherwise remain unexplored. As mentioned earlier, more than anything else place- and community-based education involves a change in perspective about how teaching and learning can proceed in and out of school.

Adopting place- and community-based educational approaches is likely to be uncomfortable as teachers push past the familiar into the unknown. Some educators will be more adventurous than others and more tolerant of uncertainty and confusion; they may be willing to take on a unit of several weeks in length at the outset. For others, small steps will be much more appropriate. We leave this up to teachers, themselves. What we do suggest is that planning for such a unit be extensive enough that the chances of success are greater than the chances of failure. Failure can never be completely sidestepped, but anticipating problems and addressing them before rather than after they occur can do much to make a positive outcome more likely. And positive outcomes are important if teachers are to gain the confidence required to persist with their instructional experiments and legitimately affirm the value of their efforts to potentially skeptical colleagues and administrators. At issue is starting. The reward can be engaged students, interested community members, and a revitalized professional life.

Websites that include useful information about curriculum projects

Alaska Native Knowledge Network: http://www.ankn.uaf.edu

Community Works Journal: http://www.vermontcommunityworks.org/cwpublications/journal/index.htm

North Coast Rural Challenge Network: http://www.ncrcn.org/home.html

Rural School and Community Trust: http://www.ruraledu.org

Vermont Rural Partnership: http://www.vermontcommunityworks.org/vrp/aboutus/index.html

Chapter 6

Impact on Academic Achievement

Place- and community-based education is a new enough approach that studies tracking its impact on students, teachers, and communities remain more preliminary and suggestive than definitive. An evaluation of the Annenberg Rural Challenge conducted by the Harvard Graduate School of Education is one of the largest efforts to explore the early effects of learning experiences rooted in children's community and region. A series of studies conducted by the State Education and Environment Roundtable have also sought to determine changes in student achievement and attitudes associated with a curricular strategy that consciously uses the environment as an integrating context. Studies conducted by researchers associated with the Rural School and Community Trust provide initial assessments of place-based educational approaches in Louisiana and Alaska and their impact on student achievement. Since 2002, a group of educators in New England has joined together to strengthen their own assessment procedures through the creation of the Place-based Education Evaluation Collaborative (PEEC). Their initial reports provide useful information about ways that teaching that connects classrooms and communities can affect many elements of children's and teachers' school experience.

Because place- and community-based education is closely allied with other innovations such as service learning, environmental education, and a form of pedagogy called authentic instruction, it is furthermore possible to draw upon related research that points to the value of educational experiences situated beyond the classroom and that involve the application of concepts and skills in "real-world" settings. Combined, all of this research suggests that the adoption of place- and community-based educational approaches does in fact hold the promise of enhancing student engagement and achievement, and their sense of responsibility for the broader human and natural communities that surround them. Additional benefits, rarely discussed in much school reform literature, also accrue to teachers who embrace this approach and to the communities that support it. In this chapter we will consider what is known at this point about the relationship between place- and community-based education and student engagement and achievement. In the following chapter we will explore its impact on student behaviors and attitudes as well as its effects on teachers and, to a lesser extent, communities.

Grappling with the Problems of Motivation and Alienation

The heart of place- and community-based education's claim to increased student achievement can be found in the way it addresses the issue raised a century ago by John Dewey about student motivation. To reiterate, Dewey observed that, in the absence of a strong connection between school and the life children lead outside the classroom, educators must set "painfully to work, on another tack and by a variety of means, to arouse in the child an interest in school studies" (1959, p. 77). In the nineteenth century, those means included corporal punishment and the ferule; in the late twentieth and early twenty-first centuries, the immediate threat of a teacher's disregard and the long-term threat of an impoverished adulthood have become the most common tools of persuasion. A proportion of students, often-times from families who themselves have been educationally successful, under-stands the implications of educational achievement and is generally willing to comply with teachers' requests and demands regardless of lack of interest in either the subject matter or class activities. For many other students, however, the division between schooling and life is so profound that most of their teachers are only inter-mittently able to enlist their intellects or passions. School—especially its academic requirements—remains a compulsory obligation but not something that touches their lives.

There are a number of potential reasons for this alienation from learning. Cognitive psychologists point to the way people fit new information into already existing schematic frameworks built upon earlier experiences of the world. In the absence of those frameworks, what teachers say or what is encountered in textbooks finds no purchase in a student's mind. Teaching in such circumstances is as effec-tive as throwing Velcro against a smooth surface. Jim Cummins (1996), noted expert on bilingual education, argues that English-language learners have more success when teachers frame cognitively demanding tasks within contextually rich educational settings. If students have the opportunity to relate new learning to what they already know or can directly experience (e.g., through a demonstration, exper-iment, or research project), they will be more likely to attend to and master the skills and knowledge presented to them. Although clearly valuable for students who are still mastering any foreign language, Cummins's insight is appropriate for many students for whom the intellectual abstractions of many academic disciplines remain largely impenetrable without this form of contextualization.

Sociolinguists and anthropologists point to another factor that can inhibit learn-ing. If students' communication or cultural patterns are significantly at variance with what they encounter with their teachers, engagement can again be precluded. Shirley Brice Heath's (1983) famous study of questioning strategies in low-income Black and middle-class White communities in South Carolina showed how both teachers and students misunderstood one another and inadvertently reinforced behaviors that favored some children while discriminating against others. Once teachers and students understood what was going on, they were able to set aside incorrect assumptions about people unlike themselves and embark on a set of learning activities aimed at overcoming these differences. Deep knowledge of one another's communities allowed this to happen.

Finally, students' motivation to learn can be diminished if they believe that teachers do not have their best interests at heart. This may be one of the primary reasons behind the forms of resistance that Ogbu (1978) encountered among students from discriminated-against groups both in the United States and elsewhere. Such discrimination can also be directed against students from working-class communities as well as ethnic and racial groups, leading to similar forms of resistance and disengagement (Anyon, 1981; Willis, 1981). Place- and community-based education can help deflect these sources of student inattention by bridging differences between home and school, by situating learning in such a way that children and youth feel as though their and their families' experiences are legitimate and worthy of attention and positive regard, and by creating meaningful contexts within which new information, concepts, and skills are conveyed to students.

Enhancing Motivation to Learn by Linking School to Community

James Coleman and Thomas Hoffer's study *Public and Private High Schools: The Impact of Communities* (1987) describes how, when the messages conveyed to children and youth from their homes, communities, and schools all converge, academic performance and achievement improve. This is the primary lesson they take from a study of public and private schools (both secular and Catholic) in Chicago. As one might expect, given the relationship between income and achievement, student performance is higher in private than public schools; what was of interest to Coleman and Hoffer, however, is the way that less affluent and more diverse students in Chicago's Catholic schools frequently outperformed their wealthier counterparts in the city's secular private schools. In their effort to determine why this might be the case, they discovered that children in Catholic schools were generally much more connected to their neighborhoods and churches than was the case for the primarily White students in secular private schools, whose parents' work lives left little time for either family or community. Coleman and Hoffer argue that lower-income students in Catholic schools had access to a form of social capital (here defined as the presence of supportive social networks) that was often absent for both public school students and students in non-Catholic private schools.

Although place- and community-based education is unlikely to have any impact on the amount of time that parents spend with their children, it can affect the degree to which students experience the different domains of their lives as integrated rather than separate. It is this integration of messages and values that Coleman and Hoffer believe can have such a profound effect on children's learning and sense of identity. When educators in public schools reach out to their students' communities, they can help create the conditions within which a convergence similar to what Coleman and Hoffer saw in the Catholic schools can take place. This convergence will not be predicated on shared religious beliefs and values, but it will be based on shared community interests and concerns. And students ideally will come to see that activities valued by their teachers are also valued by their families and neighbors, a powerful form of affirmation that can engender students' motivation to learn.

That such motivation is a critical precursor to achievement is well supported in the research literature. In his 2003 volume *What Works in Schools: Translating Research into Action*, Robert Marzano cites over 40 studies from the 1970s through 2002 that demonstrate this relationship. Several quantitative studies reveal correlations between motivation and achievement ranging from 0.19 to 0.63, and effect sizes that range from two-thirds to one and two-thirds standard deviations of improved achievement. Studies regarding place- and community-based education that are able to demonstrate increased motivation arising from the meaning and value students ascribe to their learning activities can logically be linked to potential increases in student achievement (Duffin, Powers, & Tremblay, 2004).

Research completed at the Center on School Organization and Restructuring at the University of Wisconsin-Madison in the middle 1990s points to another set of factors that can influence student motivation and achievement. This national study focused on eight elementary, eight middle, and eight high schools that had embarked on a process of school reform involving shifts in organization (from an individualistic and bureaucratic model to one in which teachers shared collective responsibility for student success), the regular and consistent expression of high expectations for student learning, and the incorporation of instructional practices that required students to master complex tasks and information connected in some way to the world beyond the classroom (Newmann, Marks, & Gamoran, 1995). For our purposes, the third characteristic of restructuring schools is most relevant.

Called authentic instruction or pedagogy, this approach to teaching and learning has many similarities to place- and community-based education. It requires students to deal with complex information, consider alternatives, apply forms of inquiry and communication associated with academic disciplines to real-world settings, write reports and speeches, and convey their findings and ideas to people beyond the school. While not every place- and community-based educational experience will display all of the elements of authentic instruction, there is enough correspondence across these approaches to view them as closely related.

Over the five-year period during which the Center on School Organization and Restructuring was in operation, data were collected regarding instructional practices in the different schools and student achievement in math and social studies, subjects that were the study's central focus. The degree to which authentic instruction was taking place varied from classroom to classroom and school to school. Researchers associated with the project evaluated classrooms and ranked them according to whether low, average, or high levels of authentic instruction were in evidence. They then estimated the contribution of this form of instruction to student performance across the sample. Even though the most successful teachers scored significantly below the top rating for authentic instruction according to researchers' standards, students in the classrooms of highest-ranking teachers still performed more successfully on tests based on items from the National Assessment of Education Progress. According to Newmann and his associates:

We found that authentic pedagogy helps all students substantially. However, it provides an extra boost for students already performing at higher levels. In other words, if a low-achieving student moved from a class low in authentic pedagogy to a class high in authentic pedagogy, that student's performance would be enhanced significantly. But a high-performing student making the same move would improve even more.

(Newmann, Marks et al., 1995, p. 7)

To summarize, in schools where what happens in the classroom parallels experiences that students have in the broader community or where teachers create lessons characterized by authenticity and real-world applications, student achievement is higher. It is important to remember that most educational research focuses more on correlation than causation, and this is true here, as well. But the positive relationship between educational experiences that are meaningful and responsive to students' life outside the classroom and learning seems to be clear.

Place- and Community-based Education, Engagement, and Achievement

What about research that explicitly addresses place- and community-based educational reforms? Gerald Lieberman and Linda Hoody's 1998 study *Closing the Achievement Gap: Using the Environment as an Integrating Context for Learning* is widely cited as one of the first efforts to link what in effect is place- and community-based learning to a variety of student outcomes including academic engagement and achievement as measured on standardized tests. The environment referred to in the title of the study includes both natural and social settings; at issue for the authors is the way teachers seek to contextualize learning through the use of local lived experiences of many kinds.

This 1998 study involved site visits to 40 schools where teachers were using the environment as an integrating context (EIC), interviews with more than 400 students and 250 teachers and administrators, and the completion of four instruments aimed at uncovering additional information about student and teacher participation, student engagement, instructional practices, and effects of the program on students' knowledge, skills, retention, and attitudes (Lieberman & Hoody, 1998, p. 3).

Much of the information presented in *Closing the Achievement Gap* is drawn from the reports of teachers and principals, and so is one step removed from direct observations of student behavior. With that limitation in mind, what Lieberman and Hoody discovered parallels research from the Center on School Organization and Restructuring about the impact on engagement of learning activities that involve inquiry and have real-world applications. They discovered, for example, that 98 percent of educators reported a notable increase in student enthusiasm and engagement in school activities after the adoption of EIC approaches (Lieberman & Hoody, 1998, p. 25). Eighty-nine percent reported that students were more willing to stay on task when learning in this way. Especially important for respondents was the way that EIC was more responsive to students with varied learning styles, particularly those considered at risk of school failure. Educators at all of the 40 schools involved in the study reported that learning in outdoor settings provided opportunities for many of these students to function more successfully. As one teacher from Kentucky commented, "When they get out there, they tell the teacher, 'I know what this is.' They just get to feeling better about themselves. You're in their territory out there. They like it. They buy into it" (in Lieberman & Hoody, 1998, p. 26).

Not only do educational experiences in the natural world or community help students feel better about themselves, but learning in this way can also enhance their ability to solve problems and think critically, ideally one of the predictors of academic achievement. Teachers involved with the PRISM program on Molokai described in Chapter 5 observed of their students that "We have parents and community members telling us, 'They're really learning. They're analyzing this stuff. They're not just transcribing something or pulling information out of books and putting it together in a composition. They are actually engaged in thinking about why this is important'" (in Cheak, Volk, & Hungerford, 2002, p. 36). A student commented that "before PRISM I could not do problem-solving or critical thinking. I had a really hard time with that. After PRISM and the investigation and stuff, I had to do a lot of it and I became better at it" (in Cheak et al., 2002, p. 34).

Findings from teachers who use the environment as an integrating context parallel those from Molokai. Lieberman and Hoody (1998) report that 97 percent of teachers who responded to the Learning Survey used in their 1998 study said that students in EIC classrooms "were more capable of solving problems and thinking strategically than their traditionally educated peers" (p. 50). Athman and Monroe's 2004 investigation of 400 ninth- and twelfth-graders in 11 Florida high schools where EIC has been implemented reported that "Controlling for grade point average, gender, and ethnicity, EIC programs significantly raised students' scores on the Cornell Critical Thinking Test at both grade levels" (p. 507). Teachers who worked with these young people believed that their growth occurred as a result of the exploration of common issues across different disciplines; the use of open-ended projects that required hypothesis-making, investigation, and research; the encouragement of student choice and voice; and regular invitations to students to reflect on their learning and its implications for their communities. These elements are encountered where students engage in locally meaningful research projects regardless of the label assigned to this process.

Similar findings are encountered in studies of college-age students who are given the opportunity to apply ideas learned in the classroom to field settings. Biology professors at Central Washington University (Quitadamo, Faiola, Johnson, & Kurtz, 2008) investigated the critical thinking skills of students in different sections of introductory biology courses at their institution. One set of sections was taught conventionally, with lectures alternating with laboratory work. Another set of sections focused on a pedagogical method called community-based inquiry (CBI). A third set incorporated mixed methods. According to the authors:

The CBI instructional model consisted of four main elements that worked in concert to foster gains in critical thinking. These elements included: (1)

authentic inquiry related to community need, (2) case study exercises aligned to major course themes, (3) peer evaluation and individual accountability, and (4) lecture/content discussion.

(Quitadamo et al., 2008, p. 330)

Significant for our purposes here is the way the CBI method's focus on inquiry projects related to community needs such as water quality or amphibian decline, projects that parallel those seen in K–12 schools that have adopted place- and community-based approaches. The authors found that inviting students to participate in community-based inquiry led to markedly higher scores when they retook the California Critical Thinking Skills Test (CCTST) at the end of the class. Students in CBI course sections demonstrated gains nearly three times greater than their pre-test performance when compared to the scores posted by students in traditionally taught and mixed sections. The authors believe that this growth is related to the way that CBI builds on students' prior knowledge, engages them in authentic scientific research, and demands ongoing reflection and self-awareness. In CBI sections, students had the opportunity to try on the role of scientist and engage in research activities that were meaningful and significant to both themselves and their community.

Early findings about the impact of place- and community-based education on student achievement are also positive but more circumscribed. In Lieberman and Hoody's 1998 study scores from standardized tests including the Iowa Test of Basic Skills (ITBS), the California Achievement Test (CAT), the Texas Assessment of Academic Skills (TAAS), and others were available from only 10 of the 40 schools, and even these data were not consistent across all study sites. Their assertions that students in classrooms and schools where EIC is being practiced demonstrate higher scores on standardized measurements of academic achievement in reading, writing, math, science, and social studies are thus less convincing from a methodological standpoint. Evidence for this claim is available from only one-quarter of the schools, and the statistical significance of students' higher performance when compared to peers in classrooms where the environment is not used as an integrating context is never assessed.

Lieberman's Pew Charitable Trusts-supported institution, the State Education and Environment Roundtable, conducted similar studies involving fewer schools in 2000 and 2005. In the 2000 study (State Education and Environment Roundtable [SEER], 2000), scores on tests in the same academic domains from eight paired sets of students were compared, some in the same school but different classrooms, and others in different schools. In 101 out of 140 assessments (72 percent), academic achievement in reading, writing, math, science, and social studies was better (i.e., demonstrated higher scores). The establishment of comparison groups, however, did not take into account other factors that could have also influenced student performance, such as teacher experience and skill or student family backgrounds. The tests, as well, were not always equivalent, making it impossible to determine whether the higher scores were once again statistically significant.

In the 2005 study, four matched treatment and control pairs of schools were investigated. Pairs this time were selected from a statewide ranking of similar schools, and the scores were all from California's STAR (Standardized Testing and Reporting System) exams. A comparison of five years of scores revealed that:

- In 100 percent of the reading assessments, treatment students [students in schools where EIC was practiced] scored as well or better than control students
- In 92.5 percent of the math assessments, treatment students scored as well or significantly higher than control students
- In 95 percent of the language assessments, treatment students scored as well or significantly higher than control students
- In 97.5 percent of the spelling assessments, treatment students scored as well or significantly higher than control students
- In over 96 percent of all cases treatment students scored as well or significantly higher than control students
- In only 4 percent of the cases control students scored significantly higher than treatment students
- In 42 percent of the cases treatment students scored significantly higher than control students in reading, math, language and spelling

(SEER, 2005)

Although this most recent study is methodologically more credible than SEER's earlier work, it still does not provide enough detailed data for readers to determine whether students' higher scores were in fact statistically significant, diminishing the persuasive power of this research, as well.

Another study of the EIC approach was completed in 2004 regarding the Bay Schools Project in Maryland (Von Secker, 2004). This three-year project focused on using Chesapeake Bay and its watershed as the context for integrated instruction. Clare Von Secker, an independent evaluator, sought to answer three questions at the conclusion of the project, two of which related directly to issues of engagement and achievement:

- Was student engagement in learning related to the amount of emphasis teachers placed on EIC?
- Was students' environmental knowledge related to the amount of emphasis their teachers placed on EIC?

Teachers in five schools in five Maryland counties participated in this project. Classroom observations and interviews allowed Von Secker to rank them according to the degree to which they incorporated project-based, interdisciplinary activities into their classrooms. She found that, within each of the five schools, students self-reported significantly higher levels of engagement when they had the opportunity to work with teachers who made extensive use of EIC practices. While Von Secker did administer tests aimed at assessing students' environmental literacy as it related to Chesapeake Bay, she did not attempt to gauge other forms of academic achievement. With regard to environmental literacy, students in the classrooms of teachers who emphasized EIC outperformed their peers at a statistically significant level, suggesting that more methodologically credible studies of other EIC sites could potentially affirm findings presented in the SEER reports.

A handful of studies associated with the Annenberg Rural Challenge have also attempted to gather comparative data regarding the impact of place- and community-based education on student achievement as measured by standardized tests. Emeka Emekauwa's study "They Remember What They Touch: The Impact of Place-based Learning in East Feliciana Parish" (2004a) describes changes in student performance over a three-year period in three Louisiana elementary schools. Funding from the National Science Foundation and the Rural Challenge supported three consecutive summer training programs that showed teachers how to integrate the study of local natural resources into the teaching of science, math, and technology. Students in Feliciana Parish public schools are largely African American (80 percent) and economically underprivileged (84.8 percent qualified for free or reduced-price lunch during the years of the study). Baseline data were collected regarding the percentage of students who posted unsatisfactory scores on the fourth-grade Louisiana Educational Assessment for the 21st Century (LEAP21) tests for language arts, math, science, and social studies. District- and state-level scores demonstrate the way that, over the time students had the opportunity to learn in this way, the number of low-performing students came increasingly close to the state average. In math and social studies, for example, gaps of 10.7 and 15.6 percentage points in 1999–2000 were reduced to 0.2 and 7.5 percentage points respectively by 2001–2002.

It goes without saying that altogether too many students in East Feliciana schools are failing to learn at a desirable level. Still, educational experiences that are more grounded in the context of their lives appear to be having an impact on the learning of formerly low-performing students when compared to their peers across the state. Dr. Knight Roddy, district director for place-based learning, maintains that the incorporation of local phenomena into classroom teaching "is serving as a hook to get students excited by learning" (in Emekauwa, 2004a, p. 8). A seventh-grade teacher also involved with this district initiative observed that students in his classrooms are "remembering facts from last year about the critters they netted. When other students and adults come to my class, my students can talk articulately about what they are doing ... they remember what they touch" (in Emekauwa, 2004a, p. 8).

Table 6.1 Percentage of fourth graders scoring unsatisfactorily on state tests in 1999–2000 and 2001–2002

	1999–2000		2001–2002	
Grade 4	District	State	District	State
English-language arts	32.6	19.7	18.4	14.2
Mathematics	39.0	28.3	24.9	24.7
Science	27.5	18.2	19.4	14.5
Social studies	39.4	23.8	28.1	20.6

Source: Emekauwa (2004a, p. 5).

Emekauwa (2004b) has also reported on the impact of place- and community-based education on the achievement of Alaska Native students in schools associated with the Alaska Rural Systemic Initiative (AKRSI). This project, again supported by both the National Science Foundation and the Annenberg Rural Challenge, worked for a decade from the mid-1990s to improve the educational performance of Alaska Native students through the incorporation of indigenous values and knowledge into educational programs encountered in rural schools. This was done through the integration of Native and non-Native knowledge and skills in curriculum development, the compilation of a knowledge base documenting the cultural and ecological knowledge of the state's five groups of Native peoples, the establishment of elders and cultural camps that linked students and teachers with local experts as they pursued inquiry-based activities, and the development of village science applications that exposed students to the work of scientists in field and laboratory settings.

The culminating report from Alaska Rural Systemic Initiative (2006) describes changes in the number of students performing at the advanced or proficient level on the eighth- and tenth-grade mathematics benchmarks from 2000 to 2005. During these years, the science assessment system was still being piloted, and no reliable data on achievement in science were available. Data compared the achievement of students in AKRSI schools with those in other village schools. AKRSI worked with 20 rural districts that included 176 schools; nearly 19,000 students—60 percent of all rural students and 90 percent of all rural Alaska Native students—were enrolled in these districts. As Emekauwa notes, "These school districts ... have historically posted the lowest student achievement scores in the state and the nation" (Emekauwa, 2004b, p. 6). Non-AKRSI rural schools are almost always located on Alaska's road system and include a much higher proportion of non-Native students. These include towns such as Homer, Seward, Kenai, Delta Junction, and Tok. Student scores in non-AKRSI districts are approximately the same as or slightly higher than state averages.

For eighth graders, the number of AKRSI students meeting the benchmark has doubled, while the proportion in non-AKRSI schools has increased by slightly less than 1.5 times. Tenth-grade scores at the advanced/proficient level in AKRSI schools are 2.5 times as great as what they were in the 1999–2000 academic year compared to slightly less than 2 times as great in non-AKRSI schools. Scores in AKRSI schools still obviously lag behind those in schools with fewer Alaska Native students, but as in East Feliciana the achievement gap is closing. Also notable are

Figure 6.2 Percentage of rural students as advanced/proficient in the eighth-grade mathematics benchmark and tenth-grade high school graduation qualifying exams

	1999–2000		2004–2005	
	AKRSI	Non-AKRSI	AKRSI	Non-AKRSI
Eighth grade	21%	41%	42%	60%
Tenth grade	20%	32%	50%	63%

Source: Alaska Rural Systemic Initiative (2006, p. 23).

increases in first-time enrollments between 1995 and 2002 at the University of Alaska by students who had attended AKRSI schools. This number nearly trebled, growing from approximately 110 to slightly more than 300. In comparison, increased enrollment by non-AKRSI schools grew from approximately 150 to 200. It is important to note that both increases in student enrollment were affected by the implementation of the Alaska Scholars program, which allows the top 10 percent of every graduating class to enroll in the University of Alaska system tuition free. Once again, these research findings are strongly suggestive of a positive, albeit small, link between place- and community-based education and enhanced academic achievement as measured by standardized tests and, in the last instance, rates of college attendance.

Research Regarding Environmental Education and Achievement

Another set of studies regarding the impact of environmentally focused initiatives that demonstrate many characteristics of place- and community-based education also point to the impact that learning experiences that involve inquiry, field studies, and work in or for the broader community can have on student achievement. The National Environmental Education Training Foundation (NEETF) published a study entitled *Environment-based Education: Creating High Performance Schools and Students* in 2000. In it, the authors present information about ten elementary schools and one high school in various states that have created strong offerings in environmental education, including some that work closely with the State Education and Environment Roundtable (SEER). Hallmarks of the educational practice that was the focus of this study include integrating learning across disciplines, problem-solving, decision-making, independent and group learning, issues-based instructional activities, and a balanced variety of perspectives. Some, although not all, schools serve low-income and diverse students. Information about achievement varies from site to site, sometimes tracking tests scores in a single school over a number of years following the introduction of an environmentally based approach, sometimes comparing a school's scores to statewide averages, sometimes comparing scores of students in a single classroom to school-wide averages. It is difficult from the data to ascribe improved achievement to environmental education per se, but in most instances students in classrooms or schools where the practices listed above are in evidence are outperforming their peers in other schools.

The most methodologically convincing study regarding the impact of environmental education on student achievement is Oksana Bartosh's *Environmental Education: Improving Student Achievement* (2004), one part of a broader research effort conducted by Washington state's Environmental Education Consortium. Bartosh's five-year longitudinal analysis compared 77 schools that were systematically integrating environmental education across the disciplines with 77 other schools where this was not happening in as substantive a manner. Although Washington state law requires this incorporation of environmental issues into all academic domains, implementation varies from building to building and district to district. The 77 "treatment" schools were chosen on the basis of their commitment to integrating environmental education across the curriculum, years engaged in this activity (at minimum three), number of students and teachers participating in integrated courses, frequency of team teaching, degree to which students are encouraged to construct their own knowledge, innovative assessment practices, and efforts to link the school curriculum to the community. These practices have much in common with both authentic instruction as defined by Newmann, Marks et al. (1995) and place- and community-based education. Treatment schools were chosen on the basis of scores received on an Environmental Education Rubric completed by external environmental education providers and experts familiar with schools in Washington state. The comparison schools did not have an environmental education program or were just starting to develop it. Using U.S. Census data and information from Washington state's Office of the Superintendent of Public Instruction (OSPI), schools were paired on the basis of size, students' economic status, ethnic composition, and geographic location.

Student achievement measures included scores on the Washington Assessment of Student Learning (WASL) and the Iowa Test of Basic Skills (ITBS) collected from the OSPI website. In addition, a survey with the Environmental Education Rubric and questions about school building programs and implementation was made available on the Internet for personnel in participating schools. All totaled, 84 teachers, 19 principals, and 10 others completed this survey, the majority of whom were from buildings where environmental education had become more firmly rooted. Bartosh reports that:

> According to this research, schools that undertake systemic environmental education programs consistently have higher test scores on the state standardized tests over comparable schools with "traditional" curriculum approaches. The mean percentage of students who meet standards on WASL and ITBS tests are higher in all six areas [i.e., WASL-Math, WASL-Reading, WASL-Writing, WASL-Listening, IT-Reading, IT-Math] in the schools with environmental programs. According to the statistical analysis, schools with EE programs performed significantly better compared to non-EE schools on the state standards tests. There were no schools that had lower percentages of students who meet or test above standards in all six areas. Overall, 73 pairs out of 77 project schools had higher scores in **at least** [emphasis in original] one subject.
>
> (Bartosh, 2004, p. 117)

Bartosh also notes that quantitative and qualitative evidence drawn from reports from survey respondents indicates that "EE schools use natural areas more regularly; receive more support from parents, administration and community; teachers have more EE professional training and value EE higher compared to respondents from comparison schools" (Bartosh, 2004, p. 118). She is careful to acknowledge that these effects are correlational rather than causal, but still believes that environmental education "provides tremendous opportunities for schools, teachers and students" (p. 118).

It improves students' behavior and motivation to learn. It encourages parents and members of the community to take part in the school learning activities. Also students have a unique opportunity to participate in the real-life projects and try to solve issues and problems in their communities. They see the relationships between knowledge and skills they receive in the classrooms and the real world around them. Environmental education can help students to believe that they can *make a difference.*

(Bartosh, 2004, p. 118)

Bartosh concludes her thesis with a plea for more studies about the impact of environmental education on student achievement and critical thinking skills and less reliance on anecdotal studies and reports.

As mentioned at the beginning of this chapter, in 2002 a group of non-formal and university-based educators in New England formed a collaborative to address this need. Working with Program Evaluation and Educational Research (PEER) Associates, they created the Place-based Education Evaluation Collaborative (PEEC). Findings about student achievement are still preliminary, but PEEC's work regarding other impacts of place-based education on students and teachers reiterates much that has surfaced from earlier studies about the positive effect that situating learning in authentic contexts can have on student motivation and involvement. It will form the basis of the discussion about additional benefits of place- and community-based education discussed in the next chapter.

Achievement—Only One Piece of the Educational Puzzle

Although research regarding student achievement as measured by standardized tests remains in its early stages, larger-scale studies like the one completed by Bartosh (2004) in Washington state and the national investigation of authentic instruction conducted by the Center on School Organization and Restructuring (Newmann, Marks et al., 1995) demonstrate that contextualizing learning and inviting young people to be the creators and not merely consumers of knowledge can have a powerful impact on students' willingness to attend to educational tasks and demands. Without such attention and commitment, school achievement will remain problematic. With it, existing evidence suggests that improved performance will follow. But academic achievement should be seen as only one of the outcomes of any educational process. If children learn only to advance their own self-interest in a competition for higher grades, society suffers. Schools need to prepare individuals who also perceive their membership in broader social and natural communities and then act accordingly. We will now turn to ways that place- and community-based educational experiences support this broader understanding of educational purposes, looking at the impact these can have not only on children and youth but also on those who teach and support them.

Chapter 7

Striving for More than Test Scores

In today's political environment, raising students' test scores must necessarily be of concern to teachers and principals. Without the ability to demonstrate or at minimum promise improvements in performance on standardized examinations of student learning, even the most attractive instructional or curricular proposals will be discarded. Over the long run, however, other educational outcomes may in fact be more important. The acquisition of certain forms of academic knowledge and the ability to "cipher," read, and write are certainly essential to negotiating the demands of the modern world. But, for both individuals and the society in which they live, less tangible attributes and dispositions are also necessary.

Are young people, for example, growing up in such a way that they perceive their identities as tied to the identities of others and the well-being of the broader community? Do they have an understanding of the way that human life is dependent on the healthy functioning of natural systems, and that disrupting those systems will come to erode the foundations of the social environment, as well? And do the people who teach a society's children feel as though they are supported and enlivened by their work, so that the examples they set for the young are characterized by enthusiasm, responsibility, and civic involvement? Do the communities in which these children and their teachers live benefit from the work of schools, or are they diminished in some way by what happens—or does not happen—in classrooms? In the era of No Child Left Behind, these questions have been pushed to the margins of educational discourse, much as a market society ignores the impact of economic decisions on communities and the natural world. The reality of our social experience and effects of our decisions on planetary systems, however, have a way of intruding upon our beliefs about what is of value or of little import.

In this chapter we will consider the impact of place- and community-based education on students' experience of connection to the social and natural settings in which they live, their development of a sense of environmental stewardship, and their feelings about themselves as learners and as citizens. We will also consider the way that place- and community-based education, by transforming teachers into curriculum creators and co-learners with their students, affects the experience of these critical players in the educational endeavor. Finally, we will look at some of the impact that this localized approach to teaching and learning has in the communities where it is practiced. Much of what we present will be based on anecdotal evidence, small-scale studies completed by others, or observations of our own from schools where teachers are implementing place- and community-based education in deep rather than superficial ways.

What we offer here will require more extensive and more systematic research to confirm, but, in the schools with which we are familiar, changes are taking place that point to the value of bringing the real, the tangible, and the humane into children's school experience. The principal of Portland's Sunnyside Environmental School—described earlier in Chapter 4—mentioned to Smith that her central office supervisor took her aside in the fall of 2006 and said that he had been puzzling over what it was that made her school so unique when compared to others he visited on a regular basis. He had concluded that what set Sunnyside apart was the happiness of its students and teachers. Happiness is hard to quantify and assess, but its presence speaks to something worth acknowledging and cultivating.

Educating Children to Become Self-directed, Confident, and Participating Citizens and Environmental Stewards

Observations drawn from a variety of studies as well as our own experience suggest that students involved in place- and community-based educational activities demonstrate behaviors and attitudes that set them apart from peers who have not had comparable opportunities. Children and young people who have a chance to learn in ways that connect them more deeply to surrounding communities, for example, are often viewed by their teachers as possessing more self-discipline as well as the skills and forms of attention associated with self-directed learning. Presented with projects requiring teamwork, students become more collaborative and able to work effectively with their peers. Learning experiences that push past textbooks and worksheets to inquiry and application also tend to be more inclusive of a broader range of students, many of whom remain marginalized for academic or behavioral reasons in conventional classrooms. Confronted with real-life problems from their own communities, students exhibit improved analytical and problem-solving abilities and become more capable critical thinkers. Given the opportunity to share their ideas in public settings where adults listen and weigh their research, presentations, or testimony, children develop a sense of voice and gain in self-confidence. When study and presentations are joined to action in and beyond the school, they acquire a taste for environmental stewardship and civic participation. Finally, attention to the local can nurture a sense of pride about one's community and a deepening connection to the people there and the place that supports them. In the pages that follow, we will explore these effects of place- and community-based education in more detail, providing anecdotes and occasional data summaries from evaluative and scholarly efforts to learn more about this approach.

It shouldn't be surprising that when students find learning to be meaningful their behavior and attention improve. This is one of the central findings from Lieberman and Hoody's *Closing the Achievement Gap* (1998). Seventy percent of the educators from the 40 schools using social and natural environments as an integrating context

(EIC) reported a reduction in disciplinary problems. The year before EIC was intro-duced to Hotchkiss Elementary School in Texas, for example, teachers made 560 disciplinary referrals. The next year the school reported only 160 referrals. This number dropped to 50 during the second year of program implementation. Teachers and their principal ascribed these changes to students' increased involve-ment in learning activities. Jeff Coppes, an assistant principal at another EIC site in Pennsylvania, observed that students in the STREAMS program there "truly begin to discipline themselves. I think if you keep it so it's centered around the kids and they're involved, and they're actively doing things, then there's less time for them to think, 'I'm bored and I want to do something else'" (in Lieberman & Hoody, 1998, p. 25).

A teacher involved in the IEEIA (Investigating and Evaluating Environmental Issues and Actions) program on Molokai made similar observations about the behavioral impacts of increased student engagement. "This gives our students the opportunity to really internalize their locus of control. It can be any conflict. 'If I [assuming the voice of the student] take that action then I have to take responsibil-ity for it.' Now, our students are more aware of the consequences" (in Cheak et al., 2002, p. 30).

One of the most significant ways that self-control has played out in the program on Molokai involves the degree to which children are taking responsibility for their own learning. One community member noted that "I see these kids and the ones that have graduated and gone on and they've learned how to learn. They're not afraid. They're not afraid to ask questions" (in Cheak et al., 2002, p. 38).

Comments from evaluators of the Annenberg Rural Challenge parallel those from Molokai. After visiting schools across the United States during the second year of this project, the authors of *Living and Learning in Rural Schools and Communities* asserted that "students engaged in Rural Challenge work at its best have learned to be self-directed learners, certainly a prized, longed-for achievement of students anywhere" (Rural Challenge Research and Evaluation Program, 1999a, p. 138). These findings suggest that, when students are drawn into learning experiences that tap their own curiosity and desire for competence and autonomy, they invest their energy and attention in academic pursuits. Problems related to classroom manage-ment and student motivation largely evaporate when young people are given the chance to learn about things that are clearly meaningful to themselves and their community.

One of the reasons that this happens could be tied into the role of collaboration and teamwork in many place- and community-based educational settings. It is not uncommon for teachers to serve more as facilitators of learning than instructors, allowing students the time for the kind of purposeful social interaction that in conventional classrooms must be caught on the sly. When Smith observed at Portland's Environmental Middle School (the predecessor to the Sunnyside Environmental School), he was frequently impressed with the way that classroom activities felt like sewing bees or quilting circles in which students worked on com-mon projects in small groups, quietly conversing with one another as they com-pleted their assigned tasks (Smith, 2004). On Molokai, as well, program evaluators noted that collaboration became a "way of life" for students and that joint problem-solving was common (Cheak et al., 2002).

One of the benefits of this degree of collaboration is the way it counters the individualistic tendencies of typical school settings and the disadvantage this poses for less academically inclined students. Cheak and her associates observe that:

> Many traditional educational approaches tend to marginalize students of lesser ability by their very design of promoting instructional contexts of competition and comparison. It is within these contexts of competition and comparison that students work hard at concealing their lack of ability, rather than being risk takers as they can be within this program. The IEEIA program appears to offer a safe context, where all students can participate in an atmosphere of challenge with support.
>
> (Cheak et al., 2002, p. 63)

Such a context can be extraordinarily valuable in helping students classified as lower-ability to discover their own talents. Given opportunities to accomplish challenging tasks, some special needs students are able to leave programs set up for them (Cheak et al., 2002).

Not only collaboration invites the participation of students who otherwise struggle in their classrooms or float through school without ever really applying themselves. So does the chance to be engaged in activities that tap other talents and abilities than those associated with linguistic and mathematical intelligence, the abilities most frequently rewarded in conventional educational settings. Rural Challenge teachers involved in the creation of aquaculture labs in both Maine and Alabama describe how students generally disengaged in most of their classes come alive when given the chance to work in another kind of setting that demands action and application. Brian Leavitt, a science teacher for a number of years at the K–12 school in Lubec, Maine, observed that some of the most capable and involved students in the lab were the same boys who basically paid little attention in most of their other classes (Leavitt, 2005). John Harbuck, a science teacher from Florala, Alabama, found himself similarly surprised. During a convocation celebrating the work of PACERS (Program for Academic and Cultural Excellence in Rural Schools) in the spring of 2005, he recalled students who had caught his attention in the aquaculture lab, students who oftentimes didn't excel at anything else but still wished "there was something that would get my name in the paper":

> Tom. Three years Tom was in the ninth grade. Tom made practically all F's. Tom would not do anything for anybody. Tom made straight A's for aquaculture. My principal put him in that class because he knew that Tom wasn't going to do anything. [But] Tom was one of those kids who was sitting there wanting something. If I ever had a perfect job done, he did it. The last I heard of Tom, he was obeying the law. … Matt. This young man I had when he was a senior. He was a special ed student. His mama wouldn't let them put him in special ed. He was just like Tom. He could run the [aquaculture] system just as good as I

could. When he graduated, I gave him an aquaculture award. He said it was the only thing in his life he had actually won. I said, "You didn't win it; you earned it." He got married after high school and took off to the Northwest. On the way, he passed a char hatchery. He told his wife, "Let's stop in here." They looked around. He started telling him [a person from the hatchery] what he knew. Largest arctic char hatchery there. He was hired. Special ed right into a job.

(Taken from fieldnotes recorded during the convocation, May 5, 2005)

Truly "inclusive" classrooms provide this range of opportunities for their students, assuring that every young person grows into an adult who believes, like Tom or the youngsters in the IEEIA program on Molokai, that he or she is capable of doing good work for others.

Being treated like capable and responsible learners and placed in settings where their projects have meaning and significance beyond the classroom can also enhance students' self-confidence. They come to see themselves as social actors whose voices deserve to be heard as much as the next person's. A student who had participated in Elaine Senechal's environmental justice class at the Greater Egleston Community High School in Boston said about her adventures with giving testimony in public meetings:

> I am proud of my accomplishments in environmental justice this trimester. Most importantly I have been able to gain confidence to speak in front of large groups of people. Before presenting to the City Council I was very nervous. But after watching them and my classmates somewhat debate I realized they are regular people just like my family, my teachers, and my friends, and I should not be nervous when it comes to speaking my mind.
>
> (in Senechal, 2008, p. 27)

A teacher involved with an Annenberg Rural Challenge project in Crete, Nebraska recounted a story about formerly "at risk" students at his school who were building and servicing computers for local residents and had recently secured a contract to do the same work for a local hospital. As these students earned the respect of the townspeople, "They have gained in poise, self-confidence, and credibility" (in Rural Challenge Research and Evaluation Program, 1999a, p. 137). One can imagine them, like Tom and Matt from Alabama, no longer being at risk but taking on the opportunities and responsibilities of adulthood after earning their high school diplomas. The parent of a student involved in the PRISM project on Molokai similarly commented on the surprising growth in self-confidence she had seen in her own daughter:

> Before she came into the program, she was very shy—never wanted to go in front of the public and speak. ... We never thought she would be doing what she is now. And when we went to the first symposium they had, I was just blown away with what they did ... with the information that they had, what they did in the community ... to see our daughter where she opened herself up more—it was just a shock to us.
>
> (in Cheak et al., 2002, p. 30)

Students who had participated in the PACERS journalism program described in Chapter 5 spoke of the powerful impact simply being listened to had had on their sense of identity and purpose. Laura Pittman, a senior at Oakman High School, said this about the value of this project for her and the way it had allowed her to cultivate her own voice:

> I'm not talking about me speaking to you, I'm talking about the silent voice you hear in your head, where somebody has gone out and researched an issue or investigated something. ... We help others determine what they want to believe. It has helped me feel proud when people in the community come up and say that my article helped them to decide where they stand.
>
> (in Smith, 2007, p. 20)

Fred Fluker, another PACERS student and now a staff member at the *Detroit Free Press*, observed that participating in the writing of the community newspaper transformed his and his classmates' identities. Instead of being passive students, they became "active citizens, public servants, and professional journalists, providing a voice for the community" (in Smith, 2007, p. 20).

Robert Kegan, a leading scholar of human development (1982), suggests that one of the central tasks of adolescence involves becoming a member of a community. Frequently, the only community available for many young people to join is a community of their peers (Bernstein, 1975). What is happening in schools where the boundary between classroom and town has been diminished is that students begin to fulfill this developmental need by becoming members of the broader community in which they live—something that extends their own possibilities as it benefits the community. This membership can be seen in their willingness to take on the tasks of citizenship just as their peers in Alabama did. Chapters to this point have provided numerous examples of ways that children and young people are demonstrating this kind of responsiveness.

A more formal and less anecdotal investigation of nine rural and urban schools associated with the Antioch New England-based CO-SEED program during the 2003–2004 academic year discovered that among the most notable impacts of this place-and community-based educational effort were increases in students' civic engagement and their environmental stewardship behaviors as reported by both teachers and students (Duffin, Powers, Tremblay, & PEER Associates, 2004). Students who had had the opportunity to engage in local investigations and service learning experiences on a regular basis were more likely to agree than disagree with the following statements:

- I feel like I am part of a community.
- I pay attention to news events that affect the community.
- Doing something that helps others is important to me.
- I like to help other people, even if it is hard work.
- I know what to do to make the community a better place.
- Helping other people is something everyone should do, including myself.

- I know a lot of people in the community, and they know me.
- I feel like I can make a difference in the community.
- I try to think of ways to help other people.
- In the last two months, I have done something *with my classmates* to take care of my neighborhood or community.
- In the last two months I have done something *on my own time* to take care of my neighborhood or community.
- I enjoy learning about the environment and my community.

(Duffin, Powers, & Tremblay, 2004, p. A-16)

In her study of EIC programs in the Maryland Bay Schools Project, Von Secker similarly found that students in the classrooms of teachers who emphasized project- and place-based learning reported higher levels of stewardship behaviors than their peers in classrooms where teachers did not incorporate these practices to the same extent (Von Secker, 2004).

These studies match others that speak of the link between service learning opportunities and enhanced civic outcomes. Billig, Root, & Jesse (2005) report that a

> gradually accumulating body of evidence suggests that service-learning helps students develop knowledge of community needs, commit to an ethic of service, develop more sophisticated understandings of politics and morality, gain a greater sense of civic responsibility and feelings of efficacy, and increase their desire to become active contributors to society.
>
> (Billig et al., 2005, p. 4)

They speak specifically of increases in civic-related knowledge, civic-related skills, civic attitudes, service behavior, and the cultivation of social capital, "including increased connections to schools and other organizations and increased social networks" (p. 4).

Central to the experience of civic engagement and participation is the belief that such activities can actually make a difference. For many young people and American citizens, in general, the idea that their own efforts could lead to social betterment is often viewed as fanciful. The result is that people assume "you can't fight City Hall" and withdraw from a community's public life altogether. When children are shown that their efforts can influence decision-making and lead to improvements in local social settings and the natural environment, they develop a sense of their own capacity as change agents, something that seems likely to set a life trajectory characterized more by activism than passivity. For Elaine Senechal at the Greater Egleston Community High School (see Chapter 4), this was one of the major benefits of an education that seeks to involve students in vital public affairs (Senechal, 2007).

A final impact of place- and community-based education noted by the evaluators of the Annenberg Rural Challenge (Rural Challenge Research and Evaluation Program, 1999a) is the way that learning about and becoming part of the life of one's home community can enhance students' pride of place. Rather than being embarrassed about coming from a small rural town or inner-city neighborhood, students come to see that there is value in what they had formerly disregarded. A student who had participated in a Rural Challenge-supported project in Pennsylvania that focused on nature observation, drawing, and journaling noted:

> You are looking at the flowerbed and you've never seen this bug on the leaf before, but now all of a sudden you see all those bugs and birds everywhere. And you're like, "where did they come from?" You never noticed it before. After you go through Selborne, you see all these things.
> (in Rural Challenge Research and Evaluation Program, 1999a, p. 39)

It is exactly this kind of awareness that teachers at Portland's Sunnyside Environmental School seek to nurture, as well, believing that young people alert to the natural beauty around them will invest their energies in its protection. The same kind of awareness about the human community can also take root in children given the opportunity to learn about people they might never otherwise get to know.

> Community members with traditional skills or native knowledge are finding their way more easily into school and, as a result, this traditional knowledge is being valued and passed on. After a community project day in Idalia, Colorado, one student exclaimed, "Wow, I didn't know there were all these cool people here."
> (in Rural Challenge Research and Evaluation Program, 1999a, p. 137)

Montana educator Michael Umphrey (2007) makes a powerful argument for engaging the young in the collection of oral histories and other forms of local inquiry. He believes that psychologically healthy people are those who have developed a narrative about their own lives that is meaningful and focused on living in ways that support the welfare of others. He asserts that contemporary society makes it difficult for children—or anyone, for that matter—to acquire and sustain such stories. This process, however, becomes easier and more certain when children are able to attach their lives to the stories of their own communities. This is more likely to happen if they know enough about that community's members and feel enough attachment to its places that they are proud of their own human and geographical roots. Grounded in this way, they will be both more certain of their own identities and more committed to caring for the source of who they are.

Revitalizing Teachers

One of the striking conclusions from Lieberman and Hoody's *Closing the Achievement Gap* (1998) is that the incorporation of local social and environmental projects into the curriculum is good for teachers as well as students. Educators in the 40 schools that had adopted EIC practices reported increased enthusiasm for teaching, improved interactions with students and colleagues, renewed interest in professional development and personal growth, and increased willingness to experiment with innovative instructional strategies. Similar findings were given voice by a teacher Smith heard at the PACERS convocation mentioned earlier.

Karen Bishop is a biology teacher at Fairhope High School. About five years earlier, she was just about ready to give up her position and become a full-time choir director. She had become bored with teaching high school and figured that life was too short not to enjoy what she was doing. At about this time, however, she learned about John Harbuck's use of aquaculture as a teaching tool for science. She decided to visit him. What she saw in Florala transformed her approach to instruction. She had always relied heavily on labs in her own classrooms, but these had always been cookbook labs. She now realized the value of letting students solve problems on their own without following a step-by-step procedure and modified her own teaching strategies accordingly.

She began by building a greenhouse with a recirculating water system. At the time, she didn't know much more about what she was doing than her students. Drawing on what she had seen in Florala, she and they single-handedly constructed their own system. She observed that "We built relationships that year that still exist. I learned from them and they learned from me." A couple of years later she was able to add another building and started using aquariums to breed and raise fish. Working in the lab required students to apply concepts like nitrification that in a typical classroom setting had remained largely meaningless to them:

> Now students have to use that information. They think, "My ammonia level is higher—so this is what I'm going to do about it." They know what they have to do to solve problems. They have become problem solvers. We're not teaching students how to solve problems at high school in regular classes. I *am* in my aquascience program. ... [Students] do daily water quality testing. They know what the information means. Alkalinity of 40 has meaning and demands a particular response. They know what to do. They don't have to come to me. They get their hands dirty, they get wet, every single day.
>
> (Fieldnotes taken during the PACERS convocation, May 5, 2005)

Bishop finished her presentation by observing that "My students are interested in science. When they come to class every day they are glad to be there. When I get out of bed every day I'm ready to go to work. I'm thrilled to be a teacher, and my students are thrilled to be learning."

Teacher interviews conducted by researchers associated with the Place-based Education Evaluation Collaborative (PEEC) revealed that project- and place-based efforts in New England had resulted in comparable forms of revitalization, with teachers reporting higher levels of engagement and collaboration. Echoing the words of Karen Bishop, one of these teachers commented: "CO-SEED has transformed my teaching—facilitating my development and skills. It's given me a way to truly integrate the disparate subjects I teach. My students are incredibly engaged, the learning is truly meaningful, and the academic successes documented" (Duffin Powers, Tremblay and PEER Associates, 2004, pp. 38–39).

Within the context of educational reforms associated with No Child Left Behind, teachers more often than not are treated as part of the problem rather than the source of the solution. The growing use of scripted lessons for the teaching of reading is indicative of the degree to which policymakers and school leaders have grown to distrust the capacity of those adults most responsible for the education of our young. But when teachers are deskilled in this way, the result is alienation and disengagement, not a good recipe for motivating children to learn. What often happens when teachers are invited to incorporate place into their curriculum is that they, too, must become learners and collaborators with their students. As one of the Rural Challenge evaluators noted with reference to the Selborne Project in Pennsylvania: "I see animated, even excited teachers. They say they are often learning about the place they live alongside their students" (Rural Challenge Research and Evaluation Program, 1999a, p. 61). Perhaps even more important to teachers' sense of their own capacity and self-image is the way they perceive the impact of such learning on their students. One of them commented that "The teaching and learning process is just so much more rewarding than sitting in a classroom because it has so much more significance. We go out and observe things and then we come back and write about them. With something that is meaningful, the motivation is taken care of" (Rural Challenge Research and Evaluation Program, 1999a, p. 61).

Schools that are good for children and youth must also be good for the adults who work in them. Absent adult passion and commitment, education becomes deadening and meaningless for all but the most dedicated students. Time and again, we have seen classrooms transformed when adults have been invited to bring their own intelligence and desires as learners and actors into educational endeavors. When they come to see their own lives as meaningful and valuable to the broader community, they model this possibility for children.

Renewing Communities

One of the unintended consequences of the institution of school has been the way that it has separated children from the lives of adults and the informal social networks that once constituted the matrix in which the young matured. Both children and communities have lost in this process, and place- and community-based education goes some distance toward correcting this problem. In schools where this approach has been adopted, divisions between the generations have been reduced, and young people—rather than being removed from their communities—begin to contribute their talents and energies to important local projects. As they learn about issues that affect their own lives and the lives of their families and neighbors, they not infrequently surface information that impacts decision-making and plans for the future. And, as they learn, the adults around them begin to learn in new ways, as well, stimulating the creation of what might be called a "learning community." In some respects, the young can become critical agents in any change effort since, by their very nature, they come at common problems with fresh eyes and new ideas. In communities where lines have been drawn and people no longer listen carefully to those with whom they disagree, children and youth can set the example for everyone. Adults, not uncommonly, become more careful of their own behavior and begin to act in ways that match the selves they wish to present to their children.

Bringing different generations together can have a profound impact on a community's sense of identity and shared purpose. Schools have to some extent always played this role, although this more often than not has been limited to athletic contests and musical or theatrical performances. When settings are created that allow the young and the middle-aged and their elders to speak with one another, relationships can form that initiate something new. This was one of the most encouraging findings uncovered by evaluators of Annenberg Rural Challenge projects. In the concluding chapter of their report they note that:

> Boundaries that seemed barriers between young people and town elders, school work and community work, are being whittled away, creating a new interdependence around common pursuits. This new awareness and commitment of a larger body of rural residents has become, in the most significant sense, the site of community and changed its connotation from a group of people inhabiting the same area to an interdependent collective of citizens from numerous walks of life who engage with each other and with external bodies to enhance the lives lived in their communities.
>
> (Rural Challenge Research and Evaluation Program, 1999a, p. 139)

Michael Umphrey observed similar developments in the communities with which he worked during the decade-long Montana Heritage Project. Following a meeting tied to a community visioning process, he wrote:

> At times during the discussion, grizzled veterans pondered hard questions about their community's destiny while young high school students with their gleaming skin and bright eyes stood at the white marker boards, facilitating the discussion. Outside, the cold Montana winter covered the forests with snow. Inside, people warmed to one another. "This is the first time young people have gotten involved with the old goats like me."
>
> (Umphrey, 2007, p. 81)

This kind of interaction can do much to overcome a dilemma identified over a decade ago by David Matthews, head of the Kettering Foundation, in his book *Is There a Public for Public Schools?* (1996). Matthews was concerned about the degree to which schools and communities had grown apart and what this meant for the future of an institution central to the perpetuation of American democracy. What Umphrey and others have reported from towns where the young intermingle with adults suggests that there still is a public for public schools if efforts are made to strengthen ties between classrooms and communities:

> Inter-generational teaching and learning helps rebuild trust between the community and the school, and to engage parents and grandparents in the educational mission of the school. At the most pragmatic possible level, several

schools have reported success in passing operational levies and bond issues for new buildings after extensive oral history projects that put interested teenagers in the homes of the elderly throughout the community. Older people often feel no personal connection to the schools though they still vote, and bands of teenagers one doesn't know can seem a crass and frightening lot. But most are nice people, when you get to know them.

(Umphrey, 2007, p. 108)

In these circumstances, schools become the agent through which social capital is regenerated, opening possibilities for collaboration and reciprocity that would not have existed otherwise.

Umphrey recounts a story about how this phenomenon played itself out in Corvallis, Montana. A young woman had investigated the way her community had responded to a fire that destroyed its local school in the years prior to the Great Depression. This disaster spurred the local Masonic temple, a school in a neighboring town, and several churches to open their doors to "school children in need of a warm place to learn" (Umphrey, 2007, p. 107). Patterns of mutual support emerged during this time that continued during the hard times of the 1930s. Only a few months after this student's presentation, Corvallis's middle school was consumed by fire. Umphrey writes that:

People seemed to know instantly how they should react. Their own lore, taught to them by one of their children who had learned it from one of their elders, served as a guide. Altruism, compassion, honesty, and peacefulness can be taught as surely as phonics and math, though they aren't taught in ethics classes so much as by communities enacting themselves.

(Umphrey, 2007, p. 107)

When young people are given the chance to direct their energy and intelligence to the life of their community, more than social capital and mutuality are strengthened; they are also able to make real contributions to everyone's welfare. Their work on environmental issues not infrequently contributes to safer and healthier living conditions (Rural Challenge Research and Evaluation Program, 1999a, p. 137), as clearly happened with regard to the efforts of Elaine Senechal's environmental justice class in Boston. When they direct their attention to economic concerns, as in Howard, South Dakota, new businesses can take root that hold the promise of creating sources of income and commerce (Rural Challenge Research and Evaluation Program, 1999a, p. 137). Comparable contributions occur when students update species lists along regional creeks and rivers, collect meteorological readings, conduct archaeological surveys, and hundreds of similar research projects (Umphrey, 2007).

The importance of student research regarding local issues cannot be overestimated. One of the challenges of adulthood in the twenty-first century is that the requirements of an individual's work life are such that people have little time for the reading and inquiry activities required for informed citizenship. This can be even more acute in low-income neighborhoods where mothers and fathers must often work more than one job to support their families. Yet without accurate and credible information, it becomes nearly impossible for people to make good decisions on their own or influence the decisions of local power holders. Students do have this time and, when given the appropriate support from their teachers and the commitment that comes from knowing that others will rely on their findings, they can become the eyes and ears of a community. On Molokai, for example, the research activities of upper elementary and middle school students are bringing to light data that are making it possible for their parents to develop a much firmer grasp of environmental issues that will affect the long-term health of their island. Cheak and her colleagues saw this play out in numerous ways among the island's adult community. Following a presentation by two sixth-grade boys about traditional Hawaiian fishponds:

> One gentleman, a fisheries biologist, got up and said, I just finished paying consultants $30,000 for a report on the fishponds, and their information wasn't as good as that I have just heard. From now on I guess I'll have to hire these sixth graders to do the research for me.
>
> (Cheak et al., 2002, p. 33)

Seeing children enter the public domain in this way can stimulate adults to do the same. On Molokai, Cheak and her associates believe the PRISM project has had a positive impact on the entire island, stimulating the growth of new programs and restoration activities as well as more parent involvement. In many respects, it has helped to develop a community of learners both in the school and on the island. As one parent commented, "Other parents that I know who have kids in PRISM, it's not only their children who have learned or that have had their eyes opened to what is going on, but it is as if their whole families went through the PRISM process" (Cheak et al., 2002, p. 37). Students, furthermore, set an example that adults feel compelled to follow. Another Molokai resident observed that "When adults say to people, 'Pick up litter; don't litter the land,' it goes in one ear and out the other. But when you see these kids actually researching and doing, I think that it makes an impact on the entire island" (in Cheak et al., 2002, p. 32). Sometimes, children motivate their parents to embrace new identities as involved citizens. An aunt described the shift she saw in her niece's mother: "We would come down and listen to how the research turned out and stuff like that. ... Her mom—who never got involved in community things—is now one of the Enterprise Community Board and volunteered to be on the waste management project" (in Cheak et al., 2002, p. 37).

What can be seen in schools where the boundaries between classroom and community are diminished is a kind of restorative process not unlike what happens when people participate in the restoration of damaged ecosystems. When invasive species—such as Scotch broom or Siberian blackberries—are removed from a neglected area, native plants that haven't been seen in years begin growing themselves, often through no effort of people at all. In communities where citizens engage in cross-generational conversations and projects, the simple opportunity to interact with one another can similarly induce the experience of mutuality and support that lie at the heart of humanity's common life with one another. When invited in this way, people's best selves are more likely to come forward, and everyone is the better for it. As the Rural Challenge evaluators put it:

> In an historic moment of growing alienation, isolation, self-interest, and material consumption as hallmarks of our North American culture, the lessons of Rural Challenge work that focuses on place and on a collective effort to reconstitute viable communities of people inhabiting that place are illuminating, offering an experience that is too often elusive in too many citizens of rural, urban, and suburban America. The community that is the outcome of some of the best effort of Rural Challenge work can provide a powerful answer to the demise of public-spirited virtue and disinterest in our collective welfare.
> (Rural Challenge Research and Evaluation Program, 1999a, p. 139)

This is the kind of regeneration that must become more common if the vitality of American democracy and the stability of the communities where it is practiced are to be sustained.

Educating Whole Citizens

It is common for progressive teachers to talk about educating the whole child and practicing education holistically. By this they generally denote their interest in addressing all sides of a child's personality or being—the intellectual as well as the emotional and physical and spiritual. It is not as common, however, to look beyond children to the roles they must play within broader social networks once their schooling is completed. And, although lip service is given to citizenship education in the mission and vision statements of most conventional schools, in actual practice it is the economic outcomes of teaching and learning that preoccupy many educators and policymakers. It has been our contention throughout this volume that schools must aim towards more and that the learning outcomes associated with No Child Left Behind and the accountability movement are not enough.

What has become hopefully apparent in this chapter and those that preceded it is that educators who bring communities into classrooms and their students into the community are accomplishing learning goals that include but also go far beyond higher scores on academic achievement tests. Mastery of the ability to read, write, and speak, to use mathematics, and to have in one's possession the cultural knowledge required to become employed and be viewed as competent are without question essential outcomes of schooling. But these outcomes should be viewed as the baseline rather than apex of educational goals. What human societies prior to our own have sought to accomplish through their generally non-formal educational efforts is the development of young adults capable of reproducing cultural practices essential to their long-term survival as well as the capacity to adapt successfully to changing environmental or social conditions. In focusing primarily on only one element of our common life—the economic—people in contemporary societies run the risk of failing to prepare the young for the forms of collaboration, problem-solving, social commitment, and imagination required to live not merely as individuals but as members of interdependent communities.

Data available from schools and communities where learning is situated within the broader social and natural contexts of students' lives suggest that this kind of development can in fact be fostered, and that doing so may require little more than a reorientation of common understandings about what education is and where it can happen. When this takes place, all stakeholders in the educational endeavor—students, teachers, and the communities that support them—benefit.

Chapter 8

Collaborating with Community Partners

Delia Clark

Initial research about the impact of place- and community-based educational efforts is thus encouraging, and examples of its practice, often appealing if not inspiring. But what does it take to get projects like those described earlier in this volume off the ground? Schools and communities clearly do not have to remain separated in the way they often are, and the walls between classrooms and neighborhoods and regions can be made more porous. Community members can gain meaningful access to the education of children and youth. And students themselves can gain access to their community. But how do people start? What kinds of lessons can be taken from schools and communities where this approach to teaching and learning has been implemented and gained some traction and staying power?

In the next two chapters, we will seek to provide some tentative answers to these questions, looking first at different ways that collaborative partnerships between schools and community organizations have emerged as a result of either serendipity or intention and then at the critical role that school leaders can play in jump-starting and supporting this process.

A Cascading Effect

In Littleton, New Hampshire, the catalyst for the development of a long-term place- and community-based initiative was a perceived act of vandalism. Long-time Littleton resident Bill Nichols, retired, lived up on a hill in a residential neighborhood separated from the downtown area by the small Remich Park. Bill had invested countless volunteer hours over the years in the maintenance of the Pine Hill Trail, a short trail through the park that connected the neighborhood with downtown, including building a rock staircase on the steepest part of the trail. One day he strolled into the park and discovered to his dismay that much of his work on the staircase had been destroyed and the boulders rolled down the hill.

Chair of the Littleton Conservation Commission at the time, Nichols brought his story to the next commission meeting, sure that his rockwork had been the target of youthful vandals. As luck would have it, one of the current members of the commission was Bill Church, the Littleton High School physics teacher and a highly skilled trail maintainer with ten years of experience with the Adirondack Mountain

Club. After pondering the situation, Church suggested that perhaps he could involve his conceptual physics class in rebuilding the rock staircase section of the trail. This way he could deal with the erosion problems through aspects of the physics curriculum generally taught using textbook assignments and laboratory experiments.

Walkable from the high school, the trail project would provide a strong motivation for developing a meaningful understanding of such abstract concepts as potential and kinetic energy, gravity, friction coefficients, torque, and mathematical ratios. In addition to learning specific physics concepts, students would also learn how these concepts are applied in the use of levers, ropes, wheels and axle, and pulleys to complete the very challenging task of moving 150- to 400-pound boulders. Students would also explore the fundamental causes of trail erosion and some maintenance techniques to deal with it. Finally, students would learn from the variety of unique lessons that come from working with community members on an important local conservation project. Each day of trail work would be supported by two days of class time and out-of-class assignments during which students would study the concepts being applied on the trail.

Church's idea fell on supportive ears back at school. Littleton educational leaders had already moved toward an ideology that encouraged education that integrated students into the community. The idea of combining community development with education goals had arisen five years earlier when both town and school officials were having difficulties passing their budgets with voters. Realizing that they were duplicating efforts to achieve similar goals, the two factions combined committees and presented their budget requests on a single ballot, a highly unusual strategy in New Hampshire towns. This risky proposition worked, resulting in collaboration, shared resources, and the realization that they could also work together to reach goals in areas in addition to the budget. In this atmosphere, the community had welcomed CO-SEED, the place-and community-based education initiative sponsored by Antioch University New England described in Chapter 1.

Church applied for and received enthusiastic support from CO-SEED and the Conservation Commission for the trail project. This support included contact information for community members who might be interested in helping with the project, input about ways the project could be presented to the community beyond student posters and local television coverage, suggestions regarding how the project could be sustained through future years, and financial resources for the purchase of such items as pry bars, pick mattocks, shovels, safety glasses, and materials to build a rock-hauling sledge.

The project was an unqualified success, and Church has continued with other segments of the trail in successive years. Using the physics strategies they were learning in class, students took the work seriously, conferring creatively on strategies for moving the boulders and installing them to withstand the effects of time. At one point, a student confided in Church that, though the next day had been secretly designated as "Senior Skip Day," he would be there just for physics class, knowing how much he was needed for the trail work. Volunteers from around the community turned out regularly to help with the work, and Church was able to forge valuable community connections unavailable to him before. As he said, "How else would a high school physics teacher ever have the credibility to call up the road commissioner at 7:00 a.m. and have a road crew there by 8:00 to help haul rocks? And these guys just loved the chance to work with the kids and help the school."

In addition to solving a community problem, the project has left a lasting impression on the students. Jennifer Morris commented that "the fact that we all worked together to create something that is going to last for such a long period of time gives me great satisfaction." Fellow student Jesse Emerson said, "I'm glad that I am doing something that our town and town's descendants can use." For the record, it *was* kids who had destroyed the original rock stairs, but not as an act of vandalism. They thought they were improving the trail ... for mountain biking. They now have a new route.

The visible success of this project, coupled with the development by CO-SEED of procedures and mechanisms that facilitated interaction and communication between the school and community organizations, brought about a change in attitudes toward place- and community-based learning. As the *Littleton Courier* reported, "In excited talk that frequently includes the words 'connections' and 'linkages' school officials describe how students of all ages can become involved with the town's revitalization and development projects." Town manager Jason Hoch remembers about this time: "That really started forcing a lot of the questions, pushing people toward new ways that school and community could work together on projects that would enhance student learning, achieve community benefits, and save money."

One of the most valuable things about school-community partnerships is that one connection easily leads to another. The following fall, after the new high school entry sidewalk was completed, George Broeder's wife came home one night from a meeting of the Ladies' Auxiliary at the newly built Littleton Hospital. Hospital administrators had requested the Auxiliary's help with a design flaw in the admissions area that was resulting in a lack of privacy during admissions. Administrators hoped the ladies could make some quilts to help with sound-proofing. Broeder immediately suggested going to the physics students for a solution. Church and his class took on the challenge, sought and received a $500 grant to buy ambient noise meters, and within a few months had completed several proposed designs for presentation to the hospital board.

This led to a new way of involving students in community issues. Chutters Store is a long-time fixture on Littleton's Main Street, and home of the World's Longest Candy Counter according to the *Guinness Book of World Records*. To supplement its local business Chutters was looking to expand into the world of e-commerce but lacked the staff time or know-how. This presented an opportunity to move the overcrowded marketing program from the high school vocational-technical program into the basement of the candy store, where students then spent two years of quality class time setting up an online candy business. Other students joined an annual summer intern program in the town hall, for which they used GIS technology to map catch basins, trails, and subdivisions, leading in some cases to post-college careers in planning and technology. According to town manager Jason

Hoch, "There is not a town project I do now where I don't first start with 'how can we involve the students?' ... We're genuinely enhancing stewardship of the community, helping people see students as an asset to solving community problems, not a community problem unto themselves."

Across the continent in Seaside, Oregon, city and county officials in the 1990s actually formalized Littleton town manager Hoch's approach to engaging young people in important community projects. There, memoranda of agreement were drawn up to encourage officials to turn to educators when they had research needs that could be accomplished by students. This was one of the reasons that city planners mentioned in Chapter 4 turned to young people to gather data about buildings on the tsunami plain or plants and animal species in a mill site the city hoped to turn into a park.

In Littleton, this shift toward an emphasis on place- and community-based education is having a subtle but profound effect on the lives of students and the community as a whole. As Al Smith, principal of the Littleton High School, observed:

The attitude toward education and kids has changed in a positive manner in this town because of the increased interaction between students and Joe Blow on the street in Littleton. [This] has brought people from the town into our building to work with kids and now they're not as critical of education. They think more highly of the kids. In the past these people would have never been in the building. There's an effect on the budget process. We've passed the school budget in the past three years without an issue. We create a unified budget with the town and in the past we were competing with each other. Now there are some mutual goals and more understanding.

Student Morgan Knapton mirrored this thought from the student perspective as he prepared to head off to college, the first child in his family to do so: "It's good to know you're making a difference in the community."

Littleton's experience with place- and community-based education highlights the importance of the creation of structures to facilitate and support school-community relationships. One successful strategy is the creation of a local coordinating committee consisting of teachers, administrators, local agency or business partners, and other community members. Through regular meetings, this steering committee can maintain connections with relevant community groups, scope out potential community needs that would lend themselves to service learning projects, participate in project planning retreats, and plan for project continuance. They can also solicit additional funding to distribute in the form of mini-grants to teachers and community members through an application process.

One challenge in all of this, though, is program sustainability. Hoch points out that it is an easy mistake to allow these community- and place-based education initiatives to become too personality-driven. He cautions other communities interested in adopting similar approaches to cross-pollinate projects, pulling in a wide range of participants and supporters who are capable of continuing the efforts through the inevitable shifts in personnel. The steering committee is one good way to do this. Having now moved to a new community himself, Hoch is philosophical about the final outcomes:

> We made a difference for that cadre of students at that time and they have gone on to build on these experiences in their lives. I'm still in touch with some of them and they have said that they are so glad to have had these experiences in high school. I can still hear the excitement and engagement, everything these kids got out of those projects, the incredible sense of stewardship.

Engaging city officials and citizens in the development of place- and community-based projects can often play a significant role in the staying power of this approach. If the projects are primarily tied to the energy of one or two especially committed teachers, the chances of this kind of work continuing after their departure from a school can be slight. When community members begin to have a stake in this process, however, this can change. John Harbuck, the biology teacher mentioned in Chapter 7 who had been instrumental in getting an aquaculture project off the ground in Alabama, observed that, now that the community was invested in this work, the school couldn't let it go. In these instances—Littleton, Seaside, and Florala—schools begin to adopt a more reciprocal relationship with their communities, giving back as well as taking. Citizens come to expect this, and the schools need to deliver.

Student Connections to Community Vision

Another way to foster the sustainability of place- and community-based education initiatives is to link them to community-wide visioning initiatives. The goal of a visioning process is to bring together voices from throughout the community to discuss specific assets and concerns and to collaboratively develop ideas and citizen-based action plans for community-related projects. This approach was used in Howard, South Dakota, and in community studies associated with the Montana Heritage Project. Community visioning conducted in conjunction with a place-based education program adds to this the goal of identifying community needs and opportunities that might make appropriate projects for student involvement.

In Antrim, New Hampshire, a former mill town in the southern part of the state, the visioning process, "Antrim Next: A Gathering of Ideas," was spearheaded by a diverse committee that included both school and community representatives. CO-SEED staff had pitched the idea to the local planning board, including an offer for modest funding, and the planning board had embraced it as a way to build civic engagement in local affairs and identify opportunities for student involvement in the life of the community. The planning board charged a local volunteer steering committee with event coordination. Held at Great Brook Middle School in the spring, it was open to everyone in the community and offered children's activities and transportation for senior citizens to back that claim. "Antrim Next" utilized an approach called the vision-to-action forum that moves participants back and forth between large-group and small-group discussions, spiraling ever inward from consideration of generic qualities of successful communities to very local opportunities and concerns, finally identifying and launching a few well-defined and broadly supported local initiatives.

"Antrim Next" began with a potluck supper and maintained a lively balance of convivial atmosphere and serious conversation throughout. Life-long Antrim resident Izzy Nichols launched the discussion with a presentation about the evolution of Antrim, from its agrarian days to its present incarnation as a bedroom community, concluding, "This is a rare opportunity for Antrim residents of all ages to get together for a celebration of their community and to share their visions for its future." A highlight of the program was the unveiling of a shower-curtain-sized map of the community prepared by Barbara Black's fifth-grade students. The map included dozens of small clear pockets, each displaying a card documenting the vital statistics of one of Antrim's thriving small businesses. The general buzz was that seeing this map, alone, was worth the time investment required by the forum—nobody had known that there were so many businesses tucked away in Antrim's back rooms and garages.

After a day and a half of meetings, participants settled on three key priority actions for the immediate future. One of these was sprucing up Antrim's downtown area. With a vacant mill building and a litter problem, residents also noted diminished pride in the appearance of their hometown. Hearing this, Barbara Black and her colleague, sixth-grade teacher Letitia Rice, decided to act. After a series of planning sessions over the summer, they decided to merge their classrooms weekly for the entire school year to take on the challenge of beautifying Memorial Park. Situated in the village center on both sides of the Great Brook, Memorial Park had a history of loving use but had fallen into disrepair and neglect.

With the assistance of a teacher's aide they broke their students into three multiage groups and started work. Black created a timeline that broke the whole project into pieces that were manageable for the students. In the fall they honed math skills as they measured and mapped the park; each of the three groups chose a different section on which to focus. Local landscape designers came into the classroom during science segments and taught the students how to identify trees and shrubs by leaf shape. One local resident guided them through a discussion of the meaning of "beauty"; students decided that for them in this case beauty meant colors. During the winter students researched the colors of the plants, berries, and flowers at different seasons of the year, creating a chart that wrapped high around three walls of the classroom showing with dots the color of each plant species in the park throughout the year. Local senior citizens visited the classroom and were interviewed by students about their stories of the park's history when they were young.

Over time students became clear that their goals would be to refresh the plantings in the park, including as many diverse colors and self-maintaining native species as possible. In late winter, they created a large foam core model of Memorial Park and made a formal presentation of their design to the board of selectmen, with different students presenting different parts of the plan. The select board enthusiastically approved their design. Community members rallied in the spring with donations of plant materials and loans of equipment. Planting day was a big success, with many parent and community volunteers as well as an exuberant group of high school students seeking community service credits. The local newspapers, the *Peterborough Transport* and the *Monadnock Ledger*, devoted nearly full-page coverage of the event, emphasizing the students' connection to their community and their sense of pride in Antrim.

The project has been of lasting benefit to the community. One town resident commented, "I see Memorial Park as having become more of a focal point for Antrim and [this project] has a lot to do with that." The project has also achieved the students' goals. As teacher Letitia Rice said, "It changed how kids in the community looked at Memorial Park as a place they could actually use, not just a place for their parents or grandparents." The park has now become a popular gathering place for the younger generation, and community leaders have recently installed a skate park there.

Other outcomes of Antrim Next include a group focused on after-school activities and recreation, which merged with and revitalized Antrim's existing Friends of Recreation group. As resident David Essex reported, "The ideas and energy from Antrim Next translated into stuff like the Celtic Festival, Friday night gatherings, line dancing, kickboxing, aerobics, and gymnastics classes. There was never really an after-school program for kids before." Antrim Next also resulted in the Antrim Center project, which involved students in studying a 16-acre parcel of land owned by the Antrim Conservation Commission. The students accepted responsibility for creating a proposal for developing this land as a nature study and recreation site.

The importance of a supportive school leader cannot be overemphasized in building strong school—community connections. Letitia Rice credits the open, flexible school atmosphere to then Great Brook principal Rick Nanicelli, who encouraged educators to think of their teaching in ever-expanding ways. This includes such logistical matters as permitting classes to leave the school during the day, allowing students to make phone calls, offering teachers planning time to develop interdisciplinary curricula, and establishing teachers' own personal links with the community, strategies that will be described in more detail in Chapter 9. As Rice commented, "Rick empowered us to make choices that are good for kids."

Key to the success of community visioning sessions that are linked with place- and community-based education is the support of local town and school officials, a short but intensive burst of volunteer activity in the form of a planning committee, and skilled neutral facilitation. These sessions are most successful when they are perceived as being celebratory and open-ended and when leaders from diverse sectors of the community lend them their names.

There is a need for advance training to prepare teams of adult and student facilitators, and for follow-up training and support in such areas as how to utilize volunteers, how to keep people involved, and how to delegate work to build communal ownership of undertakings. Teachers often benefit from targeted training and/or support in techniques for building student voice into the forum and the ensuing projects. Teachers also often require training in the development of projects that simultaneously address educational objectives and authentically address identified community needs.

This final point bears emphasizing. One of the challenges of place- and community-based education is that implementing these kinds of outside-of-classroom projects requires teachers to learn that acting in isolation is no longer an option. Their decisions have an impact on others and will be subject to public scrutiny. A project to remove invasive species like ivy or blackberries from city-owned properties can result in complaints from neighbors about piles of vines and thorns if they are not quickly picked up by the local parks department. Or a well-intentioned effort to explore difficult neighborhood issues such as drug use and violence—issues brought up by students, themselves—can lead to complaints from citizen activists who acknowledge these problems but are also striving to build upon community assets, something that teachers might overlook. Educators cannot simply bring their own analysis of what needs to be fixed in a community to their work with students. The projects they choose will ideally arise from needs that community members have identified themselves.

Big Partners

Educators interested in place- and community-based education should not assume that their only partners should be representatives of local governments and businesses. Partnering with state and federal agencies can also provide rich opportunities for collaboration. Local residents of Harpers Ferry, West Virginia, for example, can hardly miss the fact that the Appalachian National Scenic Trail (AT), a unit of the National Park Service, goes right through their town. Their local post office is one of the few along the length of the 2,175-mile-long AT trail that is within a quarter-mile of the trail—a perfect place for "thru-hikers" (who are doing the whole trail at once) and their support teams to send care packages, new boots, love letters, medicines, and other necessities. In peak season there is a steady stream of AT hikers trudging along the main road of Harpers Ferry with their letters and packages.

Aside from watching this odd seasonal influx of hikers through town, though, few Harpers Ferry residents are aware of the presence of the Appalachian Trail, a problem echoed in communities up and down the length of the trail. For this reason, after completing a period of 25 years of intensive focus on trail construction and land acquisition to protect the 185,000 acres of public land associated with the trail, the Appalachian Trail Conservancy (ATC, the nonprofit partner of the AT) recently turned their focus to community outreach and educational programs for the regions through which the trail passes. Their goal has been to weave connections to local communities, expanding the trail from a national treasure to a valued local educational and recreational resource. Rita Hennessy, outdoor recreation specialist for the AT, explains: "[As we looked at community outreach], one approach kept reoccurring—place-based education. We quickly realized that we did not need an interpretive staff, but enablers and resources to build education programs for the trail within local schools and non-formal educational organizations."

Lacking experience in working with schools, Hennessy immersed herself in courses and workshops about place- and community-based education and service learning, determining to launch her effort in the hometown of the trail's headquarters, Harpers Ferry. A co-worker had introduced her to the principal of the Harpers Ferry Middle School, Joe Spurges, and Hennessy went to see him with an idea. The AT was very interested in getting youth involved in the trail as part of their belief that students immersed in the interdisciplinary study of their own "place" are more eager to be involved in the stewardship of their communities and public lands—and are more likely to become trail volunteers as they mature. The AT was in need of a brochure that would encourage some of the more than 300,000 visitors per year to the Harpers Ferry National Historical Park to venture the extra one-third mile to the ATC headquarters, which currently received only 15,000 annual visitors. Hennessy had examined the sixth-grade state standards and thought there might be a fit.

Spurges instantly grasped the possibilities and invited Hennessy to speak to the entire sixth-grade faculty team. To Hennessy's surprise, the team agreed with the notion of involving all 165 students in the sixth-grade class, including getting everyone out hiking on the trail. Back at headquarters, flush with success following the meeting, Hennessy found that her trail colleagues balked, arguing against taking so many kids out on the trail, citing liability concerns and the Leave No Trace principles that limit groups to 20. Hennessy successfully countered that an unknown number of other groups were already using the trail without any connection to AT or ATC. Here was one group that they could actually connect with, assist, and influence. Why turn away from that? She prevailed and assembled a team of hike leaders.

The sixth-grade faculty decided Hennessy should open the unit with a presentation in the auditorium to the whole class. Hennessy planned a program that featured a series of speakers standing in front of a PowerPoint of rotating photos of the trail. The speakers included a past thru-hiker in hiking garb as well as uniformed park service and forest service staff, together explaining why they liked to hike, things to do on the trail, and things to watch out for. After reviewing Hennessy's proposal for the presentation, one teacher commented, "You're obviously not a teacher." Hennessy responded, "You're absolutely right. I'm a community partner. You're the teacher. I want to work with you to do this." This teacher's hesitation continued, inching toward opposition, until Hennessy finally took her out for a personal hike to assuage her fears. The teacher confided later that the personal hike had turned the tide for her. She also said that knowing that she had the support of the principal and the whole sixth-grade team built her confidence to give the program a try.

The hike came off without a hitch, with groups of students starting at several different trailheads, a northbound and a southbound group at each. They later gathered to share stories about the views, shelters, and hikers they had encountered. Following the initiation hike, Hennessy taught a section of science for each class on mapping using triangulation and GPS units, standard trail management tools. Students then went out in the field again, accompanied by parent volunteers, this time walking the loop of trail and local sidewalks for which they were developing the brochure. Although the ATC headquarters was less than a mile from the center of town, many of the students had never visited the area before. Each student got a turn tracking their exact location with the $20,000 GPS unit, taking photos with disposable cameras, and recording field notes.

The students' enthusiasm for the project was contagious, with many reporting that they had come back and brought their families, introducing them to a new healthy pastime. Hennessy's favorite story from the day concerns the father of one of the girls in the class. The girl had loved the initiation hike and came home full of talk about becoming a thru-hiker on the Appalachian Trail. Based on her enthusiasm, the father took a day off from work to volunteer with the class. He walked close to Hennessy, full of questions. He had heard of the trail but didn't know much about it. They reached the point where the loop they were mapping left the sidewalk and intersected the AT. The father hesitated, unsure about how to follow the trail once they were in the woods. Rita explained that a hiker had a choice: north or south. The father said incredulously, "You mean I could follow this trail all the way to Georgia?!" He paused a minute and then asked suspiciously, "Wait a minute. What's a thru-hiker?"

Using a template provided by the National Park Service staff, and drawing on their language arts, graphic arts, and math skills, the students completed a useful and attractive brochure, complete with color photos, a quiz, and a credit to the students. The brochure opens with an invitation:

> The Appalachian Trail through Harpers Ferry may come as a new experience for beginners as well as experienced hikers. It has a gorgeous view of an old church and trees add shady spots. You might see people on the rocks in the Potomac River. You can also see three states divided by valleys and mountains—West Virginia, Virginia and Maryland. So why don't you come and check out the scenery?

Toyota paid for the publication of 2,500 copies for distribution through the Harpers Ferry National Historical Park Visitor Center and the ATC, and the brochure is headed into a second printing.

The auditorium presentation and hike have become annual features in the sixth-grade curriculum, even with the class size up to 200, and several other projects have emerged from the partnership. One notable project was student-initiated. After seeing how cool the hike and brochure project were, the Student Council decided that they wanted an AT project of their own. The AT had a need for some interpretive posters at one critical point where the trail intersects a set of historical parks that attract 300,000 annually. The AT crosses the Potomac just above its confluence with the Shenandoah River, right beside the historical C&O Canal: village and history this way, woods and nature that way. The students did research and took measurements and photographs. A graphic artist intern from the local university and a professional park service designer then worked with them to develop some poster design options. The ribbon-cutting for the kiosk where their posters were installed attracted park service officials from Washington, DC and a host of local dignitaries as well as students, faculty, and parents.

At this celebration of school-community collaboration, one parent praised Joe Spurges, saying: "You are the most wonderful principal. All this happened because you let it happen. You got out of the way." Hennessy said that one of the most important lessons she learned from this process is that teachers can make great use of these community partnerships to achieve their teaching goals but only if they have the support of school leaders.

Making School—Community Collaboration Work

The stories above demonstrate that healthy school-community collaboration is at the core of successful place- and community-based learning. This collaboration relies on attentiveness both by people within the school and by those based in the community. As with all good partnerships, these relationships work best when they are flexible and adaptive. They succeed at effectively weaving together school and community by drawing out the best attitudes, energies, and relationships of the full range of individuals involved.

An early step in building sturdy bridges between school and community is the active cultivation of an intimate knowledge of the local community. Efforts such as reading local publications, hanging out at the coffee shop or the post office or wherever people gather, or offering to serve on community boards as time allows, nourish the development of personal relationships with a diversity of people and organizations. It was Bill Church's membership on the Littleton Conservation Commission that opened the door for all of the projects that followed. Similarly, it was Elaine Senechal's participation in some of Roxbury's citizen action groups that led to her students' involvement in the anti-idling campaign (see Chapter 4).

As a partnership between a school and a community organization begins to emerge, it is essential for school and community leaders to work together to develop a common vision big enough to inspire all partners, grounded in a sense of what is possible rather than a sense of what is lacking. The process of identifying and shaping a common vision through structured and informal dialogue will support the growth of a healthy collaborative culture with shared control and decision-making and strong mechanisms for open communication. In this atmosphere, partners are motivated to play to each other's strengths, offering support when needed, even when it falls outside the bounds of a particular project.

Beginning with a small concrete task like Church's stone steps builds credibility and a sense of the community partners' culture. A good starting point is to consult with others to identify projects that address real community needs, including plugging into existing community projects that could flourish with the addition of youthful energy and skills. Identifying organizations that are already addressing environmental or social justice concerns and drawing upon volunteer support can provide some useful initial opportunities. While offering a world of promise, partnerships are also time-consuming. It makes sense to look for flexibility, adaptability, and a strong mission fit in the local partner and the projects undertaken together.

When sustained over time, community partnerships can grow deeper and increasingly yield tremendous synergy and mutually beneficial initiatives. This requires wide-open communication lines, a transparent structure, and a sense of humor. Building in time for regular communication and coordination makes it feel like less of a burden and more a way of just doing business. It makes sense to put out useful information about the project through means appropriate to the local culture, whether through blogs and listservs or newsletters and flyers on grocery store bulletin boards. Keeping to a regular meeting schedule for the coordinating committee with regularly updated contact lists can also be helpful. In addition, developing a positive relationship with local news media professionals is an excellent idea. School-community partnerships stay relevant when they link to other local needs, social objectives, and initiatives; they stay vibrant when credit for each success is spread around lavishly in an attitude of gratitude and celebration. Frequent articles in the local press or short spots on the evening news can do much to acquaint the public with the positive impact this kind of collaboration can have on their common experience. This kind of publicity can also build the broad support for this educational approach needed to sustain and develop it.

It takes time to build strong relationships, and there will be a continual need for upkeep and maintenance as personnel and issues change, but, through welcoming these opportunities for renewal, schools and communities can pull together toward the same goals and accomplish far more than either could alone. In this way, schools and communities can work with one another to—as the Rural School and Community Trust motto encourages—get better together.

Chapter 9

Leaders as Gardeners

Creating Space for Place- and Community-based Education

> I always tell people that when you go into any classroom in our school—
> or maybe the collective classroom—you should know that you're in Oregon,
> you should know that you're in Portland, you should know what season it is,
> you should know that there was an election. You should be grounded in
> place.

These words are Sarah Taylor's, the founding principal of Portland's Sunnyside
Environmental School. She captures one of the central characteristics of place- and
community-based education: its incorporation of local phenomena into the day-
to-day details of students' school experiences. What is on the bulletin boards in
Oregon should be different from what a visitor would see in Alaska or New Jersey.
Principals and other school administrators can play a role in assuring that this happens by reminding their faculty and other staff about the learning possibilities that
inhere in the surrounding community and region.

Although the implementation of place- and community-based education rests
squarely in the hands of teachers, without a supportive institutional and cultural
environment at the school—and ideally district—these efforts not uncommonly
remain isolated and temporary. With the intention of tapping the knowledge base
of people enmeshed in the work of making place- and community-based education
a reality, Smith interviewed six school leaders in the Pacific Northwest, including
Taylor, who have been successful in encouraging teachers to move teaching and
learning in this direction. Three work as central office administrators, and three as
principals or vice principals. Together, they have been sponsoring educational initiatives grounded in local places and communities for more than 40 years. Each will
be introduced when their comments are first shared.

Their wide-ranging observations grouped themselves into six themes:
philosophy, approach to school change, staff development, structural supports and
curricular frameworks, organizational details, and partners and resources. Our
hope in presenting their insights is that school leaders will gain a sense of some of
the challenges, pitfalls, and opportunities encountered in encouraging this kind of
innovation.

Philosophy

Central to the work of all of these school leaders is the belief that learning is not contained in classrooms or textbooks or standardized tests, but in the parks, rivers, homeless shelters, and local businesses that lie just beyond the school's walls. In this, these educators have adopted one of the fundamental premises of place- and community-based education: that the best education is an education that sees schools as integrated with rather than segregated from the lives of the human and other-than-human beings that surround them. Ed Armstrong led the Annenberg Rural Challenge initiative in Tillamook, Oregon in the 1990s and now works for the school district as its grant writer and foundation director. The natural resource-focused educational efforts started in the district more than a decade ago remain alive and well in part because of his dedication and vision. He observed that, when "the school is a part of a community, part of a bigger world, you have a lot more richness for your students to look at and draw from. It's about the experiences." These kinds of experiences furthermore take precedence over the widespread preoccupation with students' scores on standardized tests. "Yes, we would like strong test scores, but we're here to do great and powerful things with kids. Place-based learning can accomplish those things."

Voicing this philosophical perspective is important because without it teachers tend to believe that, as Tom Horn said, only "a very traditional sort of pedagogical model, a nineteenth-century mode," is acceptable in the school. Horn is the principal of the Al Kennedy Alternative School in Cottage Grove, Oregon, where he has been leading an effort to transform a once floundering school into a leader of sustainability education for his district and region. He stressed the importance of explicitly encouraging teachers to take students outside the classroom and of letting them know that establishing ties with community partners is a central rather than tangential part of their work. Brian Goodwin, director of special programs for the North Wasco School District in The Dalles, Oregon, shares Horn's understanding about the need to let teachers know that it's OK to incorporate less conventional instructional strategies into their own work with students. He believes that hearing this perspective from their leaders can "give them some level of comfort to dip their toe into that pool." Without it, many teachers will engage in a process of self-censorship that too often results in the stifling of creative ideas and possibilities. Goodwin has worked to overcome this tendency by exposing his teachers to new ideas and acting as a community cheerleader for those who break down the boundary between their classroom and the world beyond it.

Part of this shift in philosophical perspective also involves leaders' beliefs about the way children learn. Do they learn purely through a process of formal instruction during which the teacher acts as a disseminator of knowledge, or do they learn through a process of exploration, invention, and play with the teacher assuming a more facilitative role? At the Sunnyside Environmental School, teachers of children in kindergarten through grades one and two regularly take their classes to nearby parks, where their students are allowed to engage in unstructured play for several hours, play that can surface new content and questions from children's explorations. Principal Sarah Taylor acknowledges that this approach to teaching and learning for young students flies in the face of contrasting trends that have led to the elimination of recess in the interest of providing more instructional time. When questioned, she is able to draw on credible research that validates educators' trust in children's capacity to learn as a result of their innate curiosity and ability to process and master new information in the same way they master language. Sunnyside students' strong performance on statewide tests gives credence to her faith in this process.

An added benefit occurs when the emotional content of the learning experience inspires children to continue investigating a topic on their own time outside of school, another facet of what it means to trust in students' capacity to learn. As Brian Goodwin observed about classrooms where more learning is grounded in the local:

> Now instead of six hours of canned curriculum, we have six hours of quality learning plus when they go home or during the summer or on the weekend. If they are inspired by what they are doing in school, that will carry forward into the rest of their lives and become organic to who they are. And then you've maximized—you've multiplied—instructional time.

For these leaders, learning is as natural and necessary as breathing. At issue is creating the opportunities that stimulate meaningful experience and that encourage children to process and extend what they have encountered with their teachers.

Although the use of outside-of-school resources is notable by its absence in many classrooms, the cultivation of citizenship and lifelong learning is a goal found in most school district mission statements. Joyce Yoder is the vice principal of a Salem, Oregon middle school that has become the home of a school-within-a-school for approximately 90 sixth through eighth graders. Called the Academy for Citizens of Tomorrow (ACT) Program, it focuses on giving young people the opportunity to become leaders both in their school and in the broader community. Yoder noted that she and the program's teachers were able to use the district framework as a validation for more place- and community-based education:

> We have not had to justify place-based learning experiences because they enhance rather than detract from our district mission statement: "In partnership with the community, we ensure that each student will have the essential knowledge, skills, and attitudes to be a lifelong learner, a contributing citizen and a productive worker in a changing and increasingly diverse world."

When first designing curriculum for their school-within-a-school, ACT Program teachers went to the state standards and used these as the foundation for their courses. They then sought out learning experiences tied into their community as the means for addressing these standards. As Tillamook School District's Ed Armstrong noted, place- and community-based education essentially involves a shift in philosophical perspective. One of the tasks of school leaders is to acquaint teachers with what that shift entails and the kinds of curriculum and instruction it allows and encourages.

Approach to School Change

Choosing to incorporate place and community into a school's approach to curriculum and instruction involves making fundamental as opposed to add-on changes (Wehlage, Smith, & Lipman, 1992). Such initiatives are much more difficult to accomplish than the implementation of an after-school program or even the adoption of a new daily schedule. As suggested above, schools that have successfully implemented place- or community-based approaches have gone through a process of cultural transformation and now see the processes of teaching and learning in different ways. This necessitates a level of buy-in and understanding from teachers that rarely accompanies the implementation of mandates originating from outside a school or its classrooms. Orchestrating this process of change fittingly requires a school leader to treat teachers in the same way that teachers will be ideally treating their students: with respect and trust and a willing relaxation of control.

Effecting this kind of change requires finesse, tact, and a willingness to allow things to develop in their own time. Brian Goodwin suggested that conversation can be a means for beginning this process. "The act of conversing and dialoguing between community, staff, and students—you may not solve the world's problems or the community's problems—just the fact that you're talking about it is the starting place." If these conversations across a school's or school district's stakeholders are happening, then there's a better chance that place-based education can "get a toe-hold with teachers and administrators and eventually work in the community." One way to encourage such conversations is to start study groups that pull together administrators, teachers, and community members and present them with ideas and possibilities that may be new to many of them. By reading books or watching films about place- and community-based education together, they can become aware of the benefits of this approach and acquainted with some of its characteristics and practices.

It has been Goodwin's experience that some principals and teachers will be drawn to the possibilities of place- and community-based education and interested in bringing elements of the approach into their own school or classrooms. His observations describe an implementation strategy well worth consideration by school leaders in other communities:

What I've found is that place-based learning is so broad, there are so many points of entry as a teacher no matter what your subject is—once staff have done it, I can't think of any staff that I'm aware of that has stopped doing it. What I've seen is a gradual and steady increase of staff that are using it. And so, the teacher is probably the most effective at spreading this practice, and so I'm—I see myself as a support system on a bigger level. If staff have ideas that they want to try—like the book group or workshops or conferences for staff—I try to support them in those kinds of ways just to let it grow naturally. I very intentionally have taken the tack of not forcing it upon anyone, but just to let them come to it and say, yes, I'm interested, how do I get involved?

Once a teacher has expressed an interest in incorporating more local issues and phenomena into their classroom, Goodwin then sits down with them individually to identify topics or projects that excite them. If teachers are passionate about a particular curricular possibility, they become willing to invest the time and energy needed to develop it and make it part of their work with students. He also encourages teachers to take risks, recognizing that, when people embark on new ventures, failure can occur in spite of good intentions and thoughtful design. When this happens, he celebrates their efforts and encourages them to learn from their "good failures." This willingness to accept occasional missteps is what relinquishing control is all about.

At the Al Kennedy Alternative School, Tom Horn has worked to make place- and community-based education central to nearly all of the program's educational activities. He observed that an important learning experience for him has involved figuring out how to "take the bull by the horns and move a whole school forward and at the same time play a supportive and an understanding role and be able to help people through some of the quandaries they are going to experience, philosophically or otherwise" as they implement this approach. He has discovered that he can't simply come back with ideas that excite him and expect teachers to accept and implement them. Ed Armstrong noted that he has learned how to present new possibilities to teachers as just that: possibilities. He acknowledges that, if teachers "don't think it's important right now, then it's not important. You can push. But you can also do it in a way that is assaultive, in a way that can destroy the work." Both leaders have clearly come to understand the importance of being facilitators of learning and implementation for their staff members rather than directors of school or classroom change. They treat teachers as collaborators rather than employees.

Another factor with regard to leadership and school change that came up in some interviews involved sustaining this effort over time. Armstrong acknowledged his disappointment when teachers he has worked with for a few years choose to leave the district for a teaching position in another community. These changes happen, and the loss of skillful practitioners of this approach can have a serious impact on a particular school or even district. The likelihood of this event points to the importance of assembling teams of practitioners in a given school and striving to increase the number of people who have embraced this approach. This way, the departure of a single person will not disrupt the entire effort. The same dilemma occurs with regard to changes in school leadership. Horn reflected on this issue in the following way: "What happens if I leave the school? Who could come in and continue this work? ... what happens if I'm not here, so that things don't just fall apart? The way to do that is to create leadership qualities in everybody." He has accomplished this task by sharing more and more of the work that he does with regard to the development of the curriculum and community partnerships with his teachers.

In addition to these strategic approaches to the challenge of school change, there are also structural issues that a school leader should take into consideration. These will influence how this change is orchestrated. On some occasions, for example, it will be possible to assemble a group of like-minded teachers to create a school-within-a-school, charter school, or special focus school. In these cases, all of the teachers participating in a school will be generally persuaded that place- and community-based approaches have merit and demonstrate an interest in implementing them in their classrooms. When this happens, school leaders will encounter challenges when working with people external to the school. With regard to a school-within-a-school, it will be imperative to create an admissions process in such a way that the school's students demonstrate demographic characteristics and ability levels that roughly parallel those of the entire student body. Care must be taken to avoid circumstances that could result in other teachers perceiving themselves to be "have-nots" when compared to the school-within-a-school's "haves."

Special focus or charter schools can encounter similar political dynamics in their relationship with other administrators or teachers if their student bodies appear to be creamed or their resources greater than those available in other schools. Even when these issues are dealt with, however, a school that incorporates place- and community-based approaches can on occasion be treated as an educational "renegade" and relegated to the margins of the district in terms of either financial or psychological support and recognition. This has remained an ongoing challenge for the Sunnyside Environmental School, even though it remains one of the most sought-after and highest-performing schools in its district. Although viewed favorably by superintendents and school boards during the years it has been in existence, its tendency to push the educational envelope has often been treated as a form of aberrant behavior on the part of middle-level management.

When working with a pre-existing school, a principal or central office administrator will be wise to begin moving forward with place- or community-based initiatives only when a majority of teachers are willing to support such efforts. In his work in New England, Sobel has found that, although not every teacher needs to have the characteristics of early adopters, enough need to be in favor of this direction to allow their more committed colleagues to try new things and occasionally be the beneficiaries of additional resources. When this happens, it is not uncommon for more people to begin experimenting with place- and community-based approaches until eventually a tipping point is reached and the culture of the entire school changes. One of the teachers in a New Hampshire school associated with Sobel's CO-SEED program has been making extensive use of a wooded area on the boundary of the schoolyard for a number of years. She indicated that, when CO-SEED came into the school, only a handful of teachers made regular use of this learning resource next to the school. Now, nearly every teacher makes at least one visit a week to the natural area.

Because deep-seated curricular and instructional changes entail a transformation of fundamental aspects of a school's culture, it is important for school leaders to see themselves more as gardeners than engineers. They can prepare the soil, make sure that there's plenty of water, and put new starts in the ground after the danger of frost has passed, but they can't make the plants grow. This approach is very different from one where observers come into classrooms to ensure that teachers are using mandated reading programs in a manner that demonstrates fidelity to the publisher's vision. This more organic process may not work as quickly, but when place- and community-based education is allowed to grow in this way it becomes more firmly rooted in a school and more likely to persist over time.

To protect the kind of cultural shift she has been supporting for a dozen years, Sarah Taylor noted that she has found it necessary to buffer her teachers from the frequently changing mandates that originate in her district's central office. "You don't want to disrupt teachers' thinking if what they are being asked to do [by the district] isn't going to stick." For example, a few years ago Portland public school teachers were required to schedule time to prepare for and write "anchor" essays as part of the district's effort to implement a common assessment procedure. Devoting what often amounted to several days of instruction to this exercise disrupted the Sunnyside Environmental School's well-established and successful curriculum framework. Taylor and her staff were unwilling to relinquish an approach that they knew was working for their students even though doing so risked conflict with their bureaucratic superiors. It is the cultivation of what *is* going to "stick"— both for teachers and for students—that needs to be foremost in a school leader's mind when attempting to encourage his or her school or district to incorporate more local knowledge and experiences into curriculum and instruction.

Staff Development

Few teachers in contemporary schools will have encountered anything like place- and community-based learning over the course of their own educations. School leaders interested in moving in this direction therefore face the task of helping their teachers develop a grounded understanding of both the opportunities and the pitfalls associated with creating learning experiences that take them beyond the classroom into neighborhoods, agencies, and wetlands. If this is not done, there is a good chance that some teachers will fail to grasp the potentialities of this approach and be unable to present lessons or units they design to students in ways that make sense and are compelling. As Ed Armstrong observed, if students don't know why "they went out here and did this, they get confused." They think, "That was fun, but I don't know why we did it." For him, if teachers use field trips as only an auxiliary activity or as an excuse to get out of the classroom, it "degrades the practice. Then people in the community say, 'If that's what place-based education or service learning or whatever the vocabulary is, then I don't want to be part of it.'" Guarding against this possibility—the idea that place- and community-based education involves little more than incorporating additional field trips—is one of the school leader's responsibilities.

The starting place for staff development activities aimed at developing effective place- and community-based educators can be found in conversations about how teaching in this way involves a shift in the roles of teachers and students. As Tom Horn thought about this issue, he observed that "teachers almost become tour guides of a sort. To do staff development around how to become a tour guide is different from how to implement a reading instruction program." This process requires helping teachers "flip the concept of what the student is in their own minds. The students are the ones that are the researchers, and the teachers help them find those answers. The teachers don't have to have all of the answers."

Teachers must next begin to explore the curricular possibilities of what lies outside the classroom and school doors. In an effort to show teachers how it is possible to meet district and state requirements while at the same time incorporating local knowledge and experience into the curriculum, Sarah Taylor takes her staff on walks around the neighborhood surrounding the school as part of professional development days. She asks her teachers to take a specific benchmark or goal and think of all of the places within walking distance from the school or local people who could be invited into the classroom that would facilitate the teaching of that benchmark. More formally, Jon Yoder, Joyce's husband and the secondary science specialist in the Salem-Keizer district, has worked to create "content specific activities/lessons that can be connected to a broad array of place-based experiences." He noted that in the natural resources area there is already a fair amount of such materials, although "they address a pretty narrow range of science content standards relating to ecosystems and human impact." He's hopeful that, with an increasing emphasis on inquiry and engineering in new standards being adopted in his state, "there may be more justification for teachers to use this approach."

Yoder furthermore observed that it is imperative to help teachers understand that place- and community-based education is "not an add-on or extra thing to do but a different way to achieve the same content goals." A superintendent in Maine said something similar to Sobel when she observed that place-based education is the basket; it's not an egg in the basket. Making this shift in thinking is something that is not likely to happen overnight or something that will take root as a result of teachers simply incorporating lesson plans designed by others into their work with students. Educators effective in using this approach will be those who have made it part of the way they think about creating learning experiences for students.

In addition to school- or district-based staff development opportunities, some leaders have also been able to make it possible for teachers to attend summer workshops or institutes that provide more focused opportunities to learn about and experience place- and community-based education. Others have created semester-long professional development courses that bring teachers and administrators together on a monthly basis, provide them with dinner, and encourage the exploration of new teaching and learning possibilities with their peers. These experiences can be valuable in helping teachers to see that they are part of a broader effort to link learning to local knowledge and concerns. The cross-fertilization of ideas that occurs in such settings can stimulate even more experimentation and innovation.

Structural Arrangements and Curricular Frameworks

The shift to place- and community-based education can be supported in important ways through the adoption of structural arrangements and curricular frameworks that make teaching and learning in this way more accessible and comfortable for teachers. This could be accomplished by moving to a block schedule or establishing regular periods of time during the week when there are no pull-outs, no bells, and the opportunity to get students out of the classroom and into the community. A second structural arrangement involves making it easy for teachers to leave the school. While emphasizing the importance of safety, Sarah Taylor felt that teachers should be able simply to "let the office know and go." Steps need to be taken to make sure that no unnecessary obstacles stand in the way of learning outside the classroom.

A third way to encourage more teachers to incorporate this approach can be found in the creation of a shared curriculum framework that informs the work of all educators in a school. Both Taylor and Horn have invested significant energy into the development of such frameworks for their teachers. The framework for the Sunnyside Environmental School, for example, is seasonally based and tied to the garden and food cycles as well as food preservation. Teachers are encouraged to always start with students' personal experiences as these relate to different curricular topics. Lessons then move on to the external environment and require students to record their observations through writing or art. The next step involves "going deeper into what the geology or botany of that place is," giving students the tools to look beneath the surface of what they are seeing to explore roots and relationships. Final elements of the framework consider the experiences of indigenous peoples who lived in the region and their use of its natural resources. The aim of this process is to ground "the kids in story" and make sure that learning experiences match what is happening outside in the community and region. Interviewed in December, Taylor noted that "We're being really clear that the winter phase of learning at our school is about storytelling and service and coming inside, whereas the fall was much more about exploring our landscape."

At the Al Kennedy Alternative School, the curricular framework centers around five aspects of sustainability: forestry, agriculture, energy, architecture, and community. Much of the coursework at this school is tied into projects located in the community and region. With regard to forestry, the school recently received a five-year grant from the Weyerhaeuser Foundation to implement a monitoring project that will involve students in assessing the health of a forest's microbial environment. The school is also working with the School of Architecture at the University of Oregon to develop a prototype housing kit for low-income families that would incorporate solar panels, a rainwater catchment system, and composting toilets. Students are already involved in propagating vegetables in the school's large greenhouse and caring for a sizeable garden on the school site, the produce from which is distributed to people in need through the local food bank. Future plans include involving students in the creation and maintenance of community gardens at local school sites and trailer parks in an effort to encourage more people to grow some of their own food. The framework provides a template that directs teachers at the school to different projects that become the vehicles through which the conventional disciplines are taught. With it, making curricular choices from a potential world of possibilities is made easier. Having the framework also directs teachers' attention to areas they might also be potentially neglecting.

Finally, school leaders can advance this work and deepen its effectiveness by systematically providing opportunities for teachers to team with and mentor one another. Sarah Taylor emphasized the value teachers in her first- and second-grade team find in being able to visit one another's classrooms: "Just that openness, feeling that classrooms are open, you can go from classroom to classroom to get ideas." She has also been successful in encouraging her more experienced teachers to move from grade to grade to mentor teachers less familiar with place- and community-based approaches. Former middle school teachers, for example, are now teaching in elementary school teams, lending their expertise to teachers new to the school. Jon Yoder spoke of the importance of bringing teachers with similar perspectives together to meet periodically "to provide mutual encouragement." Brian Goodwin observed that "the peer support network is huge. This year, for example, we have more and more staff coming on board in just a few schools." As in CO-SEED schools in New England, this has led to the formation of a "critical mass. The staff start to take a leadership role, not as individuals but as teams, and that's pretty neat to see."

Nuts and Bolts

In addition to these organizational changes, school leaders can also develop a variety of more immediate tools to enable their faculty to make place- and community-based educational approaches their own. One aspect of place- and community-based education that lies outside the experience of many educators, for example, is the task of approaching people who work in other agencies or businesses to form partnerships with the school. Some schools overcome this challenge by hiring special staff members who can serve as brokers between the school and the community to develop and sustain these relationships. To some extent, all of the district leaders interviewed for this chapter devote part of their time to this chore, as well. But when teachers can take on some of the responsibility for forming partnerships, the range of possible projects can increase dramatically. Tom Horn at the Al Kennedy Alternative School has developed a template with a phone dialogue narrative to help teachers feel more confident about initiating contact with outside agency resource professionals. He has also worked with his staff to develop sustainability symposiums at the school that involve both agency staff and teachers. "The intent of those was to bring all of these people together, so that we're not all working in isolation and we're able to put faces to names. The more that we do that, the better understanding we have of what the whole picture is." To make this process even more accessible for teachers, Horn will fill in for them as a substitute or find a substitute when they need to meet with potential or ongoing partners off campus to work out the details of specific projects.

He will do the same thing if teachers have learned about a particular site that appears to be promising for a potential teaching unit or project. In order to help a teacher become comfortable about taking students to a new location, he will give them a chance to spend time at the site without young people in tow so that they can acquaint themselves with both the possibilities and the challenges of working there. "One of the best things I've done at Kennedy is to ... let them go work a day or two days or a week with a Forest Service employee to get a project started. So then the teacher gets to experience the project beforehand." Similarly, Sarah Taylor will encourage teachers at the Sunnyside Environmental School to visit sites they think they might want to incorporate into their curriculum on the weekend with their own children so that they can become familiar with it. If this is not possible, she will also give them a school day to scout it out.

Figuring out how to best match the learning opportunities outside the classroom to the needs of different students can also be a challenge for teachers. Horn has worked with his staff to develop a chart aimed at identifying ways that:

> each student can feel empowered by their involvement in a project. [The chart] looks at the pieces of a particular project and where we feel they fit, so that we know that they are going to feel empowered and involve themselves in the parts of the project that they can do. For instance, if a student is having difficulties with reading, we might not have him work ... with some of the planners, because some of what they might have to read is pretty high level ... . But they can feel valued, and the amazing thing about this kind of place-based activity is that the kids have no clues about levels. They don't feel less than or better than [as a result] of their involvement in a particular part of the project. And so the idea of differentiated instruction and training teachers how to do that creatively within the context of the project is really important.

What these different practices and strategies demonstrate is the importance of staying in close touch with teachers who are in the process of learning how to implement place- and community-based approaches. When school leaders are aware of difficulties that their teaching staff are encountering as they attempt to incorporate the local into their classrooms, they will be more able to invent tools or make programmatic modifications that can enhance the likelihood of teacher and student success. Place- and community-based education demands real instructional leadership and a hands-on approach to teacher support from principals and central office administrators.

One final detail important to keep in mind when implementing place- and community-based education is the value of an up-to-date contact list and an accurate calendar. Tom Horn noted that he's realized that he can't keep all of the information he's got to juggle in his mind. He has to write down dates and keep good records. The consequence of not doing so is teachers finding themselves three hours away from school at a project location with a group of students ready to work and no partner in sight. Or vice versa. The result is either wasted learning opportunities or disgruntled partners. Place- and community-based learning requires a different kind of organizational routine, which includes but goes beyond set schedules and ringing bells.

Partners and Resources

At the core of place- and community-based education is the belief that children and youth learn best when the wall between classroom and community has become permeable—with people from outside the school making classroom presentations to students and students interacting with adults in the places where they work. Enacting this vision means that school leaders need to include in their own job descriptions the cultivation of partnerships with people generally given scant attention by the school. Horn described this part of his job—something he estimates as taking 15–20 percent of his time—as social networking. Among those partners, he includes students' parents. Without these outside ties and relationships, place- and community-based education won't work, so it is imperative that principals and district administrators responsible for implementing this approach—as well as their school boards and teachers—understand the significance of time spent away from school.

One of the first tasks of leaders interested in implementing place- and community-based education is to inform parents and community members about what they are doing, about why students aren't in the classroom and are out on city buses going to wetlands or collecting oral histories at a nearby retirement home. The leaders I spoke with were in general agreement that the best way to share this information was informally or through student presentations. Effective place- and community-based learning projects often speak for themselves. At the Sunnyside Environmental School, the school holds regular celebrations of student work to which parents and community members are invited. People visit classrooms throughout the building filled with student work and then share a meal and enjoy a musical or dramatic presentation. During these events, student learning is on display for everyone.

School principal Sarah Taylor noted that the reason her school and its approach

> got as far as it got was because we had people who were able to talk about how this worked really well with their kids. And I think seeing high school principals and teachers [who'd] say you could really tell kids who went to that school— they act different from other kids.

She went on to observe that in the past dozen years three of the student representatives to the school board were graduates of her school (from more than 30 other K–8 or middle schools), something that demonstrated to the board and the community as a whole the impact of the school's approach on students who went there.

When Ed Armstrong from Tillamook does intentionally introduce people unfamiliar with this approach to its practices and benefits, he asks them about memorable learning experiences from their own careers as students. What he finds they remember is original research opportunities, a teacher who really cared about them, or unique projects. He then asks them what experiences they would like their own children to have in school. They generally begin by saying that they don't want their children "to have the experience that I had," sitting in rows, and never having any fun. He then describes place- and community-based learning activities. People respond by saying "Wow, that's really cool. I wish we would have done that." As mentioned earlier, Sarah Taylor also draws upon research about the effectiveness of more holistic approaches to education and their positive impact on student learning.

For some of these school leaders, reaching out to the community has meant becoming active in civic organizations like the Chamber of Commerce or Rotary. They give presentations to these groups and speak informally with people about current projects or needs. Horn noted that:

> one of the things that I've had to do as a leader is really market the concept to the community. And in doing so, we have garnered a tremendous amount of support from the Chamber of Commerce and other folks that maybe wouldn't have thought about this as a viable option.

As mentioned earlier, part of that marketing can involve developing ties with reporters from the local newspaper or television station. In small communities where journalists are on the lookout for story ideas, this can quickly result in regular news coverage, something that can significantly raise and potentially improve the profile of a school. Such stories can also have a beneficial impact on students. When young people see articles about their work and efforts publicized in the local newspaper, they become more easily persuaded that what they are doing is valuable and worth their time and energy. Academic engagement can often quickly follow.

Over and beyond teaching people outside the school about what place- and community-based education is, school leaders also need to acquaint the public with the roles they might play in extending and deepening children's learning. The starting place for this activity is believing that there are untapped educational assets in the community. Ed Armstrong talked about the importance of seeing the glass as half-full. He consults with educators in other districts who hear his story about what has been accomplished in his own community and then say, "We couldn't do that here," believing that resources that exist in his town don't exist in theirs. He mentioned the relationship he has built with a local lumber company that now underwrites the training of graduates of the local high school interested in operating and maintaining the state-of-the-art equipment found in its twenty-first-century mill. "Hampton Lumber was there for 30–50 years, and you never asked them for anything, so you never had that resource before. And now you do as your partner." Taylor recalled speaking with a colleague in another school who had never thought of inviting members of a thriving community of neighborhood artists into her building. Thinking back on this conversation, Taylor asked, "How could you be at that school and not have a relationship with [the community]? For me, it would be impossible."

As discussed in Chapter 8, once potential partners have been identified, the task then is to explore areas of common interest, places where potential school projects could dovetail with a partner's mission. When this happens, outside agencies or businesses become much more willing to consider providing staffing or resources that will allow teachers to implement place- or community-based projects. Looking at the implementation of projects in this way can oftentimes obviate the need for external funding. Three of the six leaders interviewed actually spoke of their belief that relying on external grants was a mistake. Armstrong said:

It's not about the money. If you have a compelling vision, the resources will show up. If it's the right vision that's aligned with the community or some values out there that other people hold, it really isn't going to be strange that resources show up. The surprise would be if the resources didn't show up.

Brian Goodwin observed that he sees grants as:

> kind of the last resort. If we really need to go out for a grant then we've got the project very concretely in our minds ... and we've got the partners all lined up. The success rate for acquiring grants with this type of operation is much higher than it used to be.

Taylor felt that grants could be useful in getting projects off the ground, but that it was completely possible to implement place- and community-based approaches without additional financial resources.

Although Jon Yoder did not argue against pursuing grants, his experience developing the Straub Environmental Learning Center—a building on the campus of North Salem High School that became the hub of his efforts to embed teaching and learning in his city and region—mirrors the experience of his colleagues elsewhere. The Straub Center cost over $500,000 to construct. Because school district and city officials believed that the kind of partnership the center represented was desirable, they and some community benefactors were willing to make significant contributions to its creation without any of the hoops associated with requests for proposals. By doing so, they created ongoing opportunities to transform students into genuine assets and resources for the Salem-Keizer area.

For the two remaining school leaders, however, grant writing has been central to making a transition to place- and community-based learning in their schools. Tom Horn in Cottage Grove intentionally decided to emphasize environmental sustainability knowing that grants were available to address forestry, energy, and water issues. These additional resources have been essential in developing what had formerly been a seriously underfunded school. And Joyce Yoder has found small grants to be invaluable in supporting the work of the team of teachers in her own building who have created the school-within-a-school that focuses on hands-on learning and citizenship education. Dollars went to planning time and staff development. In each of these instances, it must be noted that Horn and Yoder possess exactly the kind of clear educational vision that their colleagues who are more skeptical about grant writing stress is essential in developing partnerships that are productive and long-lasting.

What seems critical to keep in mind is that school leaders interested in incorporating place and community into their buildings or districts don't need to pursue this agenda by themselves alone. There are many potential allies beyond school doors who can make their own and the teachers' ideas reality. The formation of such relationships can bring both resources and legitimacy to the school. Funders look for school projects that have roots in the community. And community members can be assured about the value of new educational directions when they see respected individuals, businesses, or agencies joining with the school in these endeavors. The value for public schools in such communities can be found in the way that the work of teachers and students contributes to the common good, a factor that can positively impact voters' attitudes toward school bond and other tax measures. When schools partner with communities in this way, they truly serve the public as a whole and not only families with school-age children.

Stepping Up to the Challenge

School leaders drawn to place- and community-based educational approaches should realize that implementing this kind of reform agenda will be challenging and take time. In many respects, it is not an approach that can be imposed on teachers. Its success depends upon their willingness to bring their own interests and passions into the classroom, to share these with their students, and to ensure that the pursuit of what is fascinating to them will support students' mastery of important knowledge and skills. Brian Goodwin in The Dalles suggested that the most important thing he can do is to pay attention to teachers interested in moving in this direction and then to create as "rich and fertile" an environment for them to work in as possible. He has found that thoughtful listening, the acceptance of well-meaning failures, and the willingness to simply show up when teachers and their students are in the middle of learning experiences or involved in public presentations has helped to create the foundation of the trust upon which this kind of educational experimentation and risk tasking can be built.

It's also important for school leaders to understand that this approach—as compelling as it may be for many students—will not necessarily reach everyone. The success of learning experiences grounded in inquiry, exploration, and action depends to a large extent on the degree to which teachers and students feel safe—both emotionally and physically. For some students, early experiences in or out of school with adults and peers may have been so damaging that opportunities to learn in this more open-ended way may seem unreasonably threatening. Other kinds of learning experiences—still humane and caring but more tightly structured—may be necessary before they are ready to make the best use of projects located in the community. And leaders need to also realize that not all adults will necessarily be supportive of their efforts, as well founded and considered as these may be. Tom Horn talked about people's excitement about his plans but their tendency to focus on the reasons that following through with them would be impossible. He observed with regard to a project that eventually gained the support of a major funder:

> if I would have at any point said, "Yeah, you're right, it's not possible," it wouldn't have happened. I think that as a leader you have to hang on to the dreams and the hopes you have for what you're doing. And so, if you believe in it, go for it. Otherwise, it just won't happen.

Horn also spoke of the danger of getting caught up in the tendency to do place- and community-based learning projects just to do the projects. He felt that it was imperative to keep an eye on the broader purpose of what a school is trying to accomplish, both for its students and for the community. Attending to his own growth and activities that tap compelling personal passions and interests has been essential to this process. He seeks out opportunities to speak with like-minded people and volunteer in organizations that address issues close to his own heart. He commented: "If I didn't do that, I wouldn't have the creative juices to continue doing the work that I'm doing. I'm sure of that." So, just as leaders need to be thoughtful about supporting teachers, they need to nurture themselves.

There is no question that moving learning from the classroom into the community creates new complications and obligations for school leaders. Embracing this more comprehensive vision of education, however, can bear important fruit both for students and for the places where they live. By using communities and regions as sites for vital learning experiences and by engaging more partners in the task of preparing children for adulthood, the resources brought to bear on their development and maturation can be significantly enhanced, strengthening both the young and the communities that will eventually depend upon them. In this time of growing environmental and economic challenge, expanding the boundaries of the classroom and bringing more people into the educational process may be one of the wisest investments we can make.

Chapter 10

No School Is an Island—Except on the Coast of Maine

No school should be an island, isolated from the world around it. But, off the coast of Maine, a small number of year-round island communities, reachable only by boat, strive to preserve their schools as the soul of their communities. Without the school, there is no island community. Ranging in size from a handful to 220 students, these island schools face a unique set of environmental, cultural, and curricular challenges that are representative of isolated rural schools throughout the country.

In the later part of the nineteenth century, coastal commerce kept as many as 300 year-round island communities alive. Granite from the quarries of Penobscot Bay Islands—Deer, Vinalhaven, Swan's, Hurricane, Green's—built many of the public libraries, churches, and federal buildings from Buffalo to Washington, DC. Fishing stocks were ample and supported a diverse fishery. Schooners carried herring, farm products, lumber, and horse nets to Eastern coastal markets. Sheep were pastured on grassy islands, free from predators and the need for expensive fencing. Maine's island communities flourished, and so did a wide array of island schools. As quarrying ceased and fisheries changed, many of these communities became ghost towns, unable to support stores, businesses, and schools through the long Maine winter. Many survive as summer communities, reborn each May, but the schools have been converted to rental cottages or historical museums, no longer the center of community life.

Fifteen year-round communities survive, supported by regularly scheduled passenger and automobile ferries. Half a dozen are in Casco Bay in the Portland area, some dependent on jobs in the city for their economic livelihood. Four are way out—Monhegan, Matinicus, Isle au Haut, and Frenchboro—with infrequent winter ferry service, tiny schools, small fishing fleets, and stalwart populations of 50 to 100. In the closer reaches of Penobscot Bay, Swan's Island, Islesboro, North Haven, and Vinalhaven support larger year-round communities and schools—even three small but vibrant K–12 schools. One eighth grader recently described Vinalhaven in a My Place essay for her seventh-grade English class:

> I live in a place where the ocean waves crash on the shore and the lobster boats sway in their grasp. The fish swim under the influence of our silver shining hooks. There are boats everywhere from the shore to the red ferry buoy out in

the harbor. ... [When] summer rolls around, the people come like ants to honey for the lobster that we sell—the sweet butter-dipped gem that basically holds our island together.

(islandgirl, 2007)

On Vinalhaven, community and school leaders have been working to improve their school over the past decade.

It's a long way from Young Achievers in urban Boston to the Vinalhaven School—culturally and geographically. Students at Young Achievers are 95 percent children of color, representing a wide range of ethnic heritages; a high proportion of them receive free and reduced lunches. The natural world they explore exists mostly in cemeteries, urban parks, and the Arboretum. At the Vinalhaven School, the student population is 99 percent white, the ethnic diversity is a bit French Canadian, many students work with their parents in the fishing industry, and the natural world plays a prominent role in everyday life. But the challenges of engaging students in learning and connecting school and community are similar. And both communities are actively involved in weaving place- and community-based education into the ethos of the school. Exploring the evolution of place- and community-based learning in Vinalhaven and comparing it to Young Achievers allows us to see the core principles that characterize this approach in its many manifestations around the country. We're reminded of the rephrasing of an old John Donne quote in a Jefferson Airplane song, "No man is an island; he's a peninsula." This has been the goal of place- and community-based education in Boston and Maine—connecting the school to the mainland of the community so that the school becomes less like an island and more like a peninsula.

The Vinalhaven School

Walk in the school doors in Vinalhaven and it doesn't feel like many nameless and placeless schools in the United States. Straight ahead is a rough-cut granite wall, hewn by island craftsmen. The drill holes and shear marks testify to the hard labor needed to shape stone. Last year Tristan Jackson's students in the Alternative Education program learned the same skills while cutting slabs to line schoolyard garden beds and for a road barrier on a bridge up by Vinal Falls. They also learned that granite weighs 160 pounds per cubic foot and that seemingly impossible things are doable if you put your hands and minds to them.

Up above the granite wall floats a small fleet of lobster boats suspended from the ceiling, each about two feet from stem to stern, each one a bit different. Artist Diana Cherbuliez worked with a number of local craftsmen to create an installation that mirrored lobster boats at anchor down in Carver's Harbor. Owing to more than a bit of foresight and ingenuity, the boats in the school face into the wind, just like the boats in the harbor. They're all connected to a weathervane on the roof of the school that keeps the boats, and everyone in school, attuned to the wind direction, which you can decipher from the compass rose inlaid in the floor, directly beneath the boats. When it blows out of the southwest, lobster fishermen prepare themselves for a rough day, and people riding the ferry to Rockland consider taking Dramamine.

The surround of the sea is a constant presence. In the poem "Island Born," Harold Vinal wrote:

> My mother bore me in an island town,
> So I love windy water and the sight
> Of luggers sailing by in thick moonlight;
> I wear the sea as others wear the crown.
>
> (Little, 1997, p. 14)

Nowadays, it's lobster fishing that many of the students wear as a crown. The students' dads, uncles, or aunts fish, their teachers' spouses work at the lobster co-op, and their cousins go seining for herring on summer nights to lower the cost of lobster bait. Starting early, children often work on their parents' boats. Another recent eighth-grade My Place essay captures the island work ethic:

> When me and my dad get up in the morning, it is dark and a little cold out. We jump in to the truck to go to the store. We stay and talk for a while, then we get our coffee and head off. We get our oil gear at the shop and then get the skiff going. All you can hear is the seagulls flying overhead looking for an open bait box. You can feel the water hitting you in the face but it feels good.
>
> We get to the boat, tie the skiff up on the mooring, and start the boat. We check if we have any bait and we head off and all you can hear for the rest of the day is the engine, seagulls, and other boats. We get to the first string and haul it up. We check to see if the lobsters are the right size, throw back the little ones, then reset the traps. We haul a couple hundred traps a day. We stay out all day until around supper time and then head back to sell our catch. We tie up on to the mooring and we are on our way home with a hand full of money and sleepy eyes and ready to do it again tomorrow. Just another day on a lobster boat.
>
> (Montana94, 2007)

By the time they're in high school, some students make more money lobster fishing than their teachers make at school. This can be a boon or a curse. Talking about a student placed on suspension for not doing his homework, one teacher commented, "He doesn't care if we suspend him because he's planning to go haul tomorrow." Since the fishing season stretches from about April to December, many students have their own boats and fish after school and on weekends during the spring and fall as well as full time in the summer. And when push comes to shove and they've had their traps in the water too long, or they've got to get them out of the water because winter's coming, students can be tempted to haul instead of working on those Algebra II assignments. In the past, keeping them in school with their sights aimed on college has been challenging when it's reasonably easy to make $50,000 a year fishing without a college education. But things are changing.

The Challenges

Ten years ago, the Vinalhaven School was in rough shape. The building was old, cold, drafty, and not conducive to learning. Administrators came and went. Some teachers did the same or, if they stayed, they were there forever, and then no administrator could work with them. There was little coherence in the school—no agreed-upon curriculum, not much collaboration among the faculty, a ragged discipline policy. There wasn't much parental faith in the school—why should students, especially boys, stay in school if they weren't going to college and were planning on fishing? And there wasn't much connection between local businesses, the environment, the fishery, and the curriculum. Graduates either didn't apply to college or, if they went to college, stayed only for a few semesters and returned to the island. It was a different situation than characterizes many small rural schools throughout northern New England. The common complaint is that students graduate, go to college, get jobs in the city, and never come back. There's a net loss of young community members. But, in Vinalhaven, the opposite is true. High school graduates stick around, or they return home after being away for only a few years.

To summarize, the facilities were sub-standard, high administrator turnover led to a lack of faculty collaboration, no clear vision and mission existed, coherent discipline and attendance policies were lacking, many graduates were unmotivated to pursue higher education, and there was little connection between the school and the community. As a part-time teacher from those days said recently, "The school was like an old jalopy—it barely held together."

With the arrival of George Joseph, a new superintendent, in 1998, however, the school began to turn around. Joseph started down the long road of pulling the school together. He required teachers to collaborate, and he collaborated with the Island Institute, a nonprofit organization that has served the islands and communities of the Gulf of Maine since 1986, by bringing interesting young teachers to Vinalhaven. He worked with the community to convince them that regular attendance and higher education were important goals. And, to give students, teachers, and community members pride in their educational endeavors, he launched a campaign to convince islanders and the state education department that Vinalhaven needed a new school building. Many years of negotiation, finagling, and extra fund-raising on Joseph's part led to construction of one of the most learning-conducive facilities in the state.

Four classroom wings, or islands, provide classroom space for the K–2, 3–5, middle school, and high school students and teachers. The comfortable library and media center serve as the architectural heart of the school. An ample gym, an excellent technology lab, a science lab, and a life skills room surround this center. There's also a teacher-designed art studio/classroom and one of the finest theatre facilities along the coast of Maine. The main building is complemented with an applied technology workshop where some of the most innovative place- and community-based education projects have flowered in the past five years—student-built rowing dories, a completely refurbished 30-foot sail boat, and alternative energy collection devices. Vinalhaven students do real work, grounded in the cultural heritage of working waterfronts.

Once the building was complete, Joseph recruited an energetic young teacher to serve as school leader rather than principal. The task was to build a collaborative leadership team rather than to simply impose order. Mike Felton had gotten his start on the island as a high school history teacher through the Island Institute's Island Fellows program. As a Bowdoin graduate and captain of the football team, Mike had the leadership skills, savvy, and drive to take on the 14-hour-a-day job of creating a new school culture that was as promising as the new facility. Together, Joseph and Felton worked to find innovative and energetic teachers who both understand how to make the curriculum come alive and have the integrity to live in the raw physical climate and pressure-cooker social context of an isolated community.

When place- and community-based education facilitators from Antioch New England came knocking at the door four years ago, the school building was still brand new, the curriculum was still looking for coherence, the students were still unruly, and the community was still wondering if the end product justified the vast amount of money they had spent to build the new facility. Community complaints about the cost of the school were a part of the daily discourse on the fish wharves, in the checkout line at the IGA, over beers at the Sandbar. A comment at the annual meeting of the Vinalhaven Land Trust in 2008 is illustrative. When the Land Trust director proudly announced that the new Land Trust offices had been built on time and under budget, one member of the audience yelled out, "Maybe you should head up to the school and lend them some of your expertise." Another overheard comment at one of the island quarry swimming holes came from an off-islander who owned a house on the island: "I wish I didn't have to rent it year-round, but that school is so darned expensive that I can barely afford my taxes."

In trying to convince the Antioch New England CO-SEED facilitators that the school was a good candidate for the school change facilitation and professional development services it offered, George Joseph said, "We've built this beautiful building and we've gone way out on a limb to try to convince these folks that education deserves this support. Now we've got to deliver a program that lives up to these increased expectations." CO-SEED took on the challenge.

The Teachers Care Too Much

It's important to tease out the different strands that have made a difference in the culture change at the Vinalhaven School. The paradigm and methods of place- and community-based education have provided one strand. We will focus on these below. But the administration and teachers in the school have also worked hard, in a variety of ways, to foster a more positive culture. These culture changes are illustrated by comments from a recent evaluation conversation about the way the school has evolved in the last four years. Sue Dempster, the school librarian for the past ten years, reflected:

> Part of the change is that we've moved from having lots of good players on the staff to having a really good staff team. Now, the school is much more community-based and connected to the strength of the community.

And the students are starting to notice. In the past, when we tried to have a student council, it never worked. Now, the students are really invested in the student leadership team. They recognize that the teachers and administration are listening to their concerns and they're willing to step up and take responsibility. They like that the curriculum is more challenging.

Before, the students knew they could get away with stuff and they played one teacher against each other. Now they realize that we talk to each other and know what's going on. One student noted this change saying, "The teachers care too much about us."

I realized things were different this year after the first two weeks of school. All the sudden it dawned on me. I hadn't heard one student say, "This school sucks!" We've gone from being a school that just exists to a town and school that really cares about its kids. It's a different school and the students have self-esteem. They're proud to be from Vinalhaven.

(SEED team evaluation discussion, November 28, 2007)

The cultural evolution over the past decade in Vinalhaven has been from community engagement to creating a culture of responsibility to collaborative leadership to solidifying curriculum to becoming grounded in place. This is obviously an oversimplification, as many of these changes have been overlapping. But the school leadership has been savvy in holding to a first-things-first mindset, recognizing that change is incremental and that some changes need to precede other changes. Sue's comments provide a useful framework for looking at the contributions of place- and community-based education in Vinalhaven.

Connecting the School to the Strength of the Community

Superintendent George Joseph recognized the value of a building project to pull a community together. He called on all aspects of the community, from parents to local contractors to designers to artists to the summer community, to visualize and build a new school. He advocated with the state to understand that the Vinalhaven situation was different and that state guidelines therefore needed to flex to provide for the right solution. There hadn't been a new K–12 school built in Maine in 30 years, so all the design parameters didn't quite fit. He was the advocate with the State Department of Education for what the community needed. He stretched the community's resources, but he did it in a way that built common purpose. The result was a facility they could be proud of if the other pieces fell into place.

Simultaneously during this period a number of parents and townspeople realized that the community needed to complement the educational program at the school. Vinalhaven is first and foremost a fishing community, but it also has its share of seasonal and year-round artists. Community members wanted to make sure that the core curriculum was complemented with arts education and after-school programs. Thus, over the decade, Partners in Education (PIE) and the school enrichment committees emerged to enrich school programs. From funding a full-time art teacher to funding a full-time drama teacher to then raising almost $2 million to create a top-shelf performing space in the school, these committees have made a wide range of artistic opportunities available to students and community members.

The Vinalhaven Land Trust (VLT) has also played a serious role in connecting students to the local landscape. Unlike many land trusts, which focus primarily on land acquisition and protection, the VLT has put substantial emphasis on education programs that connect students with the land and sea. It supports curriculum-based Land Trust field trips, before- and after-school Outdoor Explorers programs, issues-focused problem-solving (e.g., studies of saltwater intrusion into drinking water wells), and summer sailing and camping programs. In addition, the Land Trust provides funding to support field trips to Tanglewood Environmental Learning Center on the mainland, multi-day trips to hike Mount Katahdin, marine research, and professional development for teachers. The hope is to enhance the curriculum, increase academic learning, and develop a love of the land that will foster long-term stewardship of Vinalhaven resources.

This diverse set of school–community collaborations provided the rich soil in which place- and community-based education has grown on Vinalhaven.

A School that Really Cares about its Kids

One of the preconditions of an effective academic program is a culture of order, respect, and responsibility in a school. We don't mean to suggest that a law-and-order mindset is necessary, but rather that there is a sense of clear expectations, appropriate consequences, and follow-through that everyone understands. When Mike Felton arrived as school leader, he inherited a culture rife with casualness. Because dentist appointments and shopping and sports often required being away for the day on the mainland, students and parents treated attendance casually. There was also an unspoken understanding that the needs of lobster fishing often trumped the need for high school students to be in school. In addition, in-school conflicts between students weren't treated in a consistent fashion, and parents often sided with the students rather than the administration. One of the major tasks in the first few years after moving into the new building was the creation of a culture of clear expectations and responsibility.

New policies for attendance and in-school behavior were hammered out, explained to students and parents, and then enforced conscientiously. The casual tolerance for alcohol consumption on the senior class trip was curtailed. Suspension for inappropriate behavior was implemented consistently. A homework club was created to make it clear that "Yes, everyone has to do their homework" and that the teachers were there to help make that happen.

To demonstrate that the school was responsive to all manner of learners, the school also invested in a sophisticated vocational technology program to complement its college prep programs. This led to the creation of a comprehensive shop facility and a full-time voc tech staff person and more recently the creation of an alternative education program for students who have a hard time staying in academic classes. These program developments, in addition to the support of the arts, means that there's a place for everyone at the school. Taken together, this has led to a school where "the teachers care too much" about the students. Students may sort of miss the laissez-faire days when they could get away with poor behavior, but they also feel recruited into serious educational pursuits as a result of higher expectations.

From Lots of Good Players to a Really Good Staff Team

Once the new school opened, the superintendent recognized the need for a collaborative leadership model to draw all teachers into shaping the culture of the school. In addition to hiring a school leader rather than a principal, the superintendent simultaneously created a leadership team with representatives from the four school islands—the K–2, 3–5, 6–8, and 9–12—and the school counselor. One teacher from each of the islands serves on the leadership team, which meets on a weekly basis, for a two-year term. School leader Mike Felton handles many of the day-to-day problems, while the leadership team develops long-term policy and culture and serves as a vehicle of communication with all the staff.

To address the isolation of teachers from each other, the administration created a schedule that allows for grade-level team meetings on a daily and weekly basis. Each team of four to six teachers has a short daily meeting and a longer weekly meeting to coordinate logistics, integrate curriculum, and discuss students. At each level, teachers share some responsibility for teaching all of the children in that grade-level island. For example, in the third- through fifth-grade island, teachers provide math and reading instruction for students in their own grade and then coordinate language arts, social studies, or science for all three grades.

In the two years 2006–2008, as part of pulling the curriculum together, curriculum teams were also created. So there's a science curriculum team with the science specialists from K–2, 3–5, 6–8, and 9–12. Similar cross-grade curriculum teams exist for social studies, language arts, and math. The challenge for these teams is to look vertically across the grades to eliminate redundancy and create developmentally appropriate learning sequences. For instance, the social studies team recently created a plan articulating how research projects should get conducted at each grade-level island. And the language arts team created a chart specifying the writing product expectations in narrative and expository writing across the grade levels. Arts, technology, and health/physical education teams engage in similar cross-grade planning. As a result, most teachers are part of at least two collaborative teams, one with a horizontal and one with a vertical focus.

More recently, each grade-level team has taken responsibility for a monthly curriculum presentation. In September 2008, the third- through fifth-grade team presented its Vinalhaven granite unit from the previous year. In October, the sixth-through eighth-grade team presented the red tide testing unit that happens in the spring. In November, the K–2 team presented the field trip program done in conjunction with the Vinalhaven Land Trust. Each team portrays the project on the entranceway bulletin board and also creates a PowerPoint to present the project at the monthly school board meeting. This both pulls the members of the team together and communicates the rich, often place-based curriculum to community leaders.

After a recent beginning-of-school professional development day, fifth-grade teacher Gloria Smith and vocational technical coordinator Mark Jackson organized a late-afternoon rowing outing for new and old staff. Jackson is the coach of the high school rowing team. The 16-foot dories were handmade by voc tech students and are manned by eight rowers and a coxswain. Made for ocean rowing, the boats are much wider and sturdier than sculls, and the oars are similarly beefier. The Vinalhaven team competes all around New England, and their co-ed team often beats all-male

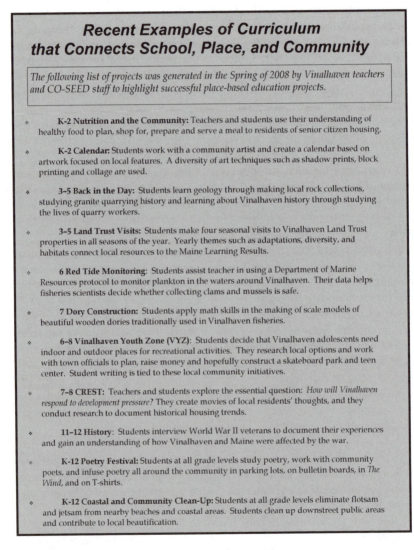

Recent Examples of Curriculum that Connects School, Place, and Community

The following list of projects was generated in the Spring of 2008 by Vinalhaven teachers and CO-SEED staff to highlight successful place-based education projects.

❖ **K-2 Nutrition and the Community:** Teachers and students use their understanding of healthy food to plan, shop for, prepare and serve a meal to residents of senior citizen housing.

❖ **K-2 Calendar:** Students work with a community artist and create a calendar based on artwork focused on local features. A diversity of art techniques such as shadow prints, block printing and collage are used.

❖ **3–5 Back in the Day:** Students learn geology through making local rock collections, studying granite quarrying history and learning about Vinalhaven history through studying the lives of quarry workers.

❖ **3–5 Land Trust Visits:** Students make four seasonal visits to Vinalhaven Land Trust properties in all seasons of the year. Yearly themes such as adaptations, diversity, and habitats connect local resources to the Maine Learning Results.

❖ **6 Red Tide Monitoring:** Students assist teacher in using a Department of Marine Resources protocol to monitor plankton in the waters around Vinalhaven. Their data helps fisheries scientists decide whether collecting clams and mussels is safe.

❖ **7 Dory Construction:** Students apply math skills in the making of scale models of beautiful wooden dories traditionally used in Vinalhaven fisheries.

❖ **6–8 Vinalhaven Youth Zone (VYZ):** Students decide that Vinalhaven adolescents need indoor and outdoor places for recreational activities. They research local options and work with town officials to plan, raise money and hopefully construct a skateboard park and teen center. Student writing is tied to these local community initiatives.

❖ **7–8 CREST:** Teachers and students explore the essential question: *How will Vinalhaven respond to development pressure?* They create movies of local residents' thoughts, and they conduct research to document historical housing trends.

❖ **11–12 History:** Students interview World War II veterans to document their experiences and gain an understanding of how Vinalhaven and Maine were affected by the war.

❖ **K-12 Poetry Festival:** Students at all grade levels study poetry, work with community poets, and infuse poetry all around the community in parking lots, on bulletin boards, in *The Wind*, and on T-shirts.

❖ **K-12 Coastal and Community Clean-Up:** Students at all grade levels eliminate flotsam and jetsam from nearby beaches and coastal areas. Students clean up downstreet public areas and contribute to local beautification.

Figure 10.1 Documenting community-based curriculum

teams from other schools. On a hot, still, late-August afternoon, Sobel joined teachers and learned to feather blades and synchronize strokes. As the group glided through an islet-laden bay, they stopped for an exploration of Wharf Quarry, where some of the largest granite columns ever carved in the world were crafted.

This rowing outing is the kind of professional development that illustrates Sue Dempster's comments about culture change in the school. Handcrafted rowing dories and the sport of ocean rowing emerge out of centuries-old island traditions unique to the coast of Maine. Engaging students and teachers in preserving these traditions **connects the school to the strength of the community**. Similarly, rowing together is a great metaphor **for moving from lots of good players to a really good staff team**. In the beginning our oars clacked together, a rhythmic cadence eluded us, and we couldn't track a straight course. By the end of the afternoon, paddling back towards the landing with the sun at our backs, we were a synchronized team, just as the teachers in the school now experience themselves. And a **school that really cares about its kids** also needs to care about its teachers. What better way to show this care than to support hearty physical exercise and exploring cultural heritage as an integral part of professional development?

Curriculum Grounded in Place and Community

Three simultaneous curriculum initiatives are serving to improve the quality of education in Vinalhaven. First, Mike Felton has put primary emphasis on stabilizing the curriculum and connecting it to the Maine Learning Results. In the past, the curriculum was too much based on the whims of the teacher. Then, when that teacher left, the new teacher had to make it up anew. Now there's an emergent curriculum that everyone agrees on. Second, to connect high school students to the wider world and provide increased academic challenge, the school now offers a few Advanced Placement courses and provides access to synchronous and asynchronous online courses. Third, with support from Antioch New England facilitators and a half-time place- and community-based educator, there's been an increased effort to ground the curriculum in the unique character of the Vinalhaven environment and culture. All three of these initiatives serve both to increase the rigor of the curriculum, improving academic achievement, and to increase the community's understanding of and satisfaction with the school program.

With regard to the initiation of a place- and community-based curriculum, it's important to recognize the excellent pre-existing projects that had already set the tone in the school and community. The most grand and impressive was the total overhaul and restoration of a 30-foot sail boat by the voc tech students over the course of two years starting in 2003. Mark Jackson led this project with vision and grit. He and his students stripped the donated boat down to its hull and then built it up from scratch, from carpentry to electronics, to installing the engine, from plumbing to navigation equipment to designing the sails. Jackson and his students accomplished this monumental task, learning with one another as they proceeded from one step to the next. The capstone was sailing the boat, the *Freya*, from Vinalhaven to Florida in the fall and back north in the spring (2006–2007 school year), with student crews rotating in for three- to four-week stints. The students documented their travels, and their reports were integrated into the curriculum back at the school. On a smaller scale, Pat Paquet, the middle school math teacher, often has her seventh-grade students construct model rowing dories as an application of geometry and algebra skills. Both of these endeavors stem from the long history of boat design and building on Vinalhaven and throughout Penobscot Bay since the early nineteenth century.

Let's look at some of the other innovative curriculum projects unfolding on the island. Many of these projects emerged out of a summer professional development institute that involved CO-SEED teachers, students, and community members from across New England. All participants were involved in content area workshops and courses in mixed groups. Then each school/community worked together to identify goals and projects for the year. Other projects emerged during in-school professional development days facilitated by the Antioch New England place- and community-based educators. Still others just emerged out of teachers' independent spirit and became rooted in the school because its culture supports innovative projects that ground learning in the community.

Nutrition and the Community: Grades K–2

The five food groups, the food pyramid, and healthy snacks are often part of the early grades social studies and science curriculum. But it's still hard to make this content relevant to young children. Carbohydrates? Proteins? Maybe not. But certainly fruits and vegetables are graspable. The Vinalhaven K–2 teachers' solution was to engage students in eating healthy snacks and preparing healthy meals. Research on changing school lunch programs has found that one way of encouraging children to try new goods—think spinach salad, couscous, potato and leek soup—is to give them the opportunity to prepare these things in the classroom or a school kitchen. If students have a hand in preparing things or seeing how different foods are prepared, they're much more likely to taste them and like them. Engaging students in this process can have a positive effect on learning science content as well.

The teachers first focused on healthy snacks. What are examples of healthy snacks? Why are they good for us? Where can we find them? What's the difference between having a candy bar versus an apple for a snack? The teachers created a bar graph to show the number of healthy snacks during snack time each day. During this unit, one parent indicated to a teacher that her child was demanding that Mom should shop for more healthy snacks so her snack would go up on the bar graph during the math activity. What a great example of good curriculum shaping healthy eating habits in the community.

Additionally, teachers wanted to extend the learning into the community through serving a healthy meal to seniors at the assisted living center. This gave the curriculum a higher purpose, built relationships, and spread the message of eating better throughout the community. Children planned meals, composed ingredient lists, went shopping at Carver's Market, helped prepare the meal, and served it to island elders. To practice for the trip to the market, the kindergarten teacher set up a classroom store so children could practice shopping within a budget and use money to buy groceries.

What started out as a science unit now involves reading and language arts in choosing menus and preparing lists, math in figuring out quantities and costs, and social studies in understanding how different aspects of the community work together to take care of its citizens.

Back in the Day: Grades 3–5

Learning geology is part of the Maine State Learning Results. One specific guideline states:

> *Students will gain knowledge about the earth and the processes that change it. Students will be able to:*
> Elementary Grades 3–4 1. Describe differences among minerals, rocks, and soils.
> Middle Grades 5–8 5. Classify and identify rocks and minerals based on their physical and chemical properties, their composition, and the processes that formed them.

The problem with much geology instruction is that it often stays classroom- and book-bound. Teachers and students rarely go outside to actually see rocks *in situ*, and most students learn the definitions of metamorphic, igneous, and sedimentary rocks and then quickly forget them. Encouraged to adopt a more place-based approach, the grade 3–5 teachers wanted to use Vinalhaven's history to connect the learning to the real world. Moreover, they recognized the value of integrating social studies and language arts into the study. The result was a unit entitled "Back in the Day: Exploring Geology and Vinalhaven's Quarrying History."

In the classroom, students used textbooks to learn the basics about rocks and minerals, how rocks are formed, and how to use simple tests to identify specimens. Moving outwards, teachers then required students to become rock hounds and create their own personal collections, noting physical properties, dates when rocks were collected, and locations. Since many of the students wound up collecting granite, the teachers turned to focusing on the history of granite quarrying on the island, using students' first-hand experiences swimming in abandoned quarries to help them understand how building stone was extracted by quarrymen.

The next phase was to collaborate with the directors of the Vinalhaven Historical Society to use their resources to expand the historical components of the curriculum. Students found the headstones of quarrymen in an island cemetery, posed for photos modeled after historical photos, and wrote historical fiction based on the lives of workers. A writing prompt tied to this unit was designed to give students experience analogous to the prompts on the state learning assessments. One third grader wrote:

> A new granite worker was hired to cut granite at Boom Quarry. They paid him a salary of 75 cents a day, which was enough to provide food for his family and live a good life.

Connecting the Curriculum to the Community

* Using a graphic organizer developed by our writing teacher Mrs. White, students spent time sitting on the large granite rock behind the Historical Society framing their thoughts and writing about the day in the life of a granite worker with Ms. Smith.

*Students were given 35 minutes to complete this task – a complete piece of writing with a clear beginning, middle and end. This is similar to the timed writing prompts on the Maine Educational Assessments.

Name:_____

Date:_____ - _____ - _____

35 Minute Independent Writing Prompt

Directions: Choose a character, plot, & setting. Write a story using all three of those elements and any other ideas you can come up with. Have fun!

Story Check-list:

	Circle one choice for each element:
character	Quarry Worker's names *Choose names from the list of quarry workers found buried in Carver's Cemetery*
plot	A day-in-the-life of a quarry worker A piece of granite is almost finished being cut, and something happens A group of quarrymen get an order for a very important granite job Your idea:_____
setting	Booth's Quarry Lawson's Quarry Sand's Quarry Your idea:_____

☐ Does your story have a beginning middle and end?

☐ Did you use each of the character, plot, and settings that you chose?

☐ Is your story clear and easy to follow?

☐ Did you check for capitals at the beginning of a sentence?

☐ Did you use your spelling journal to check your spelling?

Quick Story Mapping:

BEGINNING	MIDDLE	END

Figure 10.2 Writing prompt for grades 3–5 Vinalhaven granite unit CO-SEED/Vinalhaven School evaluation report

Once he was working with some polishing tools at the bottom of a ledge when a cutting tool was unintentionally kicked off a ledge and headed straight for Arthur. The man yelled to Arthur to get out of the way. Arthur had just enough time to get out of the way, but the cutting tool hacked into his leg as he was moving away.

He cried out in pain and the sharp tool was lodged into his leg. He was rushed to a doctor. The doctor said he could take out the tool and it had hit his bone and there was nothing he could do about his broken leg. Arthur later moved to Alabama to live a non-dangerous life.

(Max Morton, 2007)

The teachers found that the writing-in-place experience, with stimulation derived from historical photos, videos about quarrying, and first-hand explorations of the cemetery and quarry, tended to increase the volume and quality of the students' writing. This finding resonates with findings from many other place- and community-based education initiatives.

The geology unit ended at the Historical Society with a student presentation attended by many parents, some of whom were visiting the museum for the first time. One parent went home and returned later with an artifact to donate to the museum. The use of a community resource to enhance the curriculum led, in small ways, to students and parents understanding more deeply the heritage of Vinalhaven.

Marine Science and Red Tide Monitoring: Grade 6

Oceans serve as the integrating theme for the sixth-grade science curriculum in the middle school. Amy Palmer covers numerous aspects of physical and biological sciences throughout the year. One central feature is a refrigerated saltwater tank in the classroom that allows her to have marine creatures on hand for investigation. Students collect organisms on after-school tidepool adventures conducted by the Vinalhaven Land Trust on a section of rocky coast about a mile from the school. Sixth graders lead introductory mini-touch tank investigations with first graders so that all students start to learn their marine neighbors.

To introduce scientific protocols, Palmer has the students do grid square surveys of schoolyard organisms to prepare them to do similar surveys of intertidal zones. Some students also get to go off island to participate in the Mount Desert Island Youth Watershed Forum, a project sponsored by a local water quality coalition that supports environmental research and community education. In the spring, students get to apply all their learning about marine systems when they participate in Maine's Department of Marine Resources volunteer monitoring program, with its focus on important health issues in Maine's coastal communities.

Red tides, for example, are caused by four species of phytoplankton—tiny plants in the water. When nutrient levels, water temperature, and weather conditions are just right, these four species of phytoplankton can grow voluminously. Some evidence suggests that high levels of organic pollutants and agricultural run-off from rivers into coastal bays are increasing the frequency of red tides. When these phytoplankton (*Alexandrium, Dinophysis,* and *Gonyalux* to be specific) become abundant, filter feeders like clams and mussels concentrate them in their tissues. Eating

Figure 10.3 Red tide monitoring project at Vinalhaven
Photo by David Sobel

contaminated clams and mussels can cause severe problems for consumers, including diarrhea, amnesia, paralysis, and in some cases death.

Maine Department of Marine Resources trains volunteers to collect water
samples and microscopically survey them for the offending phytoplankton.
Amy Palmer is a trained volunteer, so she has her sixth graders participate in the
challenge of collecting samples, analyzing them, and then sending reports in to the
state. Since red tides are most common in months without Rs (May, June, July,
August), this project appropriately fits into the last six weeks of the school year and
serves to pull together many parts of the curriculum. It also provides a valuable
opportunity to look at real data. By graphing data on dissolved oxygen, salinity, and
temperature in relationship to the population density of specific phytoplankton,
students start to understand how ecological factors affect populations. Good
curriculum and service to the public health community go hand in hand in this
project.

"Remember Me" at Roberts Cemetery: High School Integrated Arts

Each fall, the arts teachers at the school—there's a half-time music teacher, a full-time visual arts teacher, and a full-time drama teacher—and the French teacher collaborate to do an integrated project. This year, because of the school's increasing focus on the Vinalhaven community, they based their project on one of the local cemeteries.

Drama teacher Irene Dennis and art teacher Erica Hansen knew they wanted to create learning opportunities that would connect students to island history and give them an opportunity to express and enhance their own sense of place. After

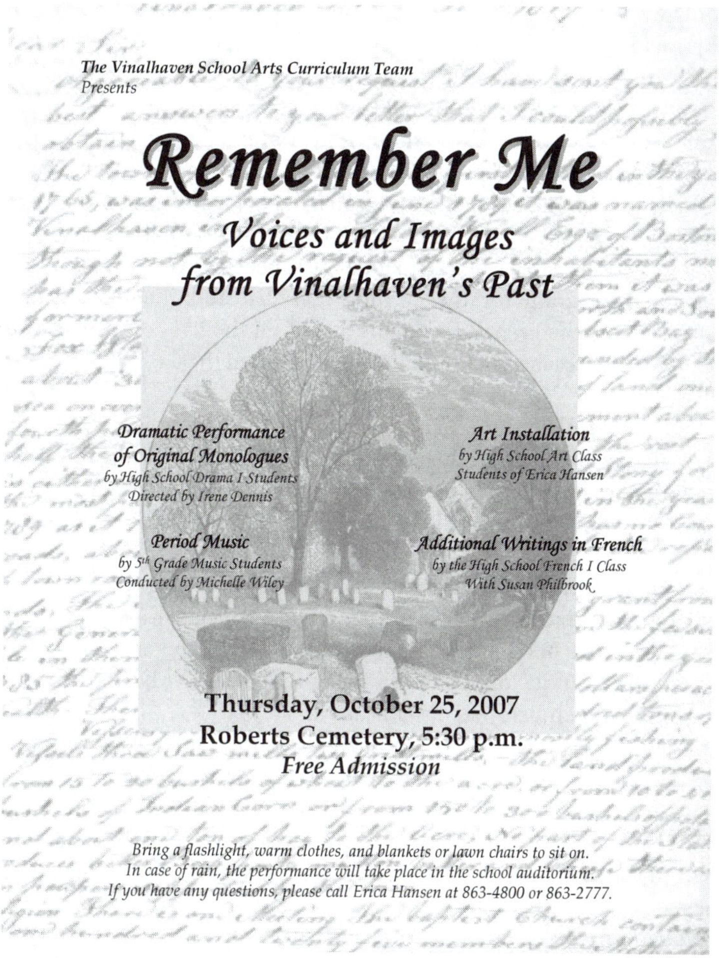

The Vinalhaven School Arts Curriculum Team
Presents

Remember Me
Voices and Images
from Vinalhaven's Past

Dramatic Performance
of Original Monologues
by High School Drama I Students
Directed by Irene Dennis

Art Installation
by High School Art Class
Students of Erica Hansen

Period Music
by 5th Grade Music Students
Conducted by Michelle Wiley

Additional Writings in French
by the High School French I Class
With Susan Philbrook

Thursday, October 25, 2007
Roberts Cemetery, 5:30 p.m.
Free Admission

Bring a flashlight, warm clothes, and blankets or lawn chairs to sit on.
In case of rain, the performance will take place in the school auditorium.
If you have any questions, please call Erica Hansen at 863-4800 or 863-2777.

Figure 10.4 Program for theater production based on local history and art
Used with permission of Vinalhaven School faculty

collaboration with the Historical Society and a logistical assessment of cemeteries to determine ease of access for an outdoor event, they settled on Roberts Cemetery. They then focused on a subset of people buried there. Parameters of choice included gender, a range of occupations and industries, and individuals whose stories were dramatic or touching. Students did historical research about their character and, through a series of well-scaffolded writing prompts, developed a monologue in the first person for that character.

The idea was to choose a fictional day in the life of their character and convey the significance of that moment to the audience. Students critiqued each other's accounts, decided who would perform which ones, and then created costumes germane to the late nineteenth century. The theatrical performance happened at dusk, with the full moon rising, on a crisp October evening. Each performer was illuminated only by candle and moonlight. Some students showed sides of themselves that others had never seen. There was the shy, reticent girl who portrayed her character with compelling drama. The class clown took on a very serious demeanor and found new ways to impress an audience. Provocative stories emerged, based on the historical record: a 16-year-old girl shot while ironing, tragic deaths of young children, quarrying accidents, disappearances at sea. One character was named Aunt Lizzy, Queen of the Horse Net Factory, which led everyone to wonder, "What are horse nets and was there really a horse net factory that employed 100 people on Vinalhaven?" Good drama can lead to good historical learning.

The printed program for the evening included additional monologues, in French, written by the French I students, based on the lives of Quebecois immigrants. The French teacher, Susan Philbrook, observed that:

> Initially, the students said, "You want us to write a monologue in French? No way! This is just French I." But because we used the set of writing prompts from the drama teacher, they came together and in the end the students said, "Hey, that's pretty cool, we really did it."

Interspersed between the performances of the monologues, the music teacher directed the fifth graders in a performance of an original song written by an islander. It described her relationship to her grandfather and his work in the granite quarries. This was one of the few times the song had ever been performed, and most community members had never heard it.

After the monologues and music, audience members followed candlearia-lined paths to find candle-illuminated silhouette installations based on the lives of the characters in the play. These images were set at gravestones scattered throughout the cemetery—hands reaching up out of water representing a character who had drowned, or granite quarrying tools for a quarry worker. The images resonated with the narrative from the monologues.

There's genuine enthusiasm at school and in the community for curriculum that has real audiences, with content drawn from the fabric of the lives of students' ancestors. Best of all, the project served to address the school's two stated goals for the year—an emphasis on increasing the academic rigor of the curriculum and a commitment to increased connections between the school and the community. The connection to the community was demonstrated by the size of the audience—more than 200 people showed up and attended the reception in a nearby renovated schoolhouse. The quality of writing, use of historical resources, and commitment to refined presentation are illustrative of the increasing rigor of the curriculum.

Vinalhaven Youth Zone (VYZ): Making a Place for Adolescents

For more than five years, teens on the island have been lobbying for both a skateboard park and some kind of away-from-school and in-town teen center. There have been many false starts, but in 2007 things began to look up. At the CO-SEED summer institute in 2007, the Vinalhaven Youth Zone rose to the top as one of the primary goals for the year. Tristan Jackson, the Alternative Program teacher and place-based educator in the school that year, assumed leadership. He had grown up in Vinalhaven, had long been active in community affairs, and knew the networks; he was well positioned to actually get things done.

Jackson convened a group of middle school students who were invested in making things happen and commenced regular in-school and after-school meetings. Though they started out focusing on the skateboard park, the idea about an indoor meeting place—a teen center—also emerged as a priority. Simultaneously, a community arts organization with a building known as the ARC was deciding whether to close or reinvent itself. Its building needed work to be brought up to code and to become suitable for winter events. Furthermore, membership on its board of directors had waned. Tristan recognized that the ARC was a suitable location for a teen center, and the real-world challenge of bringing the building back to life was just the focus students needed. Students envisioned an Internet cafe/indoor sports and meeting space that could serve both the teen and the adult community in town. They set to work creating a series of events that would raise money for the building rehabilitation and model the kinds of purposes a revitalized ARC could serve. During the rest of the school year the VYZ team of students carried off a Halloween ball, a Thanksgiving supper, a Valentine's dance, a spring fling, and an arts and activities auction to raise money for the renovations. Ping-pong tables were donated and a set of skateboard ramps were constructed to provide a temporary indoor skate park. Skateboarding now happens three afternoons a week, and a teen center has been born.

Work on the outdoor skateboard park also proceeded. Possible sites were scouted, and one option in the center of town was explored in depth. Tax maps were located, and a community member who is an architect and surveyor worked with students to survey the area and create a site plan. This work was done in conjunction with the seventh-grade math curriculum. One student—generally turned off to math—created alternative designs for the actual features in the park, an excellent applied geometry project for him. In late September, the VYZ students made an initial presentation to the selectpersons board and the town manager. The students prepared testimony, practiced it, got feedback and modeling from Jackson, and then performed admirably in front of the board. Selectpersons expressed concern about the location and the need to relocate some public works functions to accommodate the park, but at least things were rolling. Audience members at the hearing were enthusiastic about the idea and offered support and other location ideas.

One of Jackson's challenges has been to figure out ways to have this community activism work dovetail with the requirements of the curriculum so work students are doing can replace, rather than be on top of, regular classroom assignments. For instance, persuasive writing is a component of the middle school language arts curriculum. Wouldn't it make sense to have students' testimony for why a skateboard park is necessary serve to fulfill the persuasive writing requirement in the curriculum? And, as mentioned above, making scale maps of the proposed skate park involves the application of mathematical knowledge and skills. Students might also create a questionnaire to be distributed to townspeople to assess their support of a park—another applied mathematics project. Of course, there are also social studies curriculum aspects here; understanding how to shape decision-making at the local level is a good case study for understanding how bills become law. When curriculum and community development resonate, memorable learning can be the result.

Staying the Course

The place- and community-based education school change initiative wrapped up on Vinalhaven in August 2008, but the evolution of school and community programs continues. The true test of a school change initiative, of course, is whether the change processes can become institutionalized—made permanent in the structures of the school. This appears to have occurred on Vinalhaven. During the hiring of a new superintendent, the interview protocol included a question about the candidate's experience with and commitment to place-based education. Similarly, beginning of the school year professional development made it clear to new staff that connecting the curriculum to the community was a priority. The mini-grant program, initiated with CO-SEED funding, has been continued and is now coordinated by Partners in Education, an existing community nonprofit.

During the 2008–2009 school year, phase two of the ARC renovations resulted in the ARCafe. In what was formerly an old house, the front rooms of the ARC have been transformed from a small, ill-equipped kitchen and drab living area to a new coffee bar and vibrant, comfortable Internet cafe. Student and community volunteer labor provided the elbow grease for much of the renovation. Lots of native materials were used as well—the bar was built with granite counter tops sawn from island stone and hand polished by a student, and with local cherry wood trim.

The ARCafe serves both as a teen center and as a meeting space for community gatherings, meetings, and private parties. One high school student, Izza Drury, worked there during the year, and it was planned that other students would join her. She commented, "I get to learn something I've never done before, so it's a job, but it's also an experience." Drury says she has learned a lot about cafe equipment and its maintenance, as well as how to run a food service business, including making sure food is fresh and the quality good. Drury has been a member of the ARC rehabilitation team from the beginning, and is very enthusiastic about the cafe. "It totally went above and beyond what I expected," she said.

Annie Boyden, one of the original ARC founders back in the early 1980s, echoes the students' enthusiasm. "I'm very, very happy that there's new energy there," she said. "It is reaching out to the community on different levels; that was always the dream." Tristan Jackson, place- and community-based educator, sums up his strategy in getting students involved in community projects: "Give kids the space, a green light and a little support, and they'll do amazing things." In the case of the ARC, the students, teachers, and community members have pulled off an amazing rebirth of an island resource.

At the same time, there's been increased collaboration between the Vinalhaven Land Trust and the high school science curriculum. Whereas the VLT had previously focused on working with the elementary and middle school curriculum, there's been a recent attempt to provide real-world science opportunities for the biology and chemistry classes in the high school. For the biology class, VLT scientist Kirk Gentalen is training high school students to help in assessing reforestation on a piece of property recently acquired by the Land Trust. Using a protocol developed by the Maine State Forest Service the students set up sample monitoring plots for data gathering about forest regeneration and wildlife populations on Isle au Haut Mountain preserve. The area had been heavily logged prior to being acquired by the Land Trust, and the data collection will help the Land Trust decide how to manage other similar properties. For the chemistry class, Gentalen will engage students in a water quality study of the Pleasant River estuary on the island.

All these ongoing programs illustrate the commitment to a constructive connectedness on Vinalhaven between the school, community institutions, and the environment. Vinalhaven residents understand that school isn't just about test scores; it's about developing students' sense of place and commitment to preserving the natural and cultural resources that sustain that place. School should create students who are both academically proficient and willing to engage in the hard work of community development and environmental preservation. One Vinalhaven student summarizes this nicely, saying:

> Vinalhaven has always been my home and it always will be. I love the peaceful nights and the busy mornings. The morning rumble of kids going to school. The stores and restaurants serving customers their morning coffee and doughnuts, before they set out for a long day ahead of them. The people who go out on the lobster boats work hard all day-long. Vinalhaven is little, but it is full of hard working people, which is what I plan to be when I get older. I am proud to be from Vinalhaven. ... Always have been, always will be.
>
> (midnight12, 2007)

The long-term sustainability of human communities and places depends upon the cultivation of such sentiments. This is the way to stay our course.

Chapter 11

Changing Schools to Embrace the Local

We're hoping that many of the readers of this book are now thinking, "Yes! Place- and community-based education is the answer for all the questions we've got about improving schools and moving towards greater community sustainability." It's certainly been a valuable new paradigm for many of the schools and communities described in this book. As the Maine superintendent said, "Place-based education is the basket; it's not an egg in the basket." By this she meant that place-and-community-based education is a whole new way of looking at how schools, their local communities, and the ecosystem relate to each other. It's not just a new math program or a new approach to youth sports; it's a paradigm shift based on systems thinking and community sustainability. And we hope we've articulated the valuable differences between the top-down No Child Left Behind model of school change and the grass-roots place- and community-based model of school change. While No Child Left Behind emphasizes competition, place-based education emphasizes collaboration, a "we're all in this together" mindset.

But you can't just storm into your superintendent's office and plunk a copy of the book down on the desk and say, "Read this! This is the direction our schools should be headed." Take a few deep breaths. Remind yourself that all change takes time, that patience, hand in hand with clarity of purpose and determination, is a virtue. Now think about the change process and the steps you'll have to take.

One of CO-SEED's emergent school change mantras became: the right change at the right time. Schools develop just the way people do. Just as there is developmentally appropriate curriculum, there are developmentally appropriate change initiatives. To help understand this perspective, we've started to tinker with Maslow's Hierarchy of Individual Needs in the creation of a Hierarchy of School Needs. Maslow contended that it is important to recognize that some needs are foundational and that other needs rest on top of these. For instance, it is difficult to help someone focus on self-esteem, a higher-order need, when physiological needs for food, shelter, and clothing, more foundational needs, aren't being met. Similarly, it's hard for a school to focus on place- and community-based education needs when it has an order and discipline problem. This is like asking someone to conserve energy when they are wondering where their next meal will come from.

In working with a number of schools and districts around the country, we started to notice a difference in the effectiveness of place- and community-based education school change initiatives as a function of a school's developmental stage. In some cases, our school change opportunity was the ticket—it was exactly the right change initiative at that moment in school/community history. In other circumstances, and this was true with both inner-city and rural schools, our school change initiative was like water off a duck's back. It didn't sink in. It was the wrong initiative at that moment in school/community history.

The school and community's readiness appeared to be the most important variable in the success equation. Regardless of other variables in the equation—the skill and capacities of the school administrators, the finesse of the school change facilitators, the socio-economic status of the community—the developmental stage of the school at the beginning of the process seemed to predetermine the trajectory of change.

The Hierarchy of School Needs model emerged out of our trying to make sense of where the school/community change process worked well and where it met resistance. At this point it's a conceptual model that hasn't been fully tested. Some people don't like its hierarchical structure and suggest that it should be a set of nested spheres. But others have found it to be a useful guide for how to approach change.

We've also started to use the Hierarchy of School Needs to help us assess where schools are at so we can determine what kind of school development program is most appropriate based on their current needs (see Figure 11.1).

The model suggests that physical space and social fabric needs precede the needs for comprehensive curriculum and place- and community-based education approaches. Certainly, a school works on many improvement fronts simultaneously, but, without a focus on the most essential tasks, headway is difficult. In a couple of schools and communities where we have worked, we didn't accurately assess readiness for change before we began. These schools faced significant physical space, social fabric, and staff coherence challenges. Our attempts to help them focus on inquiry-based curriculum, getting students out into the environment and neighborhood, and engaging with community organizations were premature. Those schools needed a different form of school change initiative before they'd be able to benefit from what we had to offer.

In Vinalhaven, on the other hand, the CO-SEED school change model came at the right point in the life history of the school and in the school's relationship with the community. Think back to the evolution of the Vinalhaven School described in Chapter 10. George Joseph, the new superintendent, recognized that the first step was building a new building. This process consumed much of his energy for the first five years of his tenure. Once this was complete, he and other school leaders started working on creating a culture of respect, trust, and responsibility in the classroom and throughout the school. Parallel to this, the school established both the grade-level teams and the leadership team to create staff coherence. More recently, the main task over a couple of years has been curriculum documentation and alignment with state frameworks. This was where the CO-SEED initiative came into the picture. Recognizing the importance of the "Curriculum Documentation and Focus on Inquiry" stage, we targeted our energy on supporting curriculum development and subject area integration through inquiry-based projects.

> **Individuation:**
>
> The need to adapt to the uniqueness of each student and staff member

> **Sense of Place:**
>
> The need for curriculum and policies to be grounded in place and community

> **Curriculum Documentation:**
>
> The need for a clear, developmentally appropriate plan of study with an emphasis on inquiry and problem-solving

> **Staff Coherence:**
>
> The need for a collaborative relationship between staff and administration

> **Social Fabric:**
>
> The need for an atmosphere of respect, trust, and responsibility in the classroom and at all school events

> **Physical Space:**
>
> The need for comfortable, healthy, and safe school facilities

Figure 11.1 Hierarchy of School Needs based on Maslow's Hierarchy of Individual Needs

In concert with this, an emphasis on connecting the curriculum to the community emerged, and this has now become a central goal. Too much emphasis on connecting the curriculum to the community three or four years ago would have been premature; now the students and staff are ready for it. It's also interesting to see the school starting to work on the Individuation part of the Hierarchy of Needs. The school leader, Mike Felton, has taken the lead in exploring different ways for students to take Advanced Placement courses online. With limited staff, the school can't offer a wide variety of Advanced Placement courses, but online options can make it possible for individual students to pursue advanced coursework. Additionally, the alternative program at the high school, with a focus on community-based projects, has made it possible to tailor programs to individual needs, thereby keeping students in school who most likely would have dropped out.

The same processes have been at work at Young Achievers in Boston over the past five years. Prior to the implementation of CO-SEED, the principal had put major emphasis on improving the physical space of the building and creating an atmosphere of respect, trust, and responsibility. Once these were in place, she similarly focused on the development of collaborative grade-level teams and numerous forms of shared leadership. Recall that a component of the work at Young Achievers has been changing the role of the teacher's aide to the role of community teacher. Community teachers tend to be adults of color from the community. The school aspires to providing them with professional training, increasing their responsibility in the classroom, and bringing these positions up to greater parity with the classroom teacher's position. These strategies address the staff coherence need at the third level in the hierarchy. Similarly, many community teachers have been encouraged to attend the CO-SEED summer institute, where they are placed in leadership roles working with teachers and community members from other schools to give them the opportunity to experience their own professional competence.

Parallel to the emphasis on curriculum documentation in Vinalhaven, similar curriculum work has taken place at Young Achievers. Teachers have developed a comprehensive matrix framework that tracks curriculum from month to month. These curriculum documents explicitly indicate how the math and language arts curriculum are taught through project-, place-, and community-based learning. And, when teachers move on, they leave behind a well-articulated curriculum that preserves the school's commitment to integrating academic, social justice, and place-based education. Now, with that curriculum solidly in place, more teachers are exploring ways to create sophisticated community-based curriculum. Collaborations with WBUR, one of the local public radio stations, Boston Nature Center, and local businesses are flourishing.

It's interesting to observe other parallel initiatives in Vinalhaven and Young Achievers as a way of summarizing the good things happening in many schools, in diverse communities, in all parts of the country, under the banner of place- and community-based education. Vinalhaven couldn't be more different from the Llano Grande Center in south Texas. Young Achievers couldn't be more different from schools in Howard, South Dakota. Navajo schools in Arizona find themselves in completely different settings than the far north schools involved with the Alaska Native Knowledge Network. Parish schools in Louisiana have mostly African-American students. The Warren Community School in Warren, Maine, another CO-SEED school, has mostly White students. But the principles of school change through a place- and community-based education mindset take similar forms.

Take the middle school bathroom campaign at Young Achievers and the teen center campaign in Vinalhaven. Both emerged out of students' desire to improve the quality of their own living environments. In the urban setting, in an old building, the students were offended by the quality of their sanitary facilities and thought they deserved better. In the rural setting, students were disappointed by the lack of social facilities attuned to their needs and had the energy to bring them into reality. In both cases, teachers tried to harness the genuine energy of their students to make change and tie this energy into innovative curriculum. Moving one step outward into the economic health of the community, the students in Howard, South Dakota convinced townspeople to spend more locally to support the economic viability of local businesses. This was just the first step towards many community revitalization efforts that these students helped energize. The same deep spark operating in these three completely different settings represents the synergistic relationship between school and community in place-based education initiatives from sea to shining sea.

Another parallel can be found in the use of cemeteries. At Young Achievers, the first- and second-grade teachers use nearby Forest Hills Cemetery because it's the nearest patch of nature available. On Vinalhaven, both the third through fifth grade and the high school teachers are using cemeteries to connect students with their cultural heritage. In both urban and rural areas, cemeteries are often accessible from elementary schools. School buses don't need to be scheduled to get there, there's a wealth of language arts, math, and science curriculum easily available, and there's not a lot of competing uses. We've found that a well-scaffolded, curriculum-based field trip to the cemetery, a ten-minute walk from the school, can be cheaper,

Figure 11.2 Cover of Vinalhaven community-based curriculum chart
Vinalhaven School publication

more environmentally responsible, and more supportive of physical health than putting the students on a four-hour roundtrip bus ride to the big-city science museum where they get to spend maybe 90 minutes learning precious little.

The point is, place- and community-based education isn't just a rural thing, urban thing, or suburban thing. It's a healthy, collaborative approach to making schools and communities stronger and healthier. This statement from a parent curriculum document on Vinalhaven conveys this idea nicely:

> *Connecting School and Community*
> The curriculum at Vinalhaven School takes advantage of the rich natural and cultural resources of our island community as a vehicle for teaching about Maine and the wider world. Vinalhaven's granite has built America's cities. Vinalhaven's fisheries feed America's people; Vinalhaven's people provide models of independent and self-sufficient lifestyles. The strength of our school is our community. Drawing on this strength, we use our local landscapes, businesses, fisheries, community organizations, and people to provide real life connections to the world of learning.
>
> Our approach to education is based on academic rigor, student engagement, team teaching, and multi-age learning opportunities. In kindergarten through fifth grade our core curriculum is enhanced through studying island culture—quarry studies, oral histories of community elders, coastal clean-ups. While continuing to be grounded in island culture, our middle school curriculum goes ashore and helps students elaborate new skills based on the study of Maine's place in American history. In high school, the wider worlds of literature, history, the arts and sciences, and complex mathematics take hold.
>
> Vinalhaven's unique landscape and culture shape the curriculum. Many hands and hearts built the school. Please continue to lend your hearts and hands to enhance and enlarge our shared learning community.
>
> (Vinalhaven School, 2008)

Isn't this the way education should be everywhere? The curriculum of the school, whether it's in inner-city Oakland, or in the Oregon countryside, or in Harper's Ferry, West Virginia, should take advantage of the rich cultural and natural resources of the community. Then, while continuing to be grounded in the community, the curriculum moves outward. No school should be an island, but rather a peninsula—off to itself a bit, but connected to the wider worlds of first the community, then the region, the state, and finally the big wide world.

References

Abdullah, S. (2005). Personal communication.

Alaska Rural Systemic Initiative. (2006). AKRSI Final Report. Fairbanks, AK: Alaska Native Knowledge Network, University of Alaska Fairbanks.

Anyon, J. (1981). Social class and school knowledge. *Curriculum Inquiry, 11*:1, pp. 3–42.

Athman, J. & Monroe, M. (2004). The effects of environment-based education on students' achievement motivation. *Journal of Interpretation Research, 9*:1, pp. 9–25.

Bailey, L. (1915). *The holy earth.* New York: C. Scribner's Sons.

Baker, J. (2004). *Home.* New York: Greenwillow Books.

Barton, P. (2005). *One third of a nation: Rising dropout rates and declining opportunities.* Princeton, NJ: Educational Testing Services.

Bartosh, O. (2004). *Environmental education: Improving student achievement.* Unpublished master's thesis. Evergreen State College, Olympia, WA.

Basso, K. (1996). *Wisdom sits in places: Landscape and language among the western Apache.* Albuquerque: University of New Mexico Press.

Bellah, R.N., Madsen, R., Sullivan, W.M., and Swidler, A. (1985). *Habits of the heart: Individualism and commitment in American life.* Berkeley: University of California Press.

Bernstein, B. (1975). *Class, codes, and control: Vol. 3. Towards a theory of educational transmission.* London: Routledge & Kegan Paul.

Billig, S., Root, S., & Jesse, D. (2005). *The impact of participation in service-learning on high school students' civic engagement.* Denver, CO: RMC Research Corporation.

Bishop, S. (2003). A sense of place. In R. Brooke (ed.), *Rural voices: Place-conscious education and the teaching of writing,* pp. 65–82. New York: Teachers College Press.

Blum, R. (2005). *School connectedness: Improving the lives of students.* Baltimore, MD: Johns Hopkins Bloomberg School of Public Health.

Bowers, C.A. (1987). *Elements of a post-liberal theory of education.* New York: Teachers College Press.

Bracey, G. (2006). Dropping in on dropouts. *Phi Delta Kappan,* June, pp. 798–799.

Church, R. & Sedlak, M. (1976). *Education in the United States: An interpretive history.* New York: Free Press.

Carroll, A. & Bowman, B. (2006). Learning to read nature's book: An interdisciplinary curriculum for young children in an urban setting. *Community Works Journal, 7*:3 (Winter).

Cheak, M., Volk, T, & Hungerford, H. (2002). *Molokai: An investment in children, the community, and the environment.* Carbondale, IL: Center for Instruction, Staff Development, and Evaluation.

Cody, R. (1992). *Ricochet River.* New York: Knopf.

Coleman, J. & Hoffer, T. (1987). *Public and private high schools: The impact of communities.* New York: Basic Books.

Comstock, A. (1986). *A handbook of nature study.* Ithaca, NY: Comstock Publishing Associates.

Counts, G. (1932). Dare progressive educators be progressive? *Progressive Educator, 9:*4 (April), pp. 257–263.

Cummins, J. (1996). *Negotiating identities: Educating for empowerment in a diverse society.* Los Angeles: California Association for Bilingual Education.

Dewey, J. (1959). *School and society.* In M. Dworkin (ed.), *Dewey on education.* New York: Teachers College Press.

Dick, A. (No date). *Village math.* Available online at http://ankn.uaf.edu/Publications/ VillageMath/ (retrieved June 2, 2007).

Duffin, M. (2005). *Young Achievers informal report.* Personal correspondence to author from evaluator. Unpublished document.

Duffin, M., and PEER Associates. (2007). *Sustaining the vision: Place-based education at an urban K–8 school. An evaluation of Project CO-SEED at the Young Achievers Science and Mathematics Pilot School in partnership with the Dudley Street Neighborhood Initiative: 2003–2006.* Available online at http://peecworksorg/PEEC/PEEC_Reports/S0250E977-043C01AC

Duffin, M., Powers, A., & Tremblay, G. (2004). *Report on cross-program research and other program evaluation activities: 2003–2004.* Richmond, VT: PEER Associates.

Duffin, M., Powers, A., Tremblay, G., & PEER Associates. (2004). *An evaluation of Project CO-SEED: Community-based school environmental education, 2003–2004 Interim Report.* Richmond, VT: PEER Associates.

Emekauwa, E. (2004a). *They remember what they touch: The impact of place-based learning in East Feliciana Parish.* Washington, DC: Rural School and Community Trust.

Emekauwa, E. (2004b) *The star with my name: The Alaska Rural Systemic Initiative and the impact of place-based education on Native student achievement.* Washington, DC: Rural School and Community Trust.

Finkelstein, M. (2006). Reading the world with math. In E. Gutstein & B. Peterson (eds.), *Rethinking mathematics: Teaching social justice by the numbers,* pp. 19–30. Milwaukee, WI: Rethinking Schools.

FOYA News. (2004, Spring). Partnership update. Jamaica Plain, MA: Friends of Young Achievers Inc.

FOYA News. (2005, Spring). Experiential education: Hands-on learning helps students build skills and knowledge. Jamaica Plain, MA: Friends of Young Achievers Inc.

Gould, S. (1991). Enchanted evening. *Natural History,* September, p. 14.

Gruenewald, D. (2003). The best of both worlds: A critical pedagogy of place. *Educational Researcher, 32:*4, pp. 3–12.

Gutstein, E. & Peterson, B. (eds.) (2006). *Rethinking mathematics: Teaching social justice by the numbers.* Milwaukee, WI: Rethinking Schools.

Hagstrom, D. (1993). The Denali project. In G. Smith (ed.), *Public schools that work: Creating community,* pp. 68–85. New York: Routledge.

Hawken, P. (2007). *Blessed unrest: How the largest movement in the world came into being, and why no one saw it coming.* New York: Viking.

Heath, S. (1983). *Ways with words: Language, life, and work in classrooms and communities.* New York: Cambridge University Press.

Inkeles, A. & Smith, D. (1974). *Becoming modern: Individual change in six developing countries.* Cambridge, MA: Harvard University Press.

islandgirl. (2007). My place essay, Rob Warren's learning blog at vhisland.learningblogs.org, fall.

Jackman, W. (1904). *Nature study*. Chicago: University of Chicago Press.

Kegan, R. (1982). *The evolving self: Problem and process in human development*. Cambridge, MA: Harvard University Press.

Kilpatrick, W.H. (1918). The project method: Child-centeredness in progressive education. *Teachers College Record, 19*:4, pp. 319–334.

Krafel, P. (1999). Deepening children's participation through local ecological investigations. In G. Smith and D. Williams, *Ecological education in action: On weaving education, culture, and the environment*, pp. 47–64. Albany, NY: SUNY Press.

Leavitt, B. (2005). Personal communication.

Lieberman, G., & Hoody, L. (1998). *Closing the achievement gap: Using the environment as an integrating context for learning*. San Diego, CA: State Education and Environment Roundtable.

Little, C. (1997). *Art on the Maine islands*. Camden, ME: Downeast Books.

Lopez, B. (1990). *The rediscovery of North America*. Lexington: University Press of Kentucky.

Louv, R. (2005). *Last child in the woods: Saving our children from nature-deficit disorder*. Chapel Hill, NC: Algonquin Books.

Macy, J. (1983). *Dharma and development: Religion as resource in the Sarvodaya self-help movement*. West Hartford, CT: Kumarian Press.

Marzano, R. (2003). *What works in schools: Translating research into action*. Washington, DC: Association for Supervision and Curriculum Development.

Matthews, D. (1996). *Is there a public for public schools?* Dayton, OH: Kettering Foundation Press.

Melaville, A., Berg, A., & Blank, M. (2006). *Community-based learning: Engaging students for success and citizenship*. Washington, DC: Coalition for Community Schools.

midnight12. (2007). My place essay, Rob Warren's learning blog at vhisland.learningblogs.org, fall.

Montana94. (2007). My place essay, Rob Warren's learning blog at vhisland.learningblogs.org, fall.

Morton, M. (2007). Writing assignment from Heather White's third-grade class, Vinalhaven School, spring.

Nabhan, G. (1997). *Cultures of habitat: On nature, culture, and story*. Washington, DC: Counterpoint.

Nachtigal, P. & Haas, T. (1998). *Place value: An educator's guide to good literature on rural lifeways, environments, and purposes of education*. Charleston, WV: ERIC Clearinghouse on Education and Rural Schools.

National Commission on Excellence in Education. (1983). *A nation at risk: The imperative for education reform*. Washington, DC: Author.

National Environmental Education Training Foundation. (2000). *Environment-based education: Creating high performance schools and students*. Washington, DC: Author.

National Service Learning Clearinghouse. (2007). Available online at http://www.service-learning.org/welcome_to_service-learning/history/index.php (retrieved January 9, 2007).

Newmann, F., Marks, H., & Gamoran, A. (1995). Authentic pedagogy: Standards that boost student performance. *Issues in Restructuring Schools*, Issue Report No. 8, pp. 1–4.

Newmann, F., Secada, W., & Wehlage, G. (1995). *A guide to authentic instruction and assessment: Vision, standards, and scoring*. Madison: Wisconsin Center for Education Research.

Ogbu, J. (1978). *Minority education and caste: The American system in cross-cultural perspective*. New York: Academic Press.

Orion Society. (1998). *Stories in the land: A place-based environmental education anthology.* Great Barrington, MA: Orion Press.

Orr, D. (1992). *Ecological literacy: Education and the transition to a postmodern world.* Albany: State University of New York Press.

Orr, D. (1994). *Earth in mind: On education, the environment, and the human prospect.* Washington, DC and Covelo, CA: Island Press.

Poston, R. (1950). *Small town renaissance: A story of the Montana Study.* New York: Harper.

Putnam, R. (2000). *Bowling alone: The collapse and revival of American community.* New York: Simon & Schuster.

Putnam, R. & Feldstein, L. (2003). *Better together: Restoring the American community.* New York: Simon & Schuster.

Pyle, R. (1993). *The thunder tree: Lessons from an urban wildland.* New York: Houghton-Mifflin.

Quitadamo, I., Faiola, C., Johnson, J., & Kurtz, M. (2008). Community-based inquiry improves thinking in general education biology. *CBE Life Science Education, 7*:3, pp. 327–337.

Ramsey, J., Hungerford, H., & Volk, T. (2001). A technique for analyzing environmental issues. In H. Hungerford, W. Bluhm, T. Volk, & J. Ramsey (eds.), *Essential readings in environmental education* (2nd edition), pp. 173–178. Champaign, IL: Stipes Publishing.

Riley, K. & Stern, B. (2003–2004). A bootlegged curriculum. *International Journal of Social Education, 18*:2 (Fall—Winter), pp. 62–72.

Rugg, H. (1939). *Democracy and the curriculum: The life and program of the American school.* New York: D. Appleton-Century.

Rural Challenge Research and Evaluation Program. (1999a). *Living and learning in rural schools and communities.* Cambridge, MA: Harvard Graduate School of Education.

Rural Challenge Research and Evaluation Program. (1999b). *Living and learning in rural schools and communities: Lessons from the field.* Cambridge, MA: Harvard Graduate School of Education.

Rural School and Community Trust. (2005). *Rural Policy Matters*, September. Available online at http://www.ruraledu.org/site/c.beJMIZOCIrH/b.1389103/apps (retrieved May 31, 2006).

Sand, E. (2006). Howard, Corsica students to research their communities. *Madison Daily Leader*, November 20. Available online at http://www.mccr.net/ mccr/Articles/Howard_Corsica_students.html (retrieved January 29, 2007).

SEED team evaluation discussion. (2007). Personal notes collected by David Sobel, November 28.

Senechal, E. (2008). Environmental justice in Egleston Square. In D. Gruenewald & G. Smith, *Place-based education in a global era: Local diversity.* Mahwah, NJ: Erlbaum.

Sennett, R. & Cobb, J. (1972). *The hidden injuries of class.* New York: Knopf.

Shelton, J. (2005). *Consequential education: A public approach to better schools.* Montgomery, AL: NewSouth Press.

Smith, G. (1993). Shaping bioregional schools. *Whole Earth Review*, Winter, pp. 70–74.

Smith, G. (2002). Place-based education: Learning to be where we are. *Phi Delta Kappan*, April, pp. 584–594.

Smith, G. (2004). Cultivating care and connection: Preparing the soil for a just and sustainable society. *Education Studies*, August, pp. 72–91.

Smith, G. (2007). Grounding learning in place. *WorldWatch Magazine*, March/April, pp. 20–24.

Snyder, Gary. (1980). *The real work: Interviews and talks, 1964–1979.* New York: New Directions.

Sobel, D. (1996). *Beyond ecophobia: Reclaiming the heart in nature education.* Great Barrington, MA: Orion Society.

Sobel, D. (2004). *Place-based education: Connecting classrooms and communities.* Great Barrington, MA: Orion Press.

Spring, J. (1976). *The sorting machine: National educational policy since 1945.* New York: McKay.

State Education and Environment Roundtable (SEER). (2000). *California student assessment project: The effects of environment-based education on student achievement, phase one.* Poway, CA: Author.

State Education and Environment Roundtable (SEER). (2005). *California student assessment project, phase two: The effects of environment-based education on student achievement.* Poway, CA: Author.

Stegner, W. (1957). *The big rock candy mountain.* New York: Sagamore.

Stone, M. (2005). "It changed everything we thought we could do": The STRAW Project. In M. Stone & Z. Barlow (eds.), *Ecological literacy: Educating our children for a sustainable world,* pp. 161–174. San Francisco: Sierra Club Books.

Tocqueville, A. de. (1904). *Democracy in America.* New York: D. Appleton & Company.

Tso, J. & Hill, C. (2006, Winter). *Understanding cultural competency in experiential environmental education programs: A report from the cultural competency assessment project.* Boston, MA: Barr Foundation. Available online at http://www.barrfoundation.org/resources/ resources_show.htm?doc_id=427985

Umphrey, M. (2007). *The power of community-centered education: Teaching as a craft of place.* Lanham, MD: Rowman & Littlefield.

Vinalhaven School. (2008). Connecting school and community, K–8 curriculum chart. Vinalhaven, ME: Author.

Vitousek, P., Mooney, H., Lubchenco, J., & Melillo, J. (1997). Human domination of earth's ecosystems, *Science, 277* (July 25), pp. 494–499.

Volk, T., & Cheak, M. (2003). The effects of an environmental education program on students, parents, and community. *Journal of Environmental Education, 34:*4, pp. 12–25.

Von Secker, C. (2004). *Bay Schools Project: Year three summative evaluation.* Annapolis, MD: Chesapeake Bay Foundation.

Wehlage, G., Rutter, R., Smith, G., Lesko, N., & Fernandez, R. (1989). *Reducing the risk: Schools as communities of support.* New York: Falmer.

Wehlage, G., Smith, G., & Lipman, P. (1992). Restructuring urban schools: The New Futures experience. *American Educational Research Journal, 29:*1 (Spring), pp. 51–93.

Wilkinson, R. & Pickett, K. (2009). *The spirit level: Why more equal societies almost always do better.* London: Allen Lane.

Willis, P. (1981). *Learning to labor: How working class kids get working class jobs.* New York: Columbia University Press.

Index